DEAF-BLIND REALITY

*

DEAF-BLIND REALITY

Living the Life

Scott M. Stoffel, Editor

Gallaudet University Press
Washington, DC

Gallaudet University Press
Washington, DC 20002
http://gupress.gallaudet.edu

Second printing 2013.

Printed in the United States of America

Library of Congress Cataloging-in-Publication Data

Deaf-blind reality: living the life / S.M. Stoffel, editor.

p. cm.

ISBN 978-1-56368-535-4 (pbk.: alk. paper) – ISBN 978-1-56368-536-1 (e-book)

1. Deafblind people. I. Stoffel, S. M.

HV1597.D45 2012

362.4'1–dc23

2012022984

∞ The paper used in this publication meets the minimum requirements of American National Standard for Information Sciences—Permanence of Paper for Printed Library Materials, ANSI Z39.48-1984.

Contents

Contributors

Many thanks to the following individuals who shared their personal experiences in this book:

Angela C. Orlando
Kent, Ohio

Carol O'Connor
Manchester, England

Christian S. Shinaberger
Santa Monica, California

Christy L. Reid
Poplar Bluff, Missouri

Ilana Hermes
Cape Town, South Africa

Judy Kahl
Bonita Springs, Florida

Mark Gasaway
Atlanta, Georgia

Melanie Bond
Bay City, Michigan

Patricia Clark
Wellington, New Zealand

Scott Stoffel
Lansdale, Pennsylvania

Tonilyn Todd Wisner
Opelousas, Louisiana

Wendy Williams
St. Paul, Minnesota

Glossary and Abbreviations

Following are terms and abbreviations that occur frequently in the book.

Glossary

Closed-circuit tevelvision (CCTV): A TV used as a reading aid by the visually impaired. The camera faces a platform on which printed material can be placed, and the magnified image is displayed on a screen.

Deaf-blind (also deafblind or DB): A condition in which a person suffers from both a significant hearing loss and visual impairment. A deaf-blind individual is not necessarily totally deaf and/or totally blind.

Encephalitis: A condition characterized by inflammation of the brain that is usually caused by a viral infection. Deaf-blindness and other disabilities can result from subsequent damage to the brain and nervous system.

FM system: An audio device that can link a hearing aid, cochlear implant, or earphone to a microphone.

Hemolytic disease of the newborn (erythroblastosis fetalis): A condition that occurs when there is an incompatibility between the blood types of the mother and the infant.

Hydrocephalus: A condition characterized by an increase in cerebrospinal fluid around the brain that results in enlargement of the head in infants because the bones of the skull are not yet fused together. The fluid is blocked by a congenital condition or a disease and can be drained into the abdominal cavity by implanting a mechanical device called a shunt.

Keratoconjunctivitis: An inflammation of the cornea and conjunctiva.

Keratoglobus: A degenerative, noninflammatory disorder of the eye in which structural changes within the cornea cause it to become extremely thin and change to a more globular shape. It causes corneal thinning, primarily at the margins, which results in a spherical, slightly enlarged eye.

Light perception: An optical condition in which a person can only detect the presence or absence of bright light. No shapes or details are perceptible.

Macular degeneration: An optical condition in which the central vision gradually deteriorates. It can result in a "blind spot" in the middle of the visual field that becomes wider as the condition progresses.

Meniere's disease: A disorder of the inner ear that can affect hearing and balance and is characterized by episodes of dizziness and tinnitus and progressive hearing loss, usually in one ear.

Neuropathy: A disease or disorder, especially of a degenerative nature, which affects the nervous system. It can affect vision, hearing, and/or other body functions.

Night blindness: An optical condition in which a person's eyes cannot adjust to dim settings, such as outdoors at night. The person becomes effectively "blind" when illumination is weak, even if he or she can see well in normal room lighting. This condition is a symptom of RP and Usher's syndrome.

Nystagmus: Involuntary motion of the eyes. The condition causes a person's eyes to "jump around" or quiver, distorting proper focus of vision.

Orientation and mobility training (O&M): An area of rehabilitation training for blind and deaf-blind people that deals with moving about the community, both on foot and via public transportation. It may include use of a white cane or guide dog.

Oscillopsia: A visual disturbance in which objects in the visual field appear to oscillate. The severity of the effect may range from a mild blurring to rapid jumping.

Perthes disease: A degenerative disease of the hip joint, where a loss of bone mass leads to some degree of collapse of the hip joint (i.e., to deformity of the ball of the femur and the surface of the hip socket).

Polyneuropathy: A neurological disorder that occurs when many peripheral nerves throughout the body malfunction simultaneously. It may be acute and appear without warning or chronic and develop gradually over a longer period of time. Many polyneuropathies have both motor and sensory impairment, while some also involve the autonomic nervous system. These disorders are often symmetric and frequently affect the feet and hands, causing weakness, loss of sensation, pins-and-needles sensations, or burning pain.

Retinitis pigmentosa (RP): A vision disorder characterized by progressively shrinking peripheral vision. RP can also weaken the acuity of central vision and cause night blindness and oversensitivity to bright light. The rate at which the condition degenerates differs greatly among individuals with the condition. Some suffers lose all vision over a short span, while others never become totally blind.

Rubella: A highly contagious viral disease, especially affecting children, which causes swelling of the lymph glands and a reddish rash on the skin. It can be harmful to the unborn baby of a pregnant woman who contracts it.

Tinnitus: Noise, usually ringing or buzzing sounds, which is not "real" but heard by a person when cells within the ear die. The noise may be vague or quite loud and distracting.

Tracking: Tracking is a technique employed by deaf people with low vision, especially tunnel vision, to "keep track" of a signer's hand by lightly holding the person's wrist.

TTY: An electronic device that has a keyboard and a small display screen that deaf and hard of hearing people use to communicate by telephone with hearing persons through a relay operator. The relay operator is unnecessary if both the caller and the recipient of the call use TTY machines. The concept is similar to Instant Messaging (IM). TTY use is steadily being replaced by video phones and Internet-based relay services.

Tunnel vision: When a person's field of vision is reduced by a condition, such as RP, the narrowed visual field is called "tunnel" vision, as if one was looking down a narrow tunnel or tube.

Tullio phenomenon: Sound-induced vertigo, dizziness, nausea, and/or nystagmus.

Usher's syndrome: A genetic disorder characterized by RP and hearing loss. There are several known types of Usher's syndrome, the most common of which are Type 1, in which the person is born deaf and has RP, and Type 2, in which the person is born with hearing that gradually deteriorates over time and has RP.

White cane: A long cane used by the blind and visually impaired to feel for obstacles, steps, and drop-offs. The cane is painted white with red or orange near the tip to alert others that the user is blind or visually impaired and to be more visible at night. Traditional support canes may be painted similarly to serve as identification of visual disability.

Abbreviations

ASL: American Sign Language
CART: computer-assisted real-time captioning
CC: closed captioned
CCTV: closed-circuit tv
CI: cochlear implant
DB: deaf-blind
DBC: DeafBlind Communicator
ENT: ear, nose, and throat (specialist)
FFB: Foundation Fighting Blindness
HKNC: Helen Keller National Center
NFB: National Foundation for the Blind
O&M: orientation and mobility (training)
RP: retinitis pigmentosa
TTY: teletypewriter
VR: vocational rehabilitation

Introduction

As its title suggests, this book deals with the *reality* of being deaf-blind. The goal of this book is not to tell amazing or inspiring stories about people who are disabled; it is to show what life is really like for persons with a combination of vision and hearing loss (and, in a few cases, additional disabilities as well).

Most stories about people who are disabled are written for the sake of being inspirational. *Come and see the amazing challenged person overcome all odds!* While there is nothing wrong with inspiring stories, rarely do they give a true and complete view of what the challenged individuals must deal with on a daily basis. Inspirational stories tend to focus on some achievement, such as a sporting or academic accomplishment, but don't delve into the individual's less exciting struggles. How does our "amazing" deaf-blind subject interact with hearing-sighted people at a family reunion? How does he shop for groceries? What goes through her mind when she enters a classroom full of nondisabled peers? These aren't questions you are likely to find answers to while reading that incredible tale of success. They are, however, issues that a person who is deaf-blind wishes others understood.

There is also a prevalent misconception in modern society that if a person who is disabled accomplishes some goal, such as attaining a college degree or winning a sporting competition, the disability essentially vanishes, and life becomes "normal" for the still-disabled person. This is probably the result of films and literature that conclude with the disabled main character achieving a goal at the end of the story, leaving the audience to assume the challenges have been "conquered" once and for all. Unfortunately, the reality of life for people who are deaf-blind is not so simple.

Most people truly don't understand what life is like for people who are deaf-blind, nor can they relate to what deaf-blind people go through. That is the very reason I decided to create this book. But I did not want merely to lecture the world about my own views on deaf-blindness; rather, I wanted to illustrate the real world of people who are deaf-blind through the actual life experiences of many deaf-blind individuals. That said, no attempt was made to tell extraordinary accounts of monumental achievement. The book instead deals with all of those unspectacular—but altogether daunting—challenges that never make it into the amazing stories, despite being of greater importance, because they pertain to everyday life.

Instead of having each contributor tell his or her life story, I divided the book into separate topics and asked the contributors to answer questions related to each. Thus, each chapter of the book deals with a different topic, such as early schooling, adult education, careers, and the basics of daily living. There is a certain degree of chronology to the early chapters, but the book does not intentionally tell anyone's life story from beginning to end. There is modularity to most of the chapters, so one can turn directly to a chapter on a subject of interest without needing to read all of the previous chapters.

I asked the contributors to share their real experiences with each topic, not to simply state their opinions. I provided questions in electronic form and allowed each person to take as much time as needed to write up answers. Some wrote their own articles, while others simply answered the questions and had me expand their answers into articles. I frequently had to ask for additional information and allowed the contributors to proofread the edited articles for accuracy. As one can imagine, this was a very tedious process, taking over three years to complete. I admit there were times when I wanted to throw in the towel and just write a book based on my own views.

But I realized that it was necessary to get multiple deaf-blind people to discuss their experiences, since no two of us are exactly alike. My own views alone would give a misleading perception of deaf-blind people in general. It is through the actual experiences of all twelve of the contributors to this book that a non-deaf-blind person might gain insight into the obscure reality of being deaf-blind. You will see directly into the minds of these people and learn what they think and feel in various real-life situations. You may be inclined to think a certain reaction described in one of the chapters is "wrong" or "blown out of proportion," but remember that these are the *real* thoughts and feelings of deaf-blind people. If you truly desire to better understand people who are deaf-blind, you must set aside your opinions and focus on what is actual.

Please note that not every contributor opted to tackle every topic.

One chapter is devoted to the subject of cochlear implants. This is a somewhat controversial issue, so I interviewed people both with and without implants to get both perspectives. The folks with implants share their experiences with these devices and how they have affected their lives, while those without implants discuss the reasons they prefer not to have them. There are many other adaptive aids for the deaf-blind, but none of these had the profound life-changing effects that the implants did for some of the folks. Other adaptive aids are discussed when applicable in various sections of the book.

Who should read this book? If you are a parent or other relative of a deaf-blind child or adult, if you're a teacher, social worker, employer, colleague, service provider, neighbor, or anyone that has contact with a person who is deaf-blind, you will find this book invaluable on how to effectively interact with and understand the deaf-blind people in your life. You will learn what works best and what does not, as well as what actions might be psychologically harmful. And you will discover that people who are deaf-blind are very much human and a part of *this* world, not perpetual daydreamers lost in their own world.

Genuine understanding is something that people who are deaf-blind seldom encounter in society, a society in which sight and sound are of prime importance. But if one is willing to take the time to consider the accounts and discussions herein, then a shard of that precious thing, just being understood and accepted, might yet be found.

When I began this project, I recruited volunteers from among the deaf-blind members of an Internet listserv I had joined. The people had been discussing issues like the ones in this book, and someone remarked that a book with all of that information would be a great way to educate the public about people who are deaf-blind. Because I was a writer, I offered to make it happen. Things got off to a quick start but soon stalled. A handful of the original contributors dropped out of the project, forcing me to search for new ones. I had to scour the deaf-blind world for recruits. I wanted a dozen individuals with different levels of disabilities and different backgrounds. In the end, it was worth the time and effort to find all of these folks and put this book together.

What follows is some background information on each contributor.

Angela C. Orlando, age 35

Kent, Ohio

The first clue that something was wrong happened when I was six years old and in the first grade. My older brother, Tony, was in the sixth grade at the same school. He was in a very rough class. One day, Tony got hit in the eye with a pencil. He recovered from the injury, but during testing, he was diagnosed with retinitis pigmentosa (RP). Since this condition frequently results from genetic disorders, it served as a warning for what I would experience later.

This was the first evidence that there was anything wrong in our family. The doctors looked at my medical history, too. At the time, I had 20/40 vision and wore glasses. I had to go through a lot of scary visual testing at the Cleveland Clinic. My field of vision was normal. The doctors said I might be a carrier of RP, and that was the end of it for many years.

Looking back, I can see another warning sign: Even at a young age, I suffered from night blindness (a symptom of RP). I didn't like to play hide-and-seek at night with my friends. I couldn't see in a movie theater after the lights went out. I got lost at night during Girl Scout camping trips. But no one realized this at the time, not even me; I just assumed everyone was the same way.

The beginning of my troubles started when I was thirteen. I first noticed tinnitus several months before I was diagnosed with hearing loss. [Tinnitus is a condition in which the cells of the ear gradually die, causing the person to hear odd noises that aren't real. It is most noticeable when the surroundings are quiet.] I was confused by all the helicopters I thought I heard flying over our house at night. I didn't know I was the only one who could hear that "noise."

Around this time, my parents noticed I wasn't as responsive when they spoke to me. At first, they thought I was just "being a teenager" and not listening. But as it continued, they started to fear I might be having trouble with my hearing.

I was diagnosed by an audiologist at our local hospital. After a lengthy hearing test, he told us that I had a mild to moderate sensorineural hearing loss in both ears. This audiologist believed the problem would not get any worse and that hearing aids would help. But for a second opinion, I was sent to a hearing specialist. They did a full day of testing. It was very scary. I was still hooked up to a machine that showed a picture of my inner ear when the doctor informed my mother that I had Usher's syndrome. She burst into tears right in front of me. The nurse tried to block my view, but it was too late. And that's when my life seemed to fall apart.

Today, we know that Usher's syndrome was an incorrect diagnosis. But that doesn't change the feelings and the effect of what I went through. Doctors now believe my brother and I both have mitochondrial cytopathy or a more recently discovered genetic disorder called PHARC.

I have lost all my vision, hear some noise with cochlear implants, and have to deal with a number of physical problems.

Carol O'Connor, age 52

Manchester, England

As a child, I was normal-sighted and had perfect hearing until I was four years old. I was in a nursery school back in the 1960s in my first home, which was at Miles Platting in Manchester. My teacher told my mum and dad that she noticed my eye turned in. Mum and Dad were worried by this, so they took me to my first doctor. He referred me to the Manchester Royal Eye Hospital for testing. After the tests, he told my parents I had a squint in my left eye and sent me into the hospital to have it straightened.

After that, I carried on as normal in my nursery.

As I got older, I didn't really play the same way as other children my age. I loved playing on my three-wheel bike in our street, but I never went very far. I'm not sure exactly when people figured out I had a vision problem, but this was probably the first sign of it.

When I got to nine years old, Mum and Dad and my baby sister, who was about two years old then, and my other sister and three brothers all moved to a three-bedroom house in Newton Heath, Manchester. I started at a new school there, and I wasn't hearing properly at all. When the teacher, Miss Prescott, read us stories in the corner of the classroom, I couldn't hear her. She picked up on this and had me sit at the front of the classroom, which was better. When we watched the TV in class, I had to sit at the front.

On the playground one day, I felt dizzy and sick. The teacher was worried about me and contacted my parents. Again, I was sent to the doctor and then was referred to the ear, nose, and throat (ENT) clinic. After that, I had tests on my left ear and then was told I had to go into the hospital for an ear operation. But the operation was cancelled; they couldn't find anything wrong. Go figure.

Years later I had a perforated eardrum. That's when my hearing problems really got worse.

When I was twelve, I was having an English lesson, and the teacher was drawing on the board. I felt quite funny and sickly inside my tummy. Suddenly, I got this most awful sharp pain in my left eye. Oh, it was terrible. I cried, and the teacher came running over and shouted, "Oh, my god! Your eye is all bloodshot!" The children in classroom went all silent and concerned. The teacher rushed me to the infirmary. The nurse phoned my parents, and the next day I was rushed to the Manchester Royal Eye Hospital.

I had an operation, but they couldn't save my detached retina. I lost a lot of my vision and didn't go back to school until six months later. My school life changed. I couldn't join in netball or rounders [a game similar to baseball] or swimming or hockey. I became very depressed and isolated.

In high school, I used a hearing aid fitted to the waistband of my uniform skirt, as it was a boxed hearing aid. When my vision got worse, I was transferred to a special school. That school had blind children on one side and deaf children on the other side. Because I had both vision and hearing problems, they didn't know what classroom to put me in. I ended up in the deaf group.

Over the years, my vision and hearing have diminished.

Christian S. Shinaberger, age 46

Santa Monica, California

According to my mom, I had my first eye surgery at 18 months of age in Germany. My dad, who was an internist in the U.S. Army Medical

Corps, first noticed I had an eye problem. The surgery was to remove congenital cataracts. The exact cause of the condition has never been determined. I don't remember this surgery at all.

I had enough vision as a young child to recognize my dad's car from a second-story window of our apartment in Germany. But I didn't really understand that I was nearsighted until we moved to Atlanta, Georgia. I got my first exposure to Braille there while in kindergarten. That made me aware I was different from other kids.

My hearing was probably normal for a while, since I learned to speak two different languages as a youngster, German and English. My mom told me I started talking at ten months. I don't recall exactly when I noticed I had a hearing loss. I know that I didn't start using hearing aids until about the third grade.

I have no vision today but hear quite well with bilateral cochlear implants.

Christy L. Reid, age 44

Poplar Bluff, Missouri

I was nearly three years old when my parents suspected something was wrong with my eyes. I always held things up close to my eyes or pressed my nose against the pages of picture books. I always sat right in front of the TV. And one time, I remember hugging a woman in a department store whom I thought was a mannequin. I remember, because I was so surprised and embarrassed when I realized she was a real person. My mom and dad thought these behaviors odd and took me to an ophthalmologist. But the doctor sent me home, saying I was too young and that I just liked to sit up close to the TV.

It turned out my parents' suspicions were correct. When I entered kindergarten at age five, I failed the standard vision screening required for new students. Again, my parents took me to an ophthalmologist. This time, they did a bunch of tests, and I remember having to stay in the hospital a few days. I didn't like the tests, nor did I like staying in the hospital. I remember one test in particular: I had to sit very still in a chair beside a machine full of buttons. The technician put sticky stuff all over my head which attached wires from my scalp to the machine. I remember my mom, who stayed with me throughout the hospital visit and told me not to worry, helped me wash the stuff out of my hair. The conclusion of all the tests was the discovery that I had optic atrophy and would grow up as a legally blind person. The cause of the nerve damage was unknown.

At that time, we lived in Fort Worth, Texas. The news that I had optic atrophy didn't really change much; it just made things make more sense. I continued kindergarten, had friends to play with, liked to climb trees and ride my bike, took gymnastics and dancing lessons, and I had a brand new little sister to help Mom with. My early childhood was pretty much like most happy kids. As I got older, though, my vision grew steadily worse, and things got harder.

To top it off, when I was about nine years old, I constantly asked people to repeat what they said. My parents thought something might be wrong with my hearing. They took me to see a doctor to have my hearing checked. He told my mom that the hearing problem was temporary, caused by drainage in my middle ear from allergies. I returned home from the doctor's visit, went back to my life, my friends, and my gymnastics class, and now I had a new little brother. I was the oldest of three children, and so far, my sister and brother didn't show signs of vision or hearing problems. It was believed my hearing would clear up. But it didn't; it just got worse.

My parents took me to see several more doctors, trying to find out what was wrong with my hearing and find a treatment. We were living in Poplar Bluff, a small town in southeastern Missouri, and it required some planning ahead to take me to see doctors in larger cities. I remember going to St. Louis, to Memphis, Tennessee, and one time, my sister, mom and I flew in a small airplane to Tulsa, Oklahoma, so I could see a doctor there. We met my aunt and cousins at the Tulsa airport and had lunch together after the doctor visit. All of the doctors said about the same thing: I was suffering from inner ear nerve damage. The cause was unknown, and there wasn't anything that could be done to reverse it.

My vision and hearing have continued to deteriorate. I now have very little vision and can only hear some noise with a single cochlear implant. I also have neuropathy in my feet and lower legs and major problems with balance.

Ilana Hermes, age 31

Cape Town, South Africa

My first struggle actually started before I was born. A doctor told my parents that there was something wrong with me, while I was still inside my mother. He informed them the problem was very serious and suggested they have me aborted.

It's a good thing for me they declined.

When I entered the world, I was born two months prematurely and diagnosed with congenital hydrocephalus (a condition in which fluid does not drain properly from ventricles in the brain). I received my first shunt at one day of age and spent the first two months of my life in the hospital. [A shunt is a small tube and valve inserted into the brain to drain the excess fluid out of the brain.]

After I arrived home, my parents realized I didn't react when they switched on a light. In response to this, my mother regularly took me to the toy library. This is a library for disabled children where there are educational toys to help stimulate and assess a child's abilities and try to improve disabilities, if possible. There they determined I was blind and paralyzed on the left side of my body. I had some movement on my right side.

I started immediately with physiotherapy, occupational therapy, and speech therapy. This continued until I was thirteen years old. The therapies helped me get the most out of what physical abilities I had and prevented worse deterioration.

As an adult, I am still blind but can now hear fairly well with bilateral cochlear implants. I must also deal with severe headaches caused by the hydrocephalus and problems with my shunt.

Judy Kahl, age 63

Bonita Springs, Florida

My grandmother was the first to detect my hearing loss. She explained to my mother that she called my name but I did not respond. She felt my hearing should be checked by a doctor.

We saw an ENT, and it was determined that the nerve in my inner ear was damaged, due to a high fever from German measles. But I didn't have any problems with balance and found out many years later that this diagnosis was wrong and that I was born with Usher's syndrome.

At the age of six, I was fitted with a hearing aid that was like a transistor radio worn in a harness over the shoulders and under the arms. It attached to the harness in front of the chest. I hated the way it looked, but my mother solved that problem: She got me a bra and attached the hearing aid to the center of it. With a shirt or dress over this, it just made me look a little more mature than my age, if you get the picture. She also did a great job of covering the wire from the ear mold to the collar of my garment with my hair, so I felt much more normal. The main drawback to this aid was that when the fabric of my clothes rubbed against the microphone, I heard a lot of annoying scratchy sounds. My mother also had to check the wire every time I came home from school, because it would often get disconnected from all my activity.

I didn't notice anything was wrong with my vision until much later on in life.

All these many years later, I am very happy with the hearing I receive from my two cochlear implants. But I am still searching for a way to restore my fading vision. I am very active with the Foundation Fighting Blindness (FFB).

Mark Gasaway, age 54

Atlanta, Georgia

I was an eight-year-old when I became sick with encephalitis. I do not know how I contracted the virus, but it could have been through germs of some kind going around or some form of insect bite. However, I tend to rule out an insect bite because encephalitis is mostly carried by mosquitoes, and when I became sick, it was wintertime.

I first knew I was not the same physically when I awoke from a week-long coma. I knew my hearing was affected because I was unable to hear almost anything. I also knew my vision was affected but had to deal with it. I started adjusting to the deafness not too long after waking from the coma. Adjusting to the vision loss took a couple of months longer.

I lost my hearing and vision at the same time, and went from being a hearing and sighted person to a deaf and low-vision person. I also had to learn to walk again about two months later.

I found out about these new problems on my own because I could not hear properly and was seeing a lot of blurriness, so I knew things were different. It was just a complete and sudden change in my life.

My parents realized I was not hearing or seeing like before and took me to see a doctor.

After I started back to school upon recovering from the illness, I had to return to the grade I was in previously because of missing so much school that year. I had the experience of losing friends and knew things were not going to be the same.

I have come to accept being deaf and low vision and am not worried about being cured. I'm content with who I am.

Melanie Bond, age 53

Bay City, Michigan

I didn't know I had a disability until I was eight years old and was mainstreamed in third grade. That's when I learned that I was a freak. It was quite a rude awakening for me that I was the only one with a hearing impairment in the whole school. For the first time in my life, I felt ashamed about having to wear a body aid with two long coils that connected to my ear molds. I tried my best to hide it from everyone by wearing a stretchy hair band to cover it up, even though I wasn't fooling anyone. Prior to that, I had been enrolled in an oral program for the deaf. No one told me I had a disability. Instead, I felt completely normal, and I felt comfortable being around my deaf and hard of hearing classmates. Without proper support services to make my mainstreamed experience a more pleasant one, I found myself alone and with classmates who shunned me because I could not understand the words they said to me. Desperate for friends, I found myself reluctantly hanging out with the cast-offs, which included a bed-wetter, a stutterer, and two endless chatterboxes.

I never had normal vision to begin with, since my genes had already been programmed before I was born. I became uncomfortably aware in my mid-teen years that I could not see very well when night fell or in any place where the lighting was dim. I thought that if I ate more carrots, my vision would improve. I had no awareness yet that I was also losing my peripheral vision. It wasn't until I was twenty-five years old when I learned that I had RP, which would explain why I had been somewhat clumsy as a child, a failure at playing contact sports, and unable to defend myself in a fight. When I was pregnant with my first baby, I knew then that I was losing my vision at an incredible rate.

When I told my mom that I was having trouble with my night vision, something clicked inside her mind. My mom said, "Oh, my goodness! I wonder if you might have the same condition that Uncle Bruce and Uncle Carty have! They both have been recently diagnosed with a new condition called Usher's syndrome." She looked at me and then said, "Melanie, I want you to make an appointment with an ophthalmologist right away!"

Sure enough, my mom had been right about the Usher's syndrome diagnosis. I now had a name for my deafness—soon to be deaf-blindness. I learned that I would become legally blind and, potentially, a classical deaf-blind person.

It's funny—I was normal as far as I was concerned up until I was mainstreamed. What I hadn't known at the time was that my parents began to suspect that I was mentally retarded. I suppose that was because I was oblivious to sounds and conversations. I had little awareness of my siblings. I can remember repeating my mantra over and over, which was simply a soft, "Mmmm, Mmmm, Mmmm," to bring comfort into my isolated world.

There came a point when my dad began to note an alertness and intelligence that he saw in my eyes and perhaps in my behavioral patterns. He might have begun to suspect that I could hear loud sounds. He took me to a doctor who banged away on a few pots and pans while I was playing quietly on the floor. I suddenly looked up, smiled at the doctor, then went right back to playing. The doctor exclaimed, "She heard me banging on the pots and pans just fine! There's nothing wrong with her hearing!"

My dad didn't believe him. But neither did he ever give up on me. At about the age of three-and-a-half to four, my parents drove me to the Ford Hospital in Detroit, Michigan, to have my hearing tested by a trained audiologist named Dr. Graham. That was when I first became aware of sounds. You can imagine the big surprise I felt on my face as I listened to (amplified) tones and beeps for the first time in my life.

When I was about five or six years old, I literally ran into another deaf girl who was also running. Neither one of us noticed that we were running toward each other, since we were both looking at something else. We were like two trains that collided in the middle of the night. I ended up with a bump the size of a golf ball on my forehead and was sent home. Even then, I still had no clue that I had a visual impairment.

Back in the early 1980s, I had become aware of a six-year trial program in which researchers at the Berman-Gund lab at the Massachusetts Eye & Ear Infirmary in Boston worked to find a cure for RP or to find a way to slow down the progression of RP. I willingly volunteered for the program. I loved traveling, so I didn't mind having to fly to Boston at least six times in six years. I had to submit to several uncomfortable procedures on my eyes, including having hard contacts placed into my eyes; electroretinograms, where light is flashed into both eyes to measure the electrical activity of the retina, peripheral and night vision testing; and so on. If memory serves me right, I was in one of three test study groups in which each participant was told to take an unidentified pill every day for the next six years. After the six-year trial was over, I was informed that I had been taking 1500 IU of vitamin A palmitate each day. I was also told to have my liver checked each year by my medical doctor. The second group had vitamin A palmitate along with vitamin E, and this group showed the best rate of success with slowing down RP. The third group was given a placebo. I do believe that my taking the vitamin A palmitate helped to slow down my RP.

Over the next five years when I traveled to Boston, I would stay for two or three nights in a nearby Episcopalian convent, which made walking to and from the Massachusetts Eye & Ear Infirmary a breeze. The furnishings in my room were austere but clean. I couldn't complain about the price—room and board was only $15 per night. Not a bad deal!

One year, I flew into Boston, hoping to land there an hour before sundown. I had made the mistake of not realizing that the sun set sooner in Boston than it did in Michigan even though they both were within the same Eastern Standard Time Zone. By the time I got off the train at the Charles St. Station, I was shocked to see that it was already dark out. I had intended to walk six blocks to the convent on my own, thinking there would still be enough daylight for me to walk. Unfortunately, it was wintertime with freezing temperatures, snow drifts, and ice. I was paralyzed for a few minutes, not knowing what to do. Should I ask a stranger to walk me to the convent or phone a cab or call the convent and ask for one of the nuns to come after me? I was truly afraid, because I didn't want anyone to know that I had a serious hearing problem and some difficulties with my vision, especially with night blindness and loss of peripheral vision. I simply prayed and asked for God's protection. That was all I could do. I did not have a cane with me; it would be almost ten years before I received my first cane.

Fortunately, I had memorized the route to the convent. The train station was well lit, but once I crossed the main street, I could barely see through the dim lights on the street. I used my boots like a cane to feel for any curbs or snow banks or ice. Plus, I was carrying my luggage. I managed to walk the four blocks around obstacles where snow-covered steps jutted out onto the uneven brick sidewalks and short, bare trees with low branches lined the street. I then turned the corner and walked uphill two blocks, managing to not slide back down the hill. Then it was a short walk to the steps of the convent. I had finally made it—or so I thought! I knocked on the door, but no one answered. I began to wonder if I had made a mistake. So I walked to the next door, using my hand to trail along the side of the dark building. It was pitch dark on the snow-covered street. No one answered at the second door or the third door. By the time I reached the next corner, I slipped on the ice and fell hard enough to have the wind knocked out of me. At the same time, my bags flew up in the air. I felt so scared that I wanted to cry. Instead, I picked myself back up and decided to walk back to the first door. A stranger walked by and I asked him if he could help me find the right door. He told me in a gruff manner, "You're right there!" I thanked him, then banged on the door again and this time a nun opened the door. She asked me, "Why didn't you ring the doorbell?" I told her, "I never saw one!" So she showed me where it was; then she let me in. Unfortunately, I had missed my evening meal. But I was so grateful that I had made it safely to the convent. I had learned then never to take late daylight hours for granted and to plan my trips better so that I would always land when the sun still shines.

Nowadays, I still have some useful vision, although it has continued to deteriorate. I also continue to use hearing aids sometimes but prefer sign language for communication.

Patricia Clark, age 71

Wellington, New Zealand

My parents were rhesus-incompatible and already had one child. If the parents are rhesus-incompatible, the child is born with a blood type that is not compatible with the mother's, a condition called hemolytic disease of the newborn. I was born jaundiced and sickly and spent the first two months of my life in the hospital.

When I was about ten months old, my parents noticed that my eyes were well out of alignment. I was found to have keratoglobus in both eyes. This is a severe distortion in the corneas (and is degenerative). I was fitted with corrective lenses, and the glasses were held on with elastic.

My mother was critical of my poorly developing speech from the start and shouted at me a lot for not listening or for not speaking clearly. I knew there was something wrong with me but had no idea what it was. I became quiet, afraid I would be scolded for not understanding someone correctly. If I was uncertain about what had been said, I would simply answer at random. At school, I had a reputation for being very funny, but the teacher thought I was out of my mind. She consulted with another teacher, who said I was deaf, but my mother did not want to believe that. Over time, my speech and speech-reading improved and were not commented on, except by my mother.

When I was finally diagnosed with deafness at thirteen, it was a relief for me to know why I was different. My low vision seemed not to stigmatize me, and an orthopedic problem that put me in the hospital for a year at age seven also did not make me feel different from other people. But deafness certainly did.

An eye specialist ordered me to put drops in my eyes for days before every appointment. The drops reduced my vision, and since I was speech-reading—although I didn't know it at the time—the loss of vision was terrifying. I got very upset every time I had to use those drops.

My vision has gotten worse over time. I am now preparing myself for when I will become totally blind.

Scott Stoffel, age 39

Lansdale, Pennsylvania

My parents got the first clue that I had a vision problem when I was four. They noticed that when I played with my toy cars, I would lie on the floor and hold the cars close to my face. A trip to the eye doctor revealed I was legally blind from optic nerve atrophy and that glasses wouldn't help.

But for me, the understanding that I didn't see nearly as well as other kids didn't start to sink in until a few months after my folks had been informed of the problem. My father took me and some other kids to a wooded park in Clinton, Maryland. I vividly remember this incident; it was the root of many similar incidents that would follow and marked the beginning of the end of "normal" life for me. We were playing in a little fort with a ladder and some mock mounted guns. The others pretended the fort was under attack, and we all had to escape by jumping to a pole and sliding down to the ground. The pole was only about 18 inches from the platform, but that seemed like a long jump to a little kid. I assumed I could duplicate the jump-and-slide action the other kids performed with ease. But when I jumped, my vision prevented me from getting my hands on the pole. I fell down and got laughed at. I remember crying, but I don't know if it was from injury or humiliation. I didn't understand why I couldn't see the pole clearly enough to grab it, while it was so easy for the others.

The full force of being legally blind hit me in first grade, when I had to use large-print books. I was the only kid in the whole school who had large-print books. These were huge compared to regular textbooks and usually had to be divided into multiple volumes. Instead of a book bag, I needed a library cart. It made me "weird" to the other kids, and I hated it. I also found out I couldn't see what was on the chalkboard.

But the real knife in the back was when I found out I couldn't play baseball and a lot of other sports or games. My face was a ball magnet. I probably should have taken up boxing with all the sparring practice I got getting hit with balls I couldn't see coming. My family and counselors from the state Services for the Blind regarded this as an insignificant issue, just me missing out on a few common activities. But it was a lot more than that; it was failing to gain social acceptance.

To make matters worse, my parents noticed that my hands were skeletal and that I couldn't move the thumbs properly. They feared I had the same neurological disorder my sister, who was eight years older, had been born with. So when I was five, I was sent to Johns Hopkins Hospital in Baltimore to undergo two weeks of testing. It was like being a guinea pig in a mad scientist's laboratory. They stuck me everywhere with needles, zapped me with electricity, took X-rays until my internals were cooked just the way you like them, and in the end, announced that they had no idea what was causing my problems. All they did was speculate that my sister and I shared a yet-undiagnosed genetic disorder. Well, hallelujah.

All I knew was that I wasn't as good as other kids my age, and I didn't understand why. I hated the problems because they wouldn't let me fit in and be normal. I was an outgoing little kid, always looking for a group to play with. But as the disabilities took their toll, I withdrew. Ultimately, I started hating myself.

Today, I am profoundly deaf and legally blind and suffer from polyneuropathy.

Tonilyn Todd Wisner, age 38

Opelousas, Louisiana

I was born hearing and sighted. When I was six, it was found that I was completely deaf in my left ear, but no one knew why. It was the 1970s, and my parents didn't "advertise" my problem. My schoolteachers knew, but it was never talked about. I went to public schools, hearing with only my right ear. I didn't know any hard of hearing or deaf people, nor did I know there was such a thing as a deaf community.

When I was twelve, I was diagnosed with a brain tumor (cerebellar astrocytoma). It was the tumor that had cut the hearing and balance nerve on my left side. When doctors removed the tumor, they did a lot of damage in the process, and I was left with severe learning disabilities. Other cranial nerves were cut, such as the one that controls facial movements. Because of that, the left side of my face was permanently paralyzed.

Before the surgery, I was smart and had many friends. Afterward, my friends weren't my friends anymore. I was called a "freak" and other names. I was made fun of constantly at school, and the teachers did nothing about it.

I had started ballet when I was two years old, and despite having no balance function on the left side, I excelled. I was dancing *en pointe* at age seven, five years earlier than most girls. But I had to stop dancing after the brain surgery, doctor's orders. This was heartbreaking for me, but I was able to pick it up again as an adult.

I received a facial-nerve implant when I was thirteen. This was an experimental procedure at the time. The doctors took a nerve from my tongue and routed it through the sheath where the bad nerve was. Then I could control my face with my tongue, though not very well, and it was kind of freaky! I went to physical therapy for three years to help with this and also with my balance and coordination.

Since my face was paralyzed, my left eye didn't close. Because of this, my eye would dry out and become cracked, like chapped lips. I also had many ulcers on my cornea. This is all as painful as it sounds! I developed a condition called keratoconjunctivitis, which is chronic conjunctivitis ("pink eye") due to exposure. Because of the drying and ulcers, my cornea began to wear away. I suffered a slight vision loss from this as the years went on.

At present, I am totally blind and can only hear when I use my cochlear implant. I also have Meniere's disease and problems with vertigo.

Wendy Williams, age 57

St. Paul, Minnesota

As a toddler, I did not speak clearly. My brother, who was a year older than me, was able to make sense of my speech and told others what I said. My grandmother pointed out to my mother that I had a hearing loss, but my mother denied it.

When I was four years old, my mother witnessed me coming home from a friend's house, crossing a quiet street in a residential area. A car came right at me, the driver jamming on the brakes and honking the horn. Unaware of the car, I kept going and nearly got hit. The incident convinced my parents something was wrong, so they took me to a local doctor. He said I didn't have a hearing problem; I just wasn't paying attention. Thanks to the doctor, my hearing problem was ignored for a few years.

When I was six years old, I had surgery on both eyes to fix my strabismus [crossed eyes] problem. For a week, I had to lie on the hospital bed with my eyes bandaged. I well remember not only the challenge of having to lie still for an extended time, but also the exhausting struggle to communicate without speech-reading [i.e., reading lips]. No one realized it yet, but I depended heavily on speech-reading to understand other people.

At seven years old, an eye and ENT specialist acknowledged I might have a hearing loss and ordered I have my tonsils removed to see if it would improve my hearing. It didn't, but while I was in the hospital for this surgery, I became vaguely aware of another disability that was creeping up on me. I recall reaching for a glass of juice on the bed tray, having trouble seeing the glass, and accidentally knocking it over. The room was dimly lit, but other people could see just fine in there. I was the only one who had trouble, and it really puzzled me. The nurse scolded me for not being careful with the juice; she failed to comprehend that I was actually experiencing difficulty with night vision. This problem is often the first noticeable effect of RP, which I found out I had years later.

The night vision problem made its presence clearly known to me at Halloween. When I went out trick-or-treating with friends and family, I had a hard time seeing steps and curbs. The event was a physical ordeal for me, but I wanted the goodies badly enough to endure the bumps and bruises.

Then at eight, I contracted the measles and had a 106-degree fever. I nearly died. I remember experiencing an awesome light-warmth and fighting to stay there but was sent back against my wish. After this illness, I noticed I had more trouble understanding speech. I thought my hearing was worse, but my grandmother was convinced there was a change in my vision. Perhaps it was both; I don't know.

Finally, with the support of teachers in first, second, and third grade, a diagnosis confirmed I had a severe hearing loss. Hearing aids were not recommended, so I grew up relying on speech-reading. My mother wondered if the cause was maternal rubella, but this notion was never confirmed.

I now can hear with two cochlear implants, but my vision is gone.

1
Family Reaction and Support

How a family responds to a child's disabilities has a monumental impact on the child's life. Often, a youngster's ability to accept or at least cope with disabilities is a direct reflection of the family's response to the abnormal circumstances.

For this section, I asked my contributors to discuss how their families responded to their disabilities during childhood. Please understand that these responses are not report cards for parents. It is equally important to discuss the good and the bad in this very sensitive area in order to offer insights to families who are dealing themselves with children who are disabled. One must also keep in mind that few families (if any) are fully prepared to understand and deal on every level with a child who is disabled.

Addressing the immediate medical needs of a child is one thing, but properly addressing the psychological and social difficulties that disabilities bring is a much more complex issue. As you will see, many families sought medical assistance and the advice of professionals. It is interesting to note that when families received poor advice from those professionals, they had little way of knowing it and proceeded to follow that bad advice to the detriment of the child.

Sensitivity and love are crucial in helping the kids survive and cope. But understanding is another important factor that some children who are disabled don't get enough of. Even a caring family can hurt a child when they fail to truly understand what the child is going through.

The contributors share their personal experiences here not for the sake of reprimanding anyone, but to show what a child who is disabled must face and how family members can help—as well as how they often hurt.

Angela C. Orlando

When the doctor told my mother I had Usher's syndrome, she broke down and sobbed right in front of me. I was thirteen and scared out of my mind. Her tears told me that all was lost. I felt like my life was over. I will never forget that moment.

Once at home, my parents began to calm down and find the strength needed to support me during this difficult time of adjustment. We were lucky to live in a small university town. My parents contacted the Kent State Speech and Hearing Center to enroll me in aural therapy. They wanted more than anything to help me hear again.

I don't think my parents were in denial, but they were hearing culture people, so it was natural for them to push strategies to restore my hearing. I didn't mind that; I was hearing culture, too. I wanted to hear. The problem was that hearing aids didn't work for me, and nobody would listen to me or believe me when I tried to explain that. "She's just being a teenager," they said. Those words haunt me. The specialists at Kent State told my parents they had to push me to use the hearing aids and practice listening skills. They said the hearing aids would work if I would try to use them. They convinced my parents that I was just being vain and didn't want to look different from the other kids. What could my parents do? This was all so new to them. Here was this great specialist improperly advising them on how to handle the situation. They believed they were getting the right advice and followed it.

I was miserable. I couldn't hear. What started out as a mild hearing loss had become a profound loss within three years. But I wasn't allowed to learn sign language. The specialists said that would make me lazy, and I wouldn't try to listen.

I attended hearing therapy each week. The therapists stood behind me and spoke, so I couldn't read their lips. I couldn't even hear their voices, much less, repeat what they said. And all the time they scolded me for being lazy, for not trying to hear, for being too vain to wear my hearing aids. I was "just being a teenager." My parents followed their instructions. They forced me to wear hearing aids—or tried to. They pushed constantly. They used a little blackmail: "If you want to go to the mall, you have to wear your hearing aids." We fought a lot. I stayed in my room as much as possible. One time, my mother put one of my hearing aids in her ear and said she was amazed that she could hear people talking down the street. No one understood that when I wore them, all I heard was horrible crackles of sound and static. I got nothing meaningful at all out of them.

Looking back, I would say that my parents reacted in a normal and healthy fashion. They grieved and then accepted the news. They sought out professional help and followed the guidance they were given, even though it was the wrong advice. I just wish they had listened to me about what was going on. As an adult, I had the chance to prove myself, and everyone realized how wrong they'd been about me.

Christian S. Shinaberger

When my dad realized when I was eighteen months that I had a visual problem, my mom didn't want to believe it at first. But after doctors found cataracts and removed them, and I developed glaucoma as a result of the surgery, she knew I would eventually become blind. She decided to show me everything she could, while I still had some vision. She took me to parks and let me see and touch things. She continued to do the same thing when we moved back to the United States after spending a few years in Germany.

My parents got these really thick glasses for me. I think I had two pairs. One was for near vision and one for distance. They bought me a little red tricycle, a blue walking beam pedal car and a blue wagon. I used to pull the wagon with my tricycle, and my sister rode in it. But my sight soon deteriorated to the point where the glasses didn't help anymore. I was totally blind by age six.

But I didn't get a hearing aid until I was in second grade. My parents had been preoccupied with my vision problems and hadn't noticed that I also had some hearing loss.

I think my family did the best they could in dealing with me and my disabilities. My dad didn't tend to be personally involved in my childhood. He was a good provider, and he helped through the surgeries. His being a doctor was very handy in that respect. But my mom was more actively involved in my life. She was the one who researched things, such as finding a resource teacher to start me on learning Braille when I was in preschool. She was resourceful, too. For instance, when she wanted to teach me how to swim in a plastic backyard pool and the neighborhood dogs kept tearing it up, she got a metal trough to use as a lap pool for me.

My dad's influence in my life and our friendship didn't really develop until I was in high school. He was too busy "being a doctor" and chasing fantasies to spend much time with me when I was little.

Another important influence, albeit nonhuman, was my first pet desert tortoise, which I found shortly after we moved to California. As reptiles go, she was very affectionate. She liked coming into the house, would eat from my hand, and she wasn't afraid of people. I used to tell Ginger the tortoise all my secrets. I knew she wouldn't tell anyone else.

Christy L. Reid

After my parents learned I had optic atrophy, they did everything they thought would help me as a legally blind child. In those days during my childhood, our family frequently moved to a new city and new home. My dad, who worked as a sales manager for a large, national company, was transferred to a new location almost every year. That meant I had to frequently start a new school, too. But my mom and dad carefully chose new homes that would allow me to attend the school with the low vision services I needed.

My mom took me to visit a low vision specialist when I was in first or second grade; I can't remember now. But I remember we lived in Cincinnati, Ohio, at the time. That's when I was introduced to a magnifier, a Bubble, that became my best friend for the next seven or so years. I was very particular about the kind of magnifier I felt most comfortable with. The Bubble was like a small solid glass ball sliced perfectly in half. The flat side lay on the book or flat surface I wanted to look at and I pressed my stronger eye against the rounded part. I could read about two words at a time. Whenever I dropped the Bubble, it would crack in places. My mom probably ordered four to six replacements while I could use the Bubble.

By the time I was in college, my vision had deteriorated to a point where I couldn't use the Bubble. My parents bought me a closed-circuit TV (CCTV) to use during college.

Even though my parents did about everything they thought would help me as a legally blind child, there is one thing I wish they had done when I was in kindergarten and they learned I had optic atrophy: I wish I had immediately started working with a Braille teacher. If I had started learning Braille as a young child, it would have made a huge difference in my life. I don't blame them for not arranging Braille services; they were told by teachers and doctors that I had enough vision and didn't need to learn Braille. But as I got older and reading print got harder, learning Braille became an issue. I was ten years old, in the fifth grade, and very stubborn. We lived in Poplar Bluff, Missouri, then, and I was working with a very skilled vision specialist teacher. She wanted to teach me Braille, but I refused, saying I could see good enough and could use my Bubble. Of course, that was my fault; I had the opportunity to learn Braille. But I was too old to be forced into doing something I didn't want to do.

Looking back, my childhood was generally happy and normal. My parents always encouraged me to try to do things that interested me and were reasonably safe. I had friends to play with in the different places where we lived. I would spend the night with a friend and at other times, invite friends to sleep over at my house. My mom and dad treated me the same as they treated my younger sister and brother, scolding me when I was bad, playing with me, teaching me to be responsible by cleaning my room.

The only concern related to my low vision was several biking mishaps. I got my first bike for my sixth birthday, and for the next few years, I enjoyed biking like most kids. But by the time I was ten, my vision had worsened, and I experienced the first of several biking accidents. My mom was out shopping that day, and Dad was in the house with my sister and brother. I was on my bike crossing the street at the corner near our house. As I reached the middle, a motorcycle hit me smack in the center. I crashed onto the street, hitting my head. I think I felt stupid and didn't want all that attention that happened next. I jumped up, grabbed my bike, and tried to get away. But the motorcycle rider held me back and made me sit in the grass, while a neighbor went to get my dad. I kept insisting I was fine. When my dad got there, he didn't look too happy. I don't remember what was said, maybe I didn't hear it, but the motorcycle guy drove away and Dad made me come into the house and sit quiet for a while, which I didn't like much.

That was the first of several more accidents. The last one occurred when I was sixteen and a pick-up truck crushed my bike into a piece of junk. Luckily, it happened very slowly, so I was able to roll out of the way, unscratched. But my dad, with good reasons, absolutely refused to buy me another bike. That was the end of my biking days until many years later, when my husband and I bought a tandem.

Ilana Hermes

My mom told me that she almost had a nervous breakdown when I was born with hydrocephalus and that my dad told her to be strong for me, because I could not survive without her love. She was a very dedicated parent. When I was small, she carried me around the house while she did things. I was blind, so she introduced me to things by sense of touch, like she would open the cold water tap and hold my hand under the water for me to feel.

My father, mother, and sister were (and still are) beside me all the time. My father worked shifts when I was little, but I spent quality time with both my mother and father. My sister and I had normal sibling squabbles, but now that we are adults, we're closer. But since my mother was at home more, she was the one who had to deal with my tantrums and outbursts. She also had to rush me to the hospital when my shunt broke, while my dad was working.

My mother and I also had some clashes. Because I had lost sensation in my feet, I didn't like to wear shoes or socks. I couldn't explain it to her when I was little, so she would get mad at me. Once, she shredded my socks and threw them away, because I kept pulling them off. She understands now, but back then, it just seemed to her like I was being defiant.

I was a hyperactive child, and my teachers told my parents that I should be put on Ritalin. When my neurosurgeon found out about this, he commanded that they take me off Ritalin, because it masks some early signs and symptoms of shunt malfunction. As a young child, I couldn't express how I felt when the shunt didn't work right, so the masking effect was dangerous. So my parents had to be very watchful over me and regularly consult the doctors. I'm sure it was stressful for them.

My uncles, aunts, and cousins treated me as they treated my sister, and that was with love and caring. I must say that I kept myself aside when people came to visit because of my lack of social and group-interaction skills. Now that I'm older and have two cochlear implants, I socialize more with family, but I'd rather listen than talk. My hearing still isn't perfect, so I'm paranoid that I will misunderstand someone and say the wrong thing in response.

Judy Kahl

As I look back at my childhood, I can truly say that I thought I was normal. I attribute this to my parents, as they made everything "right" for me and did everything and anything possible to make sure "their Judy" was taken care of. I was an only child, and we lived very comfortably. My father was an engineering draftsman by day, taught music in our home two evenings a week, had his own Dixieland band, and frequently played in local country clubs on the weekend. This left my mother and me alone together a lot. She always encouraged me to invite my friends over for company and provided me with a "fun and loving" home. Since we had a small two-bedroom home, my mother was always close by and kept her ears open to whatever I was doing. I think my parents were overprotective at times, but this was one way of watching over me, by allowing me to have any and all friends to my house. I grew up in Sharpsville, Pennsylvania, a small town where everyone knew everyone, so it was easy to screen out any rowdies.

I remember my eighth birthday party was a spaghetti-and-meatballs dinner in our dining room. We all wore dresses and party hats, and we all tried our best to behave like ladies! My mother always had our home decorated for all holidays and that made it fun, too. Oh, yes, a party for every occasion in our home.

Whenever there was a new activity, like dance lessons, my mother would take me early to meet with the teacher and explain about my hearing loss and hearing aid. Believe me, Judy was kindly taken care of or Judy never went back to that teacher. I realize now that my mother had been doing these special things for me, but back then, I thought it was a perfectly normal thing for her to introduce me to the teacher. She handled things in a warm way, and consequently, I felt I could do anything and everything I wanted to do. I took gymnastics and dance lessons and piano lessons from my father, and my school lessons were important, too.

I was never "in the background" but was always a "doer" and involved in a lot of things, although I was not allowed to do everything. My father said "No" to dances at Thornton Hall, because that was too rowdy and I was too young—always an excuse if he didn't feel it would be good for his "little girl."

My mother had four sisters locally, and I had fourteen cousins, so every holiday and many weekends were filled with get-togethers and fun with my cousins.

I never heard my parents argue about how to handle me or emotionally upset about my handicap. Well, not in front of me, but I remember my mother saying later in life that it broke her heart to send off her little girl to school with a hearing aid and then to discover the hearing aid had gotten disconnected when I returned from school. I know there had to be some upsetting moments for them, but they were my cheerleaders in life and were supportive in everything I wanted to do. Fortunately, I did not give them problems, so it was an "easy street" life for all of us.

I firmly believe that my childhood has given me my positive attitude and fun outlook on life.

Mark Gasaway

My family tried to help me, but at the same time, let me continue to be who I was. They did not try to tell me that I was not able to do certain things just because I was deaf with limited vision. They continued to be my family and tried to help. However, in those early years, both parents were a bit overprotective.

My siblings had some attitude changes toward me. But overall, they were good about accepting the fact I was "different" than the brother they knew before the illness.

The things my family did to help me are numerous. They took me to see specialists who were recommended by doctors to see if they could help. I saw a lot of specialists who were able to fit me with glasses that helped my vision to some extent. My hearing was another story. My family took me to see a program manager for a speech and hearing center where I took classes in speaking and lip-reading. The lip-reading was not much help with my limited vision, so I decided it was not worth it to continue.

They also took me to see rehabilitation counselors, and we were lucky enough to find one that helped me a lot. I was also introduced to a hearing specialist who had me tested for hearing aids, which vocational rehabilitation (VR) service paid for.

I feel the things my family did to try to help me were the right things to do, and these things did help. If my family had not tried to do anything to help me, I would not be the person I am today. They deserve to be recognized for the effort they put into trying to help me. Upon learning that I had become deaf with limited vision, my parents and siblings accepted the limitations and then let me attempt to go beyond them. I am forever grateful to them for letting me be me and not trying to tell me I could not do something I truly wanted to do.

Melanie Bond

I believe my parents did a good job of raising me and my siblings to become independent thinkers. No one coddled me because of my disabilities, and for that, I'm deeply grateful that I have no compunction in taking a stand on matters that are important to me, even if I must stand alone. There is strength in being independent. Over time, my parents and my siblings became more comfortable in guiding me whenever I needed a helping arm.

Thank goodness that I didn't have overprotective parents! While my siblings spent time playing and hanging out with their friends, I was pretty much a loner and not much of a conversationalist. I can imagine that others thought me a dull person. But in my mind, my world was beautiful. I would often walk several blocks to Bancroft Park and play to my heart's content for hours and hours. The giant oak trees became my sentinels who watched over me, and the playground equipment gave me hours of fun and pleasure in what I called "my home away from home." My favorite ride was a lone wooden swing that was perched on the summit of a hill. On the upswing, I felt as if I was soaring up into the sky. And on the downswing, it was thrilling to dive toward the earth.

At the age of fifteen, I met up with some of my old oral deaf friends who had been looking for me. They began teaching me how to sign, and I could not learn it fast enough! Like a child, I went around asking, "What's the sign for this?" Signing came so naturally to me! Because of my deaf friends, I began to converse fluently in American Sign Language (ASL). I was ecstatic to be reunited with them and glad that my deafness was not an issue like it had been with hearing classmates and friends.

Patricia Clark

My sight problem was noticed soon after birth, and glasses were prescribed. The glasses were put on my face daily without comment, and I just took that for granted.

Deafness was not diagnosed until I was thirteen. By this time, my mother had punished me because of my failure to hear and respond properly, but I never understood what I'd done wrong. At age thirteen, a body-worn hearing aid was acquired from the city hospital. The audiology service there was nil—nobody even told me how to turn the aid off and on or that the batteries would die. My mother did not care to know, anyway. She joined in the fiction that you turn on a hearing aid and have instant hearing. Nobody told me about the problems of clothes rubbing against the aid or background noise. Since I failed to achieve normal hearing with the aid, I was treated like a failure. It was all my fault. My father and older brother ignored the situation, while my mother was angry with me. My father was at least prepared to go with me to the hearing aid vendor to get the aid fixed. This usually meant new batteries or valves.

In 1954, there were no significant services for the disabled in New Zealand, no counseling. Disabled children and adolescents were treated as though they had no feelings or needs and had to do as they were told by some very ignorant people. The important thing was to keep your head down and not be a nuisance to others. Disability was spoken of in whispers and was a subject of shame. We had a very conformist society.

My family did not shelter me at all and left me to cope with situations that were too hard for me to deal with alone. The reason for this was that these situations were too hard for them, too. My mother may have been loyal to me when speaking to other people, but she was very hard on me in person.

These days, families sometimes get involved in disability support groups. Disabled people may find employment, such as teaching or interpreting. My family would never have done that and are ignorant of disability to this day. They still don't know where I'm coming from, what I go through.

Scott Stoffel

My sister had been born eight years before me, and her problems were evident right away, so my parents had some "preparation" for what happened with me. One key difference between my sister and me was that my disabilities did not begin to manifest themselves until I was four. By this time, my sister had lost most of her hearing, gone through an ill-conceived spinal operation that added to her problems, and she had other problems that I never developed. In the beginning, the only problems I had were severe vision loss, mild hearing loss, and neuromuscular weakness in my fingers and toes.

My parents' response to my problems was to endlessly seek a cure. After I spent two weeks as a guinea pig at Johns Hopkins Hospital, the doctors decided that my sister and I had inherited some sort of genetic disorder that could not be cured. Well, that didn't stop my mother. I lost count of how many pediatricians and eye doctors she took me to see, mostly without benefit. While I think it was a good and logical course for my parents to seek medical help, I also feel we reached a point where it became obvious that modern medicine was not going to cure or correct my problems. It would have helped me a lot if my family had focused more on acceptance and adjustment.

My parents and my nondisabled older brother were nice to me. They bought me things and took me places. I idolized my brother, who was sixteen years older, when I was a kid. But their idea of "accepting" my disabilities hurt me in some ways. Once it became clear there was no cure for me, they simply became resigned about it. They had a disabled son—accept it and get on with life. At least they had one valid son, who played every sport and had all kinds of potential. No one expected much from me, because they "accepted" I was a defective child that couldn't be fixed. It never occurred to anyone that with some help, I might have been able to compete with so-called normal kids. Instead of helping build me up, helping me develop talents to offset my limitations, they took to patronizing me and just let me go my own way. "Don't tell him he's worthless; just let him think he's good at something, even though we all know he isn't." That seemed to be their attitude. Of course, I am not a mind-reader. This is just the way I interpreted my family's attitude toward me.

I was well aware of my limitations from going to public schools and struggling to compete with other kids. I didn't have a special talent that came shining through the clouds and was perpetually outdone by the normal kids of my age. The concept of "trying harder" faded from my mind, because I discovered through numerous bad experiences that when I tried harder and still fell way short, it made me feel worse. Training, developing a skill, was a concept that had no meaning to me, so I never went in that direction as a kid. My father took me to a swimming class when I was five but decided further athletic development of his defective son was pointless. Never mind that having weak fingers made speed swimming a poor choice for me to pursue seriously, since I couldn't keep my fingers closed to properly "scoop" the water (try to imagine rowing a boat with a pitchfork). But I was told I was incredible, amazing, just fantastic at swimming. Of course, my speed was too slow to compete in races. But for me, I did great.

"For you, that was great!" That became my song at home. For someone who had zero potential, I did great. Sure, people had toenail fungus that could achieve more, but for me, that was great. I grew up feeling like nothing I did mattered, because I was *me*. Other parents taught their kids sports or crafts or whatever, but mine didn't see any reason to bother. They gave me lots of presents on birthdays and Christmas. That was nice. But as I got older and found myself falling farther and farther behind my peers, I just assumed that was automatic. I was a defect, after all. They found it easier to just do things for me, rather than trying to help me learn to do things for myself.

Whenever I struggled and complained to my parents, my father had a ready reply every time: "Look at your sister. She has it *ten times* worse than you! You don't know how lucky you are." And, miraculously, all of my problems disappeared. They were supposed to, anyway.

On the plus side, I always had a good home and people that were there when I needed them the most. The excessive gifts were probably an effort to cancel the social pains and frustrations I experienced. I can appreciate that. I think what was lacking was the knowledge of how to handle a mainstreamed disabled child. The doctors never had anything to say about how a kid like me could be mainstreamed without all the psychological woes, and the state Services for the Blind didn't seem to know much on that level, either.

Tonilyn Todd Wisner

Since I was so young, six years old, I'm not sure how my parents found out about my hearing loss, nor if they responded to it right away. I do know I saw an audiologist, and that was when we found out that my hearing nerve wasn't functioning at all. I couldn't use hearing aids because they don't help if the nerve to the brain doesn't function. I don't think I had any diagnostic tests to find out "why" my nerve wasn't functioning. If they had done a CAT scan, they would have detected my brain tumor six years earlier, and I wouldn't have had such extensive brain damage. That has always eaten at me, but as far as I know, the doctors could have talked my parents out of doing tests and just told them to accept my hearing loss.

My deafness wasn't talked about, so I had to explain it to other people whenever I had trouble understanding. I resent the fact that I wasn't involved with other hard of hearing or deaf children, that I wasn't given the opportunity to feel like I belonged. I didn't belong in the hearing world where I was laughed at for saying something off-topic because I misunderstood, or for pronouncing something wrong. I hated talking to people and avoided groups. I wasn't put in special classes or therapy. I learned to lip-read on my own without knowing I was doing it.

My teachers knew of my hearing problem, and they just sat me in the front row so I could hear them best. My mom wrote notes to my teachers every year, asking them to do this. But that was all. I almost failed a class in fourth grade because I wasn't doing the homework. It turned out that the teacher wrote the homework on the side of the board and told the class this is where it would be every day. I didn't hear that, so I didn't know.

When I was twelve, the first sign of something else being wrong was that my left eye started to "roam." A teacher told my mom about it. We saw an eye doctor who gave me glasses and ignored me when I said they hurt my eyes. Then I started waking up with migraine headaches and vomiting every morning. I don't know how many "specialists" my parents took me to see, but it went on for a number of months. I was told I had sinus problems, needed glasses—every doctor had a different opinion. Nothing helped, but the "specialists" knew what they were talking about and weren't going to listen to a twelve-year-old, even though I knew for sure there was something seriously wrong with me. I eventually went back to my ENT, Dr. Norma Kearby, whom I had been seeing since I was six. She was a very understanding lady and is the only reason I am alive today. I went to her crying, ran into her arms, and told her that something was *really* wrong with me and no one would listen. She got me in to see a neurologist right away. I had a CAT scan (there were no MRIs back then) and an electroencephalogram (it reads brainwaves). By the time we left, had something to eat, and had gotten home, the doctor had called my house and told my sister that we all needed to see her immediately. I remember my parents going in to talk with her first. Then my sister, Dawnlyn, who was seventeen at the time, and I were called in. My mom was crying, while the doctor explained to me that I had a brain tumor. Dawnlyn broke down in tears. I looked at the doctor and said, "Then take it out." I knew what a brain tumor was, but it didn't scare me; I just wanted it out so I wouldn't be sick anymore. I was also annoyed, as only a twelve-year-old could be, at the other doctors for not listening to me. There had been signs of the brain tumor since I was as young as four years old—my face would get slack on the left side, plus the nerve deafness and a lack of coordination I had on my left side. When the tumor was found, I had no more than a week to live had it not been removed.

My parents and sister were very supportive through all of this. My parents were very open with me and told me everything the doctors told them. I knew I could die. I knew I could end up a vegetable. And I knew that, if I came out of surgery alive, the doctors said I would never be able to live alone (and I really hated it when people told me I could "never" do something). But as far I was concerned at that point, what did doctors know? They'd almost let me die! Some may think it was wrong of my parents to tell me those things, but I was very mature for my age and was glad that nothing was kept from me.

I was put in the hospital that same afternoon. The surgery to remove the tumor occurred on Mother's Day. When I woke up afterward, the first thing I did was ask for my mom. When she came in the room, I said over the breathing tube, "Happy Mother's Day!" I guess the nurses reminded me it was Mother's Day while I was still groggy.

My sister was in high school and got permission to take a different bus home that passed the hospital, and the bus driver made a special stop at the hospital to drop her off. She was there every afternoon after school. One of my best memories is of her dedicating a song to me one Friday night, when a local DJ accepted dedication requests.

My mom almost never left the hospital. She ate there, showered there, and slept there. She had started making my sixth-grade graduation dress before I had the surgery, and she finished it by hand, right there in the hospital. My dad was there every day after work. I can't express enough how grateful I am for such a caring family. The nurses were awesome, too; they saved all the purple popsicles for me!

After nagging my doctor for ten days, he finally let me go home. I was determined to go to my sixth-grade graduation ceremony that year. I did, and I walked on the stage with a friend helping me.

My parents were overprotective in some ways, but underprotective in others. For the first year after the surgery, I wasn't allowed to do anything by myself—I couldn't even shower alone! My mom showered with me. When I went to color guard camp, my mom was a chaperone and followed me everywhere I went. Both of my parents, my dad especially, became very overprotective about me doing anything where I might get hurt. They didn't discourage me from doing anything, but I could tell they worried.

However, when it came to the fact that I couldn't seem to remember things after a few days or that I would sometimes "freeze up" for a moment and forget who and where I was (petit mal seizures, I now know), I wasn't taken seriously. Or at least it wasn't brought up to a doctor or dealt with in any way. I think the experience of almost losing me scared them so much that they just couldn't accept there was something new wrong with me.

We are a very close family today. I wish they had handled some things differently—I struggled with so much alone—but I have no anger or resentment toward them and love them for everything they went through and did for me.

Wendy Williams

Upon being told by my grandmother that I appeared to have a hearing problem because of my garbled speech as a toddler, my mother initially denied it. A few years later, when my mother witnessed me crossing a quiet, residential street and being oblivious to an oncoming vehicle, despite the horn honking, she was convinced I did have a hearing loss. But a local doctor dismissed it as me not paying attention. After seeing an eye and ENT specialist for corrective strabismus eye surgery when I was six years old, he supported my mother's perception of my hearing impairment and removed my tonsils the following year to hopefully improve my hearing. But it did nothing to help, and my hearing problem was left alone for a while. Finally, at age eight and with the backing of my teachers, my severe hearing loss was diagnosed, though hearing aids were not thought to be helpful, so I continued to rely on speech-reading.

I was also struggling with night blindness and a decreasing field of vision in both eyes (e.g., tripping over a bicycle lying on the ground, bumping into people alongside of me and hitting my head on tree branches). My parents kept taking me to the eye and ENT specialist, who tested my visual acuity and fields, and his only remark was that I had "tunnel vision."

The manifestations of my dual disability, still undiagnosed, both scared and frustrated my mother. I was the target of her verbal and physical abuse for the first two decades of my life. She screamed at me, called me "stupid," and hit me from head to toe. She treated me like I was being "bad." After a family friend visited us once, my mother asked me if I was scared of her (my mother), because this friend perceived it to be so. I lied and said "no," in part because I was frightened, in part because I did not want to hurt her. When I shared my abuse experiences with my grandmother, it backfired on me; my mother felt I had squealed on her.

When I woke up in the morning, I didn't know whether my mother would be calm, silent, or angry. If she was calm, she was both protective and encouraging. She reminded me over and over again I would not be "sitting at home collecting the blind pension." She could be humorous, too. If she was silent, she did not interact with the family, and I'd wonder what I had said or done to cause this response. If she was angry, then I was abused. Sometimes, my mother motivated me to want to strive in life, whereas other times her abusiveness knocked me down, making me feel unworthy and angry, fearful and distrustful of other people.

My parents tried a few times to enroll me in a deaf school to provide education and socialization, as well as an emotional break for my mother and me. The requests were denied on the grounds that I'd be bored and should continue in the public school, even though my grades were low. I grew up in a rural area, and my mother did not have the resources and supports to cope with what likely was a terrifying experience for her.

In the midst of all this, there was Lopey, the collie-shepherd family dog, who gave me the love to keep going, to survive.

When I was nineteen and still living at home, the eye and ENT specialist referred me to more specialized doctors. Behind closed doors, one doctor told my parents that I would go blind and to not share this devastating news with me. About seven years later, I started seeing a psychologist, because I thought there was a psychological factor to my worsening vision. After all, I could read small newspaper print, so why did I constantly trip over things? After struggling with my vision problem for another three years, I learned from an optometrist that I had RP. This fact combined with my deafness led to the deduction that I had Usher's syndrome. I likely had been legally blind for years without realizing my visual field was that bad. After I talked to my parents about the diagnosis, they stated they had known for years and had been advised not to tell me.

At the time I found out I had RP/Usher's, I immediately felt a sense of relief in that there was an explanation for what was happening to me. I was surprised my parents had known and for that long, but I put it on the back burner because I needed to adjust to the more critical issue of being deaf-blind. Over time, I felt mixed emotions about the withholding of information. I felt angry about all the years of struggling with what I didn't have an explanation for, while they secretly did. On the other hand, at the time my parents first knew, I was depressed with the deafness and clumsiness and the abuse, and perhaps the Higher Power knew I was not up to coping with the RP/Usher's diagnosis back then.

To her dying day, my mother blamed the "inherited component" of Usher's syndrome on my father and said it had not come from her. I told her she had no way of knowing it was going to happen. [Usher's syndrome can only be inherited if both parents carry the associated recessive gene.] I used to feel guilty and responsible for her unhappiness, but I later realized her unhappiness was much deeper; I found out she had been an abused child, too.

2

Education Part I: Primary and Secondary School Experiences

School is far more difficult for children with sensory disabilities, both academically and socially. There are many ways in which parents, teachers, and special services can help these children get the most out of primary and secondary school.

When I asked the contributors to discuss their school experiences, several important issues surfaced:

First of all, children who are disabled frequently have difficulty telling teachers what they need to succeed in class. Some are too embarrassed to speak up. Some just don't realize what they're missing or what could be done to help them get what they're missing in classes. So if parents and teachers fail to take the initiative, a child who is deaf-blind may simply sit quietly in class without learning the whole of lessons.

Another key issue is making friends in school and finding ways to fit in. This is particularly difficult for children who are disabled attending "normal" schools. Special services, such as state Services for the Blind, offer little or no help at all in this area. Should they? Is social development important to a child? Many believe it is, but to this day, the issue is largely ignored. So many children with disabilities struggle to find acceptance among their peers at school and grow up with poor self-esteem, depression, and other psychological problems.

The accounts below also reveal many little things that can help or hinder children who are deaf-blind in school.

Angela C. Orlando

I attended Kent [Ohio] public schools from kindergarten through twelfth grade. Kent is known for excellence in education. We are a small town but with many resources and services because of [Kent State] University.

Kent has a fantastic special education department. It's the best place in the area to be, if you have special needs.

So why was it so difficult for me?

I think the problem was that the school system is used to young children coming into kindergarten with special needs. They do an assessment in the early grades and then work out an educational plan for the disabled child. By middle school and high school, there is an established working plan on how to deal with each child. The new teachers just follow what has been done for years; they don't have to worry about figuring things out.

But what happens when the child doesn't begin to have problems until the later grades? I had no disability at all until eighth grade when I began losing my hearing. Then it steadily worsened, until I was totally deaf in tenth grade. Soon after that, I began losing my vision. I think the high school really had no idea what to do for me, because there was no previously developed plan for my needs. At first, the teachers were told of my hearing loss and that I was to sit up front in class. That was the extent of my accommodations. I didn't even have an Individual Education Plan (IEP). I was totally on my own in trying to get around my disabilities and pass my classes. I couldn't hear the teachers. I didn't know about homework assignments or when we were to have a test. If I failed the test, I felt it was what I deserved for being so stupid and not knowing what was going on. My grades quickly dropped, but I believed it was my fault, not the school's.

I felt like an unwanted member of the school. Teachers were instructed not to call on me, so they wouldn't put me on the spot. Some teachers never spoke to me at all. It was like I was invisible.

My father fought for me and my educational rights. In eleventh grade, I was finally given an IEP. But instead of feeling like the school and my teachers were helping me, I felt like they were smothering me. They went from one extreme to another. I was given a tutor I had to work with every day during study hall. That would have been okay, except that I was an advanced student, and the tutor didn't know my subjects. She wanted to work on things I didn't need help with. They also had me seeing the school psychologist, whom I didn't like, and working with a speech teacher.

After a few months of this, I finally got fed up. This is when I came out of my shell and demanded to be treated like a normal student.

My dad likes to tell the story of how I fired my tutor and psychologist. I confronted each teacher and told them what I needed from them. If they forgot to put an assignment on the board, I turned it in late with a note reminding them that all assignments had to be written down for me. If I failed a test because I didn't know about it, I demanded a retest.

But I still couldn't hear my teachers, so I learned to teach myself. I used the books and notes I copied off the board and studied them until I understood the concepts. It forced me to work much harder than the other students. I did homework during lunch and study hall and still had hours of work to do each night.

I remember one incident in Advanced English 12. We had just read the book *Heart of Darkness* by Joseph Conrad. Then we spent several class sessions watching the movie adaptation called *Apocalypse Now*. On that Friday, we were assigned an in-class essay to compare and contrast the book and movie. This teacher didn't even talk to me. A friend in the class would write down the topic of the essay and hand it to me, so I knew what to do. I was in a state of panic—how could I compare the book and movie when I didn't understand a word of the movie? Our school didn't have a closed caption (CC) decoder. I went up to the teacher and explained my problem. He was very firm: "Do the assignment or get an F on the essay, your choice." I finally started my essay, but I changed the topic a little. I wrote a very clear and concise paper on why a person who is hard of hearing is unable to do such an assignment and would be unfairly punished to be failed for it.

I was very nervous on Monday when I came to class. I was sure I would get a bad grade and that this teacher would be mad at me. He gave me a strange look before handing back my paper. He had given me an A+ and wrote a note that said, "I'm sorry. I didn't understand." After that he was one of my biggest supporters.

The lack of closed captions at school was a big problem. We watched a lot of movies in English, sociology, and history. In twelfth grade, I took a class called "American Pop Culture" and had to watch several movies a week. There was no textbook, so most of the information came from videos. I went to libraries to find copies of these videos to watch at home with my own CC machine. Many times, I couldn't find the videos, or the videos weren't even captioned. My teachers had to give me notes on the material.

My pop culture and sociology teacher started a two-year battle to get the school system to buy a CC decoder for the high school. The machine finally arrived the very last week of my senior year. My sociology teacher proudly showed me one captioned movie before I graduated. It didn't do me much good, but I figured it might help other students who attended the school after me.

I felt like I was on my own in school. In the last two years of high school, I did get good grades but only because I worked so hard to get them. I put more effort into my studies than my close friends, who were all Advanced Placement and top-ten students.

At the end of my senior year, I received a second-year scholar award. My friends got fourth-year scholar awards, top students' recognition, and major college scholarships. I was embarrassed. I was sitting with mostly sophomores. But my mother couldn't have been more proud of me. She knew what I had overcome all on my own to earn that little second-year award.

Although I eventually excelled in academics, on the social level, school was very hard for me. I lost all my "cool" friends in eighth grade when I started losing my hearing. After that, the only people who wanted to hang out with me were the "nerds." But even then, I had a hard time. I couldn't hear my friends when they spoke to me, so they had to write things down or finger spell to me. I couldn't talk on the phone. I didn't listen to music or go to movies. My friends never asked me to hang out with them after school or on the weekends.

I had no boyfriends in school. I went on just one date to a movie, but later on, he gave me a note saying he was really uncomfortable around me because I couldn't hear him. I didn't go to homecoming dances or to the prom—no one wanted to go with me. I felt very isolated, alone, and sad. I could spend a whole day at school, and no one, teacher or student, would talk to me. It's not surprising that I was very depressed during my school years. But nothing I tried to do ever seemed to help the situation.

Christian S. Shinaberger

I first attended Montessori school briefly when we lived in Silver Spring, Maryland. I could still see a little then. I don't know how well I could hear at that point. I think I was about three years old. My mom said

I was "just too precious" at that age, but I don't remember much about the school. I remember enjoying washing the desks and playing in an old boat outside there.

When we moved to Atlanta, I attended another private school, Lovett. My vision deteriorated rapidly, so I was introduced to my first special ed teacher there. Her name was Christine George. She exposed me to Grade 1 Braille and had a neat little wooden train you could put together and play with. I didn't stay at Lovett very long, as we moved to California after only a short time in Georgia.

We moved to California for two reasons. First, my dad had an offer to work with some other doctors at the VA hospital and hemodialysis program. Second, we learned that the Santa Monica public school system had a program for mainstreaming blind students.

In the first grade, I was very lucky and got a great special ed teacher named Denise Ecter. She taught me Grade 1 and 2 Braille, and I got two years' worth of training in one year. This proved to be fortunate, as I would receive no more Braille training from that point onward from the school system. I had to teach myself Braille after that, including Nemeth Code (a Braille code for mathematics), which I never really mastered.

I don't think most of my teachers paid that much attention to me. I had one teacher in second grade who was young and interested. She found short, high-interest stories in Braille, which had complex questions at the end to test reading comprehension. She realized I was very bright and made an effort to help me get the most out of her class. I really enjoyed those exercises and appreciated what she did for me.

This didn't last long, because the idiot who ran the special ed program for Santa Monica, didn't like teachers who showed initiative or who dealt with students differently without going through him. He used the B. F. Skinner–style training technique [i.e., using negative reinforcement or consequences for failure to do things as he dictated]. My mom got so fed up with the special ed program that she found a teacher at the school in our neighborhood where my sister went who agreed to take me. Sadly, the special ed director scared that young, smart teacher, Miss Howard, into backing off. I think she would have been very good with disabled kids, if she had been allowed to work with them on her own.

I attended sixth grade at Franklin, a new school my mom moved me to. A man named John Seal agreed to work with me there. He had a very different approach to teaching me. He had us do science projects, like growing lima beans in different levels of light, and saw to it that I got to touch things and stayed involved. We did a class report on China, and I had to read things and contribute. He got a set of Braille dictionaries for me to work with. My mom found a typing tutor, and I learned touch typing in order to do lessons for class. Each year, the sixth-grade class went to Camp Colby, an early settlement near Santa Monica. We worked on fire trails, and one night Mr. Seal came for me and had arranged a private touching tour of the Colby family museum. I got to touch everything and ask questions.

Junior high was when I really got into school. There were two other blind students in the school system whose parents hated what the special ed director was doing. They had their sons in a different junior high, but my mom learned from them. I met my first science teacher at Lincoln Junior High School. She taught me a lot. I passed all the exams in her class on the first try, even the one on how to use a microscope, despite not being able to use one. I usually did well in English and history, but I never really liked Spanish. I used bilateral hearing aids and hated trying to hear lectures and group discussions, but most teachers didn't have time to teach me one-on-one.

Science became my favorite subject from that point onward. In fact, I flunked Spanish in high school. I ended up taking Latin, which I actually enjoyed. My Latin teacher often met with me at lunchtime and helped me keep up. There was no listening; it was all reading, translating, learning conjugations, and so on. Latin is a pretty consistent language phonetically, which was helpful.

I don't recall being given any note-takers until junior high school. I mostly survived in the early grades on my mom's reading to me. I had a very good memory. In the sixth grade, I did get some notes and took some of my own. Mr. Seal and my mom got a couple of Braille typists who worked for the school district to print class materials in Braille for me. I could type answers to exam questions—most exams were done up in Braille.

From junior high on up, I had to find note-takers in my classes. They gave me carbon copies of their notes, which I then took to the Braille typists and got my notes in a form I could read. I did that in junior college, as well. I also tried taping lectures for some classes, and it usually was marginally useful. Often, the recordings weren't clear enough for me to use. In high school, for long-term projects, I'd get books from the library, and they'd arrange to get them or specific chapters recorded, so I could listen to them and get information that way.

Throughout my early years in school, I usually got "given" to other students at recess. They were assigned the task of staying with me on the playground. I had an easier time making friends with the girls, and that worked out pretty well. I got along fairly well with both genders from junior high up, but I didn't spend much time with other kids.

Christy L. Reid

I attended mostly public schools throughout my early educational experience. However, when my hearing loss made it too difficult to function in a regular public school class, I was transferred to the state school for the blind for eighth and ninth grade with the hope the smaller enrollment would help. But as it turned out, the school for the blind was not able to help, either.

As a legally blind student, I did not experience any serious problems. But by the time I was eleven years old and was attending sixth grade at a public school in Poplar Bluff, Missouri, my deteriorating hearing changed all that. I stopped paying attention to the teacher and started reading books in the classroom. I did not have other services, except spending an hour each day working with a vision specialist teacher, and I was provided with large print materials. I don't know what the teachers thought; I did not understand myself what was happening. I felt very isolated and confused.

By the time I was in seventh grade at the junior high, it was really awful. I had, as a younger girl, been socially involved with other kids. But as a twelve-year-old, I dreaded lunchtime. I felt like a stranger surrounded by hundreds of faces I couldn't recognize. I brought my own lunch and liked to buy a shake because it was easier than trying to get through the lunch line and choosing foods that I couldn't see, and I couldn't understand the workers standing behind the counters. I can't remember ever sitting beside someone I knew during lunchtime.

Academically, I was failing all my subjects. I would just sit there in the classrooms reading books, not able to understand the teachers.

I remember at one point, my math teacher stopped in front of my desk and slammed his fist down pretty hard onto the desk and said in a very loud voice, "Young lady, pay attention!" I remember hearing and understanding him because he was standing directly in front of me and spoke loudly. I put my book down and slid down into my chair, trying to hide.

During that year in seventh grade, my teachers and parents decided I should attend the Missouri School for the Blind (MSB) the following year. But at MSB, the academic problem didn't improve, in spite of the much smaller enrollment. My hearing continued to worsen, and it became almost impossible to understand teachers in the classrooms.

However, one of the best things that happened in my whole life was that I began working with a teacher who was a speech pathologist. She helped me to understand what was happening to me and taught me basic coping skills. For example, if I didn't understand a person the first time, then ask them to please repeat. Before I met her, I would usually say, "What?" Then if I still didn't understand the word, she suggested I ask the person to spell the word I didn't understand. But the best method that proved to work for me was to ask the person to please write what they were saying in large print.

The speech pathologist also took me to visit an audiologist, where I received my first hearing aid. I hated the hearing aid, complaining that it wouldn't stay on behind my ear when I did cartwheels. At that time, I was a member of the cheerleading team, and I felt embarrassed about the hearing aid. The speech pathologist merely said to tape it to my head.

In general, the hearing aid didn't help my hearing problem. It made sounds louder, but my brain couldn't always translate the sounds into words (due to auditory neuropathy).

Teachers finally understood that because of my hearing problem, combined with my vision issues, I needed more help, and I was transferred back to public school in Poplar Bluff. I entered tenth grade at the Poplar Bluff High School and was provided with a full-time class aide who accompanied me to all my classes and wrote notes in large print. I also began working with a deaf education teacher and began learning sign language. Academically, things really improved. With the class aide's help from writing notes, I was able to follow class discussions and got all my homework assignments.

Years later, my deaf-blind son, Ben, is experiencing similar problems. When he was almost three years old, he was diagnosed with optic atrophy. A few weeks later and while under anesthesia, an audiologist performed an ABR (auditory brainstem response) and discovered abnormal responses. My husband, Bill, and I were shocked. We couldn't believe this was happening to our little son. He was just recovering from a rare childhood disease and had undergone two years of chemotherapy treatment and many hospital visits. In addition, not long before Ben's vision and hearing abnormalities were discovered, he had been diagnosed by an endocrinology doctor with a condition called diabetes insipidus. This is a form of diabetes in which the pituitary gland has been damaged, resulting in excessive thirst and urination. The endocrinologist prescribed a drug for Ben that controls the symptoms and that he must take twice a day for the rest of his life.

Having to deal with all of these problems and then the discovery of his legal blindness and possible deafness was a bit too much to swallow. But Bill and I wanted our children to have a successful future, and the way to reach that goal for Ben was to get the help he needed while he was young. We were living in Tupelo, Mississippi, at that time. There were no early intervention services whatsoever that could meet Ben's needs. We decided to move to Pittsburgh, Pennsylvania, where I knew some people in the deaf-blind community and where I felt sure I could get set up so I could function independently as a stay-at-home mom. In many ways, it was a good decision to move to Pittsburgh. We got Ben involved in an excellent early intervention program through the Pittsburgh public school system. He began working with a teacher who introduced him to Braille, using a white cane and other vision-related aids; plus, she knew a little sign language and began working on tactile signing with Ben. All in all, Ben had a wonderful start in Pittsburgh.

When Ben was five years old, we moved to Poplar Bluff and enrolled him in kindergarten in the public school. At that time, his hearing loss was very mild; he could often hear and understand speech. Like me, he worked an hour a day with a vision specialist teacher, but unlike me, he was being taught to read and write Braille. He also worked with an orientation and mobility teacher once a month during the school year, practicing white cane skills. During that first year in kindergarten, things went all right. There was a hearing-blind girl in his kindergarten class, and Ben enjoyed spending time with her.

But when that first year drew to an end, Ben's vision specialist teacher felt Ben should repeat kindergarten, because as she put it, Ben didn't know any Braille before starting to work with her. I was surprised, of course, having seen Ben working with his teacher in Pittsburgh. The Pittsburgh teacher had taught Ben the concept of writing Braille by letting him "scribble" with the Brailler as a sighted child would do with a pencil. In addition, she taught him how to trace with his fingers and follow tactile lines in books, which is a technique for teaching very young children to get ready for reading Braille. But she hadn't taught him the actual Braille alphabet; he would have worked on that in kindergarten if we had stayed in Pittsburgh.

During his first year in kindergarten, Ben started experiencing behavior problems during his sessions with the vision specialist teacher. He would have temper tantrums, throw things, scream, and cry. The cause for these temper tantrums was that he did not want to do the work the vision teacher said he had to do. He was five years old at this time, and he could hear and understand her speech. But because of these temper fits, a lot of time during the sessions with the vision teacher was wasted, and by the end of that first year, he didn't know enough Braille to be successful in first grade. Bill and I agreed that Ben should repeat kindergarten; we wanted him to be successful at school.

But the behavior problems continued over the next few years. Ben continued working with the vision teacher an hour a day. He also had a full-time class aide who started working with him during the first year of kindergarten. The class aide didn't know any Braille when she started, but she was very dedicated to her job of helping Ben at school, staying with him all day, helping to modify things for him. She learned Braille with Ben during the sessions with the vision teacher. Ben became attached to his aide and saw her as his friend and helper.

By the time Ben entered second grade, his deteriorating hearing became noticeable, even though he could still often hear and understand speech. I had met the deaf education teacher the year before, and we had become friends. She was deaf herself and had children of her own. She agreed to put Ben in her work schedule and began working with him during second grade, teaching him sign language.

In addition, Ben's vision teacher, his class aide, and the deaf education teacher attended several workshops sponsored by the Missouri Deaf-Blind Outreach Project. These workshops were called Hands-in-Hands and focused on the basic tactile sign communication techniques needed when communicating with deaf-blind children. Ben made very good progress with the deaf education teacher, as they set up a good working relationship.

Unfortunately, the deaf education teacher got another job in a different part of the state and moved away. During third grade, Ben's hearing worsened, and he was having trouble following spoken speech. He had good communication at home and in the family, but at school, it was becoming more and more of a struggle, in spite of the Hands-in-Hands workshops his vision teacher and class aide had attended the year before. His class aide started learning some more sign language and started interpreting a little for him. The Missouri Deafblind Project was contacted, and the specialists there recommended more sign language.

Yet, the behavior problems during sessions with the vision teacher continued and got worse. We do not believe that these problems were caused by Ben's lack of understanding. The vision teacher could finger spell and often wrote Braille notes for Ben when he didn't understand. But these problems had started back in that first year of kindergarten and had never improved. Ben liked to be the boss and had a hard time accepting that the vision teacher was boss. For example, one day in fourth grade, the vision teacher told him to do something, but when he didn't hear her, she started to finger spell. He cut in and said that she didn't know sign language and needed to Braille it. Ben is a smart, strong-willed person who has been through much more than most kids, but his father and I and other family members have been trying to get him to understand that he should respect adults, especially teachers, even when he doesn't want to do the work.

When Ben was near the end of fourth grade, Bill and I took him to St. Louis Children's Hospital for an audiology evaluation. We had never had him examined by an audiologist, although he had visited an audiologist at St. Jude when he was about seven or eight years old, and they had not been able to get enough information to make an audiogram. I knew that having Ben evaluated by an audiologist and having a new audiogram developed would help his situation at school. During his IEP meeting, which was held shortly before his audiologist appointment, several of his teachers commented on the fact that Ben could understand their speech in a quiet room without sign language. At other times, they said, he didn't understand. I could, of course, perfectly understand this. I had experienced exactly the same thing. After examining Ben, the audiologist concluded Ben had a severe to profound hearing loss. He was eleven years old, was legally blind and almost deaf. We want so much for Ben to grow up, to be independent, go to college, get a good job, and perhaps start a family of his own. With the new audiology information in hand, we hope Ben's current school will accept the fact that he needs more help related to his hearing loss and hire an interpreter for him.

He is very fortunate to have very good Braille reading and writing skills—something I didn't have when I was his age and something that made it really difficult for me later in life. With these excellent Braille skills and tactile sign language skills, many doors will open for him, if he can overcome his behavior problems.

Socially, Ben is much more isolated than I was. He has difficulty getting involved with other children because of his hearing. And his low vision often makes it dangerous for him to participate in sports activities, although he loves to be involved. During his first two years of living in Poplar Bluff, we signed him up for soccer, which he loved to play. But after a few head-on collisions with other players, we decided that was enough. He tried to participate in Tiger Club, but Bill had to interpret for him, and it became too difficult trying to help him get involved. The same problem happened when he tried wrestling. His low vision and not being able to understand the coach made it too hard.

However, he can socialize with just a few other kids. During his eleventh birthday, the four boys he had invited from his class, showed up at his cosmic bowling party. It was dark and noisy in the bowling alley, not a great place for communicating with deaf-blind people, but the four guests from Ben's class made an effort to involve him, using tactile nonverbal gestures, like shaking his hand, clapping him on the back. It was very touching to see the young boys interacting with Ben, even though they didn't know sign language. Sadly though, Ben's best friends are his younger brother, Tim, his dad, and me.

Ilana Hermes

At a special ed school for children with neurological challenges, also called a "toy library," there were mostly children with learning disabilities. Despite this, I attended that school from age three until I was thirteen. I needed regular checkups for my shunt, and the school for the blind was too far from the hospital. I also needed occupational therapy, physiotherapy, and speech therapy, which were available at the special ed school.

Since I couldn't see what was written on the blackboard, I memorized everything I heard the teacher say. But I got bored easily and sometimes stopped paying attention. I had to listen over and over to everything in class, and it was hard to stay focused. I hardly studied, hated it, but passed for a while. But when the workload became too much for me to memorize with only hearing, I was sent to the school for the blind, an hour drive from home.

I was thirteen when I started at the school for the blind. Because I was used to being in the visual environment, I was initially put in the division for partially sighted children, even though I could only detect light with my vision. I had trouble using a typewriter because of my hands and hated them. I didn't want to learn to type. I did my exams verbally. My friend, who was in my class, was my eyes, and we studied together, until she had eye surgery.

In this way, I passed grade eight, and then it was decided I should be moved to the division for the totally blind. To make this transition, I had to sacrifice my ninth-grade year to learn Braille. That upset me. I just wanted to finish school, because I felt I didn't belong there. I had some friends there but never felt comfortable, so I played cricket with the boys and studied hard.

Judy Kahl

I had the most adorable two-room schoolhouse with a bathroom between the first- and second-grade classrooms. We had woods in the back for recess. Great fun, and since we only had about a dozen students in each grade, we got wonderful, individualized attention. Since I was hard of hearing, the teachers made sure I sat up front, so I could hear them, but they failed to realize that I missed what was said behind me, which many times was the answer to the teacher's question. That was my homework—to find the answers I didn't hear in the textbooks.

The next public school I went to was within walking distance, too. I went there for grades three through six. It was like a big house, and we had two classes per grade, so it was a much bigger school. Again, the only real help I received was getting a front seat. It was up to me to ask if I needed any other special help. During class, I was much too shy to ask a question, because I was afraid of saying something stupid, and I never wanted to embarrass myself in front of the class. I was okay with making friends, because I was active and knew I could compete in games and was decent at sports. One nice thing about being in a small school was that the teachers were aware if there was any sarcasm or picking on someone, and this was just not tolerated.

The tough years for me were junior high school, as the next public school I went to had grades seven through twelve—too many "older" kids, and that made it hard. We "little guys" were intimidated. Fortunately, that changed when they built a separate high school.

I was in the band in seventh and eighth grade. They needed two trumpet players, so my friend and I got trumpets, and my dad taught us the C scale. We made third chair. It was a social thing, but after making the cheerleader squad, no more trumpet for me. Being one of six cheerleaders was a real popularity thing, and so I was "in." It didn't matter that I wore bilateral hearing aids. Of course, going with one of the "popular" boys was another big social plus. I think that was tenth grade and "going with" meant going to the school dances and maybe a house date, but no more than that. Anyway, a few people have said that my "cuteness" and "swell personality" also helped me get around my disability on a social level. Feeling accepted is the key to overcoming any disability.

I went to speech therapy classes to learn how to pronounce consonants (sh, st, shr, str, ch, etc.). I didn't like to go, but it wasn't too bad. This was in the younger grades. My mother always helped me at home, and that was fine with me. It was words like "chocolate," which I said with "sh" instead of "ch" that troubled me the most. I memorized the right way to say things like that, so I wouldn't sound funny to the other kids.

In high school, I was in the teachers club, nurses club, drama, journalism, cheerleading—you name it—but my guidance counselor wasn't much help. When it was time to decide what I wanted to do after high school, she quickly pointed out that I could not be a nurse, as my hearing loss could be responsible for someone's death if I did not hear the "beeper." She just was not very encouraging and didn't have a direction for me. It was a bit of a scary thing for me, because I didn't think I had many options.

Mark Gasaway

I went to a regular public school in my residential school district of Wilkinson County, Georgia. However, the first two years of my life in school were when I could hear and see normally. In my third year of elementary school, I was three months shy of completing the third grade when I was stricken with encephalitis. Upon recovering from the disease, I had to return to third grade and from there went on to complete the twelfth grade and graduate.

When I was in the fifth grade my parents wanted to send me to the Georgia School for the Deaf. I told them I wanted to think about it, and then I told them I did not want to go to the school for the deaf. I wanted to stay in the same school to be with my friends. There were other reasons as well, but my parents knew what I wanted and honored my wishes to let me stay in the school that I was familiar with. They knew if I went to the school for the deaf, which was about a four- to five-hour drive from home, that I would be miserable. Being away from home and well-established friends was hard enough on a ten-year-old deaf and low vision kid. So I stayed in the same school and graduated with the class I came to know during my second stint in third grade.

My teachers responded to my disabilities quite well. They helped me with lessons when they felt I was having difficulty, but they also let me be myself and learn what I was capable of learning. The teachers knew I was a bright kid, and they did not want to limit my learning because of what I could not understand in the classroom.

Several things some of my teachers did that really helped included making me feel like I was able to do what the others in class were doing. One teacher taught me in both fourth and sixth grade. She became my favorite teacher, because she, more than the others, let me be me!

Most of my teachers had no problem with having me in their classes. They may have felt challenged, but, hey, I was challenged as well—more than they were. And I loved being challenged. My teachers knew I enjoyed school and they tried to help me when needed. But, mostly, I was able to do all my work on my own.

I had some problems with several teachers who did not try hard enough to communicate effectively with me. Some teachers talked to me with their backs to me, and that certainly did not help.

When I entered junior high, I had a choice of taking physical education (PE) or another class. I wanted to take PE because I felt I could compete with the other boys. I did OK in the PE classes and survived. While in the classes, I discovered I loved to run. These classes helped me develop my running ability. My teachers understood my needs in these classes and made me feel as good as they could. They sometimes took me out of the planned activities when my vision posed a problem, such as playing softball or table tennis. I occasionally ended up shooting hoops by myself. That made me feel a little left out, but there really wasn't much anyone could do about that.

I believe I fit in with the hearing kids as well as I could, despite not being able to hear them and understand what all they said or talked about. It did not bother me because they were not being mean or cruel. I believe they tried to accept me as one of them, and they were friendly about helping me at times. At other times, I did have difficulty working with some students. One such student was a bully and really picked on me, including one day when he deliberately slammed a chalkboard eraser full of chalk dust into my face. It made me cough and become sick because I was allergic to the dust. I ended up leaving school and going home. But for the most part, I had very little trouble with other kids. My socializing skills were good, and I developed more skills. I became a student who was well liked by teachers and students.

One trick I employed was to be as nice as I could be, and friendly. For that matter, I was always smiling when I wanted my fellow students to know I was grateful to be in school with them.

This was back in the 1960s and early 1970s, and back then there were no educational interpreters like we have these days. I did not have any accessible materials and learned on my own. I read a lot and understood what the assignments were after discussing them with fellow students and teachers. Sometimes, I was able to borrow a classmate's notes and use them to help myself. It was not a simple task, but I did the best I could with what I had.

Melanie Bond

I attended public schools from pre-K to twelfth grade, but from pre-K through second grade I was placed, along with other deaf students, in the deaf oral program at Walnut St. School in Lansing, Michigan.

In the deaf oral program back in the 1960s, I loved my teachers who worked patiently with me to help improve my language and communication skills. But once we were out on the playground, I became aware that some of the deaf students were signing secretly with each other, making sure not to get caught by the teachers who supervised the playground. Unfortunately, signing was forbidden. Anyone caught using their hands to communicate silently or gesturing with their hands in any way was immediately disciplined. Some of those disciplinary measures included forcing students to sit on their hands and/or to lay their heads down on top of their desks, rapping a ruler across their knuckles, slapping one's face or the sides of their heads to get their attention, and being sent to the principal's office.

I had the opportunity to witness firsthand the after-effects of what had happened to some of the deaf students who "graduated" from the deaf oral program at Everett High School in Lansing. Many of them simply couldn't speak well enough to be understood by most people. Though they had been conditioned to use their voices when speaking, the sounds they made were guttural, often harsh and grating and sometimes too loud, too nasal-toned, or too high-pitched. I also became aware that many of them could only read at a third-grade or fourth-grade level by the time they graduated from high school.

As far as I was concerned, the deaf oral program for most deaf students in the 1960s was an abysmal failure. I noticed that some of the oral deaf students had become bitter by the time they entered high school. No longer constrained by the public education system or the deaf oral program after they graduated from high school, most of them began to converse fluently in what should have been their first language all along—ASL. The idiom "better late than never!" is no excuse when it comes to fundamental rights, such as acquiring a first language and learning to communicate ideas, concepts, and philosophy with others, whether they are spoken or signed or transmitted through any other forms of communication. It would have been far better for most of the oral deaf students to have gone to the Michigan School for the Deaf in Flint.

Patricia Clark

I attended state schools from age five to seventeen. In New Zealand, there were checks on vision and hearing for children at age five and again at age eleven. The checks were done by a nurse at school. I knew I'd "fail" the tests, but nothing was said to me about it.

I sat at the front of the class to see the blackboard and also to be in range of the teacher speaking. My disabilities were known to the teachers, who were matter-of-fact and not punitive. The school had a good sports program, but I was never chosen for anything because of my low vision. In my first year at school, I quickly learned to read, and this was a big asset for more difficult years that lay ahead. I was a quiet and fearful child but fit in well enough, made friends, and was not bullied.

When I was six, an eye specialist looked into my eyes and said I had a bone disease. I was taken to an orthopedic specialist, who found I had Perthes disease in my left hip and must go into the hospital immediately. My leg was in traction for a year. The children's ward had a teacher, but as we kids were all immobilized and mostly lying down, we didn't do much schoolwork. I was then fitted with a caliper on the left leg and sent home and did lessons at home for another year. This may have been beneficial, as everything was written clearly for me, and although this teaching was by postal mail, it was individualized.

During these years, both my vision and hearing got worse. At the end of my seventh grade year, when I was going on thirteen, my school grades were not wonderful, and I was distressed. I don't recall any comments at home. My regular class teacher treated me well but sometimes trainee teachers or others who didn't know me were harsh when I failed to hear them.

High school was a different matter. My first two years were quite successful. The class was small (about twenty-eight girls), and the teachers seemed to like schoolgirls. The third year found me in a big class of forty or more girls. But the senior teachers were cross and bitter. Two of them had been at the school for over twenty years and thought they owned it. They bullied the girls and bullied the junior teachers as well. My hearing became much worse that year, and they gave me a very hard time. One teacher repeatedly shouted at me in class, and the other would not allow me to take part in school activities. Neither of them made allowances or helped me in any way.

I passed the state exam at age fifteen but failed the next step up the following year. I repeated this class, and much to everyone's surprise, I passed very narrowly. This pass gave me entrance to university. They had managed to convince me that I was a failure, so I thought the pass was a miracle and was quite overwhelmed. From being a backward dolt, who was at the bottom of the class due to her own wickedness, I became a very successful student. This was one of several sudden reversals of fortune that have marked my life.

My social life at school was normal. At this stage, I could still use the voice telephone. I had learned not to draw attention to myself, both at home and at school, so I didn't chase after the boys. Nevertheless, I was invited to parties and dances and had an enjoyable time. Once I could no longer use the voice phone, social life fell flat, both with girlfriends and boyfriends.

Scott Stoffel

When I went to kindergarten at a public school in Camp Springs, Maryland, I thought I was just like all the other kids. I was very social, always wanting to be a part of a group. I had lots of friends. My bad vision, slight hearing loss, and hand problems didn't become known to me until first grade. That's when everything about my life changed. Suddenly, I had to use large print textbooks and paper with wide, extra-dark lines, and I had to see a tutor to review class lessons. The school taught kindergarten through sixth grade, but I was the only kid with all of these "weird" things. Instead of a cubbyhole, I had a library cart, because my huge books came in multiple volumes.

Academically, the accommodations provided by the state Services for the Blind were adequate. The tutors were necessary, because I couldn't read the blackboard no matter how close I sat to it. That made learning math particularly hard, so a tutor would do math problems out on paper with a black magic marker for me. My grades were all right, for the most part, through sixth grade.

Unfortunately, the accommodations advertised my disabilities and made me "weird" to the other kids. In first grade, I continued to seek out the social groups but was progressively pushed out. I didn't understand my problems, nor did I understand that they caused me to do things differently from the so-called normal kids. For instance, when I wrote on paper, I had to lean forward with my face two inches from the paper, and I couldn't use my thumb to hold the pencil. The other kids saw things like that and thought it was weird. To make matters worse, my poor eyesight made it impossible for me to do a lot of things in gym class, like baseball or hurdles, and that counted as another strike against me. Adults kept telling me to "try my best," so I did and got hurt and humiliated time and again. Soon, the kids started calling me "the freak."

One incident sticks in my mind as the point where I officially went from being a regular kid to being a freak. During a recess period, the teacher on monitor duty decided to have all the first and second graders play kickball. This game is like baseball, except you roll and kick a soccer ball. I could see a soccer ball and really wanted to play this game. Then an argument broke out between the teams about who got "stuck with the freak." The teacher forced one team to take me. The kids on my team were mad and said a lot of nasty things to me, while we were in line to kick. I didn't understand what was so bad about me; I just wanted to play and "try my best." But the name-calling came from all around me, while the teacher said nothing. I finally broke down and ran off crying.

The others laughed, but the teacher shouted at me to come back this instant. I ignored her and ran around to the side of the building to be alone. The next thing I knew, two of the "in" boys came around and informed me that I "had" to return to the game. I told them that nobody wanted me there, and they said that was too bad. One kid grabbed my arm. It was like a volcano erupted in my head. It wasn't enough that I was scorned and rejected by all, but I had to go back and endure further abuse. I tackled the surprised kid and flailed at his face with both fists. I probably hit him a dozen times without even knowing what I was doing. When I heard him crying, I stopped and saw his nose was bleeding like hell. I got off him, and he ran to the teacher. She took him to the nurse's office.

There was an awkward time until she came back, alone. She walked up to me and said, "Jimmy has the worst bloody nose I've ever seen! How can you be so mean?" I can still hear the words like it had happened yesterday. How could *I* be so mean? I learned it from you, lady.

I was the freak from then on. Friends disappeared, and the lack of positive social interaction retarded my development of basic social skills. Teachers and family blamed this on me and told me to be nice and try my best. Every time I did something in a way that wasn't normal because of my disabilities, someone would insult me. I unconsciously turned my head slightly to one side in order to center my better eye, and kids mocked it. My bad eye constantly looked off to the side, seeing only vague images, and kids accused me of staring at them out the corner of my eye. Everything about me was wrong. I started insulting other people in retaliation to the constant put-downs, and that only made my social woes at school worse. Ultimately, I began to hate myself.

Junior high school was the worst time of my school years. My family relocated to an upper-middle-class town in Connecticut, where I had to adjust to a very different environment from the elementary school that had been mostly for kids from military families. I was introduced to a guidance counselor and told she was going to "help me every way she could" at the new school. I never saw her again after that introduction and have no idea what her function was. My seventh- and eighth-grade years were characterized by endless attacks, both verbal and physical and usually by bold groups pitting themselves against the lone freak. I dreaded the schoolbus those years, but my mother refused to drive three miles to take me to school. She told me to be nice and try my best. I also had a gym teacher who seemed to get a kick out of humiliating me. Once, she told me I could skip the boys' hurdle race and do something easier with the girls' gym class. It wasn't optional, either, and I was the laughing stock of the whole school.

Later in life, I asked my parents why they left me to flounder in public schools like that. They said that the only other option was to put me in a school for disabled kids, which would have hurt me academically. My sister had gone to the special schools and hadn't learned nearly as much as I learned in public schools. There was no local school for the blind. They also said that a counselor from Services for the Blind had told them to leave me alone in the public school system. To all concerned parties, academics was first, last, and only. The social trauma caused by my disabilities was of no consequence. Be nice and try your best.

I nearly failed math in seventh grade. The teacher spent every class writing long problems out on the board, which I couldn't see at all, despite a front-row seat. I just listened to him babble meaningless statements like, "We move this here down to here, and we end up with this right here." You don't say? I sure learned a lot from that garbage. I think a key problem here was that I was so self-conscious by this point in my growing years that I was afraid to speak up and tell the teacher I wasn't getting anything out of the class—I didn't want to be put on the spot as a weirdo yet again. Instead, I just daydreamed during class. I didn't want to fail, but I had no reason to want good grades, either. Grades didn't win you friends. The only reward for getting good grades was some empty praise at home, so I had no motivation to study the books hard and try to learn the material. Besides that, I felt like bad grades were appropriate for a worthless freak.

After I hurt my neck in gym class, my parents finally had me removed from that hell-spawned teacher's class. She demanded I do a run-jump-flip exercise and didn't care that I had poor depth perception. She felt if I could see to walk around, then I could see to jump over a bar. On the spot again, I tried my best. I ran, hit the springboard, and tried to flip over that bar as instructed. I was high enough, but I'd misjudged the distance and jumped too soon, landing directly on top of the bar. That caused me to come down right on my head. I felt an electric shock rip down my spine and was terrified I'd broken my neck. The gym teacher was totally disgusted with me and asked sarcastically if I needed an ambulance. Luckily, I only suffered a strain.

I had a growth spurt just before my junior year in high school that made me less of a target for bullies, although I still had no social skills at all and didn't even try to make friends with other boys anymore. I was a little more comfortable talking to girls, since I didn't have to worry about things like baseball with them. In my adult life, I continued to feel more comfortable around women.

In my last two years of high school, instead of attending regular classes, I had two tutors. One was strictly to teach me algebra and trigonometry. Apparently, it finally dawned on someone that I got zero out of math class lectures. The other tutor helped me with everything else but was especially good with English. At the time I started eleventh grade, I tested at an eighth grader's grammar skill level. With her help, I scored 630 in English on my SAT exam. She had a knack for motivating me, made me feel I had some talents and could succeed in life if I pushed myself harder. Other tutors had patronized me, and I sort of had a crush (if you can call it that) on one I had in fourth grade, but none of them made me feel like there was a reason to work harder. Mrs. A. was different: She made me want to do better, like I wasn't a total loser by default.

I finished high school in the top 10 percent of my class after barely passing my first semester as a junior.

Tonilyn Todd Wisner

My hearing loss wasn't discovered until right before I started first grade. So I was always being yelled at in school to pay attention, and my mom would get mad and say I only heard what I wanted to hear. I was a bit of a goody-two-shoes and tried to be perfect, so those things hurt and made me feel like I wasn't good enough. But those were normal reactions from parents and teachers. I don't think I really gave much indication that I was having trouble hearing, so how were they to know? I don't know what prompted my parents to get my hearing checked; maybe it was just the exam they did every year before school began. But that's when they found the loss. I was completely deaf in my left ear—the hearing nerve didn't work, so a hearing aid couldn't help.

Because of the times, 1976, things like deafness were not openly talked about. It was sort of a shame to the family and kids were treated differently. I guess that is why my parents decided to raise me as a hearing child. I was already speaking very well and very plainly for a six-year-old, so I could pass as having normal hearing. I attended public schools all my life. I didn't have any special classes or teachers. The only help I got was that my parents gave each teacher a note about my hearing loss and asked that they sit me in the front row. This helped some, but the teachers moved around a lot during lectures, so I missed things. I learned not to ask "what?" because I was told I wasn't paying attention, nor did I ask my classmates what the teacher said, because then I got in trouble for talking in class. I felt isolated, and every day was a big stress, because I knew the struggle would begin again.

I had a bad experience in fourth grade, when a teacher told the class to look in a corner of the board for daily homework assignments. I didn't hear that and found out about it later on. The teacher never said anything to me about it, didn't ask to be sure I was aware of it.

In fifth grade, I wanted to play the flute. I was tone-deaf (yes, that's a real thing, not just a joke!), but both my doctor and the band teacher told me that, if I couldn't hear pitches, then I *couldn't* play an instrument. I resented them telling me I couldn't do it, because I was determined to play. And I did; I played the flute. I was in harmony; my hearing problem didn't show. But then they started changing practice times and announcing the changes over the loudspeaker. I couldn't understand most of what came over the loudspeaker, so I missed many practices and fell behind. I stopped playing after that year, but later in life retaught myself.

I did everything as a hearing person—I had no choice. I didn't know any other hard of hearing or deaf people and didn't even know about sign languages. Necessity made me learn to read lips on my own. When I discovered ASL at thirteen, my parents bought me a book, which turned out to be Signed English, but I didn't know the difference back then. I didn't learn much sign language and never really took an interest in learning until I was eighteen and took ASL classes. Then I fell in love with ASL!

In my senior year of high school, I got a cross-aid. This was a hearing aid that had a behind-the-ear microphone and transmitter on the deaf ear and a behind-the-ear receiver on the hearing ear with an earpiece that went inside the good ear. The purpose was to allow me to hear sounds from the bad side. I really hated it, because having the earpiece in my good ear blocked sounds coming from that side. Wearing that thing didn't last very long!

I was teased a lot at school and made fun of for not hearing something or misunderstanding something. I avoided groups because of this. Mostly, I was made fun of for the paralysis of the left side of my face from the brain surgery—this was done openly and constantly, and teachers did not do anything about it. I was—or I felt like I was—left to fend for myself in every way, socially, academically, and psychologically. I feel like I should have had a lot more support from my parents, teachers, and health care professionals.

Despite all of this, I was in the Gifted and Talented program, took honors and accelerated classes, and graduated from high school with honors—a 3.55 GPA.

Wendy Williams

I attended our local public school, and I was the only hearing-impaired student. About the only consistent accommodation I was given in the first seven years was having my desk placed near the teacher's desk. Some years, a certain student sat behind me to let me know what seatwork and homework we were to work on.

I spent a good part of first grade in the corner for "misbehavior." It was hard to pay attention when I couldn't hear what the teacher said. I became so bored with the alphabet and number drills that I would blabber nonsense. I recall kicking an eraser around while at my desk. I don't remember knowing rules, and I did not know what was happening or what to do at times. A worksheet was placed before me, and I cried. Sometimes, my brother was called from his second-grade class to sit with me and help me do some of the tasks—or he just did them for me.

In second grade, I loved spelling and earned a perfect grade every week till near the end of the year. On one lesson, the words "much" and "must" were on the same list. I tried with all my might to speech-read (lip-read) the teacher in hopes of getting these words in the right order, but to my dismay, I couldn't tell the two words apart with speech-reading and ended up spelling the wrong one first. So I did not achieve 100 percent for spelling that year, despite my effort.

The teacher enjoyed reading books she kept on a shelf that only the above-average readers were allowed to get to. I so much wanted to get my hands on those books but wasn't allowed because I was a below-average reader. Trying to follow when she read them to the class was impossible, since I could not speech-read her, unless she looked in my direction.

In third grade, much to my embarrassment and humiliation, I was placed with the slow learners for English-related lessons, because I was delayed in the acquisition of language and missed out in incidental learning. It was this school year that my hearing loss was confirmed, but hearing aids were not recommended by my doctor, so I continued to rely on speech-reading. The principal told my parents I would not make it past fourth grade in a regular school.

By fourth grade, I became silent, preferring not to communicate, unless I absolutely had to. I also wanted to stay in my seat and not stray from it, lest people witness my clumsiness. I didn't know it at the time, but the cause of my clumsiness was deteriorating visual fields resulting from RP.

Sometimes, I would sit in class, but my mind would be far away. Memories of recent abuse at home haunted me and made it difficult to focus. It was hard to concentrate on my class work, but I scraped by with passing grades.

Up through seventh grade, I had a homeroom teacher and remained in her room most of the time. But when I entered eighth grade, I had multiple teachers and had to move from one room to another for different subjects. I had a difficult time adjusting to the different lip movements of all these teachers and understanding what they said. I failed grades eight, nine, and eleven. Between the summer of repeating ninth grade and going into grade ten, I attended a month-long camp for deaf and physically disabled children and teens to receive speech therapy. I came in contact with wonderful staff people who boosted my self-esteem and confidence. Back home, I soared for a short time, only to return to my depressed state.

From third grade onward, French was a required language taught by the same teacher my first five years. I applied English pronunciations to French words without knowing there was any difference. In eighth grade, we had a new French teacher. I well remember that teacher repeatedly trying to get me to correctly say "je" for "I" right in front of my classmates on the first day, and I couldn't grasp it and was so humiliated. My father wrote a note to the teacher explaining I had a hearing problem, and then the teacher apologized. My mother left it to me to tell the teachers in high school I was hearing-impaired, but I was too shy and embarrassed to do so. When I had to take the final French test prior to graduation, my first French teacher managed to excuse me from the mandatory dictation, because I simply could not speech-read French and write it on paper.

Once my clumsiness started, I hated PE, for obvious reasons. If we played team sports, with a student picking the players, I usually was the last one chosen. In high school, I was excused from some PE classes when contact sports, such as basketball, were played. I sat on the sidelines, bored. On my own initiative, I decided to brave track, faithfully attending the weekday workouts. During the tryouts, the coach suddenly appeared beside me and tried to correct my poor habits, but I didn't understand what was said. I didn't even notice the coach was standing there, at first. Consequently, I didn't make the school's track team.

In high school, I had to write an essay on school spirit. My mother tried in vain to explain this concept to me, but I simply couldn't get it. Finally, as a last resort, she wrote the essay for me. The essay earned an "A" grade, and it was the first and only time something of mine appeared in the school's yearbook.

I had lots of friends the first three years of school. After that, I withdrew, seldom talking to anyone. I was very lonely, yet I wanted to be a hermit. Between the difficulty I had communicating with other kids and the problems caused by my deteriorating field of vision, I felt like an outsider and couldn't find a way to fit in.

When I was eighteen and repeating grade eleven, I was fitted with my first set of hearing aids. Adjusting to these aids was very difficult; I was going from a relatively quiet world to an overwhelmingly noisy one. I was prone to outbursts from startling sounds. The first time I entered the girls' restroom during recess I was astounded to hear the girls doing what they do behind locked stall doors. I laughed so hard! Then I remembered I came for the same reason. I was self-conscious at the sound I started to make and tried to be ever so quiet, so no one could hear me.

I managed to graduate from high school, but my marks were low.

3
Transition to Adulthood

Making the transition from childhood to adulthood can be a challenge for anyone. For a person with multiple disabilities, the challenge is even greater. The key difference between these two phases in our lives is the level of responsibility and independence expected of us. Whether "the next step" is going to college, getting a job, or becoming a homemaker, most people find themselves needing to take more charge of their lives, while parents assume a less dominant role.

Children with disabilities need more guidance, as well as physical help, and are prone to depending on parents and teachers more than average children do. This circumstance can make the road to becoming independent adults more difficult. As the contributors have shown in previous chapters, many children with disabilities do not receive any real help with their social and psychological development, which often leads to problems, such as poor self-esteem or a major lack of confidence, which further complicate the transition to adulthood.

The contributors followed many different paths after finishing secondary school. What is interesting here is the attitude and self-perception of each person as he or she struggled to become an independent adult. Also note how many of the supports these people had known as children changed or vanished when they become legal adults, and how this affected them.

Angela C. Orlando

I knew exactly where I was headed after high school, even years before graduation. I was extremely goal-driven. I knew most of my life that I wanted to be a teacher. And I knew—since I was twelve—that I wanted to teach special education.

I loved living in Kent, Ohio, and had no desire to leave, so I was proud to enroll at Kent State University as a special education major. I lived at home with my parents while attending college. I never even considered the idea of living in a dorm. We lived on the other side of Kent, so I rode the bus to campus each day.

My life really didn't change much when I started college. I think this was because I continued living at home with my parents. Instead of getting on a public school bus and going to high school, I got on a campus bus and went to college. I came home, had dinner with my parents, and studied. There really wasn't much difference.

I did like that going to college gave me the chance to explore the campus on my own and shop by myself in the university bookstore. If I had a cold, for example, I could just go in and buy what I needed, so I felt a little more independent. Sure, my parents would get me whatever I wanted, but I liked the independence. I never had that before. Eventually, they opened a food court in the university student center, so I could get my own McDonald's and Subway food whenever I wanted. People who drive don't realize how hard it is for those of us who can't. You get a craving for a Big Mac, and there's nothing you can really do about it, unless you happen to live next to a McDonald's. At least the campus gave me easy access to some things. I liked being on my own between classes, instead of stuck in a high school. When the weather was nice, I loved to walk across campus to classes that were in different buildings. Or just sit outside the student center and do homework. I felt free and on my own there.

While I did well academically, I totally missed out on the social side of college. I had no friends at Kent State. I ate lunch alone every day and went home on the bus by myself. I didn't attend sports events or social activities. I didn't go to parties or anything like that. I suppose I was avoiding social life in college, but it wasn't anything I consciously tried to do.

I remember trying to hold on to my friends from high school by writing letters to them and arranging get-togethers during break. For example, during Christmas break of my first year at college, I nearly typed my fingers raw on the TTY [or teletypewriter, a device that enables the user to type messages to a relay operator or another TTY over the phone, now being replaced by Internet-based relay services and texting] to invite our old high school group out to a big lunch. We had a large group of friends who were now in college and some who were still in high school. But they all mostly ignored me at the lunch. They no longer had the time or patience to write things down or finger spell to me. The restaurant was loud, so I couldn't hear them speaking. It hurt me deeply that none of them ever called me to go out or even just to talk. I realized I was putting in all the effort to hold on to those friendships. I got sick of it and just stopped. And none of those "friends" ever made an effort to touch base with me. They just disappeared from my life.

My hearing loss had always hindered social interaction, but my degenerative vision loss began to have a stronger effect. By the time I started college, I had a field of vision less than 20 degrees and suffered from night blindness. But most people had no idea I had any vision problems. The pressure to be "normal" was so much that I began avoiding activities that would place me in tricky situations. For example, one Fourth of July I went to downtown Akron to see fireworks. It was a nightmare. We had to walk several blocks in the dark, and there were a lot of steps I couldn't see. My friends teased me and yelled at me to hurry up. I never enjoyed fireworks after that experience and never went out to see them again.

I didn't go to movies anymore, either. If we were late, I wouldn't be able to see to get to the seats with the lights turned down. If I had to go to the bathroom, I wouldn't be able to find the seats in the dark theater when I returned. It was too embarrassing, so I just stopped going to movies.

I spent a lot of my free time watching TV during these years. I used a closed-caption decoder, so I could read what was being said on the screen. I really liked watching TV and movies this way.

Two of the most important things that happened during my early adult life were my introduction to the computer world and my first boyfriend.

I got my first computer during my second semester in college. That was certainly helpful for school, but it's not what I'm focusing on here. One day, my father brought me some software that I had never heard of before. He said, "I think you will like this. Try it out." It was Prodigy (a dial-up service), and that was my introduction to a world that would later be the center of my social life. At first, I liked to post on the *Star Trek* message board. I wasn't a die-hard "Trekkie," but I did like the show. Mostly, I liked talking about TV, and this was a place where you could find people to talk to. I met a lot of good people there, including someone who is still a close friend. Then the Internet began for real, and I was able to write emails to anyone on any service. I moved to different services before I found my "home" on Delphi. I found friendship with a group there. We shared common interests. We wrote about anything and everything. We sent each other greeting cards and gifts. It was a world that a person who was hard of hearing with low vision could easily fit in. Disabilities didn't matter. I didn't have to worry about understanding what was being said. And there were no steps to fall down or things to bump into. And this is where I found my first boyfriend, Greg Howard.

I wasn't looking for a man; it just kind of happened. We met on a *Star Trek* board. He offered to send me some *Star Trek* tapes. We started flirting in email and talked in private text chats together. It was a lot of fun. He made me feel special. I did tell him about my hearing and vision loss. He didn't seem at all concerned. He confessed to me that he had problems with clinical depression and was overweight. We eventually met in person. It was awkward at first. Neither one of us knew what to say. I was shy and nervous beyond belief. We just sat on the couch holding hands and not saying a word.

The next day I took him to Kent State where we finally talked . . . and kissed. We sat outside the student center for hours that afternoon. Every fifteen minutes, the library bells would chime. After that day, I always thought of Greg whenever I heard the chimes. We continued our online relationship for years. We got together during school breaks or on weekends. He would drive here for short visits, and I would fly to Maryland where he lived during longer breaks. But our relationship was kind of rocky. His mother didn't approve of me because of my disabilities. She actually told him that I would give her "damaged grandkids." She put him under so much pressure that he would break up with me every summer shortly after break began. And then we'd get back together in the fall. This on/off behavior broke my heart. At times, I felt severely depressed over our break-ups. But then we'd get back together, and I'd feel like the world was perfect again, because I had my boyfriend back. I was very naive and didn't realize I was just setting myself up to be hurt again.

My boyfriend really encouraged me to be independent and do things on my own. For instance, he got me to ride my bike to classes and around town, so I could do things on my own. And instead of calling my dad for a ride home after night classes, I started riding the bus and learned how to manage the walk home from the bus stop safely in the dark. I had never thought to do anything like that until Greg brought it up. He was the one who first suggested I should move into my own place.

I told my parents I wanted to move out shortly after my twenty-first birthday. They burst out laughing at me, thought I was joking. That reaction really hurt me. I knew that other people my age were living on their own; why should it be so funny that I wanted to do so, too? I absolutely didn't want to live in a dorm. The idea simply disgusted me, so that was never an option. I went to Commuter Services and got information about off-campus housing. I didn't know anyone who would want to share an apartment with me, and I was afraid to live with total strangers. I didn't even know how to go about finding a roommate. The prices for a single apartment or studio were shockingly high. There was no way I could afford that. My only income was SSI payments. So I stayed with my parents a while longer. About a year later, my brother's girlfriend, Kerri, told my parents she was looking for a new roommate. My parents felt more comfortable with this, since I'd be moving in with someone they already knew and trusted.

The place was a townhouse located right off campus. I lived with Kerri and two other girls. It wasn't a major adjustment for me. I was still in the same small town with my parents and saw them often. They helped me with grocery shopping and drove me places when I needed a ride. I had to cook for myself, but I had already been doing that a lot while living with my parents. For some reason, I quickly got in the habit of living in my room, instead of the house. I mostly only came out to make meals, and I ate those in my room most of the time. I had my computer, TV, desk, and cat in my room. I felt comfortable there. I did leave my door open and my roommates could come in to talk to me. But they didn't do that very often. This habit of being a social hermit in my room stayed with me everywhere I lived. Kerri pretty much stayed at my brother's house, so she was never around. I got along okay with the other two girls, even if we didn't socialize much.

A roommate tried to get me to go out with her and her friends. We went to a frat party, but I couldn't manage the walk to and from the house. It was dark, and there were steps and broken sidewalks. Another time, she asked me to go to a KSU basketball game, but I wouldn't go. I knew there were all those steps outside the gym, and it would have been too hard to get around. After awhile, she stopped asking me to do things with her.

Then Kerri and one of the other girls got in a big fight. Suddenly, lines were drawn, and I was in the middle of a feud that had nothing to do with me. Since Kerri was rarely home, I became the resident bad guy, and I hadn't even done anything. I ended up moving with Kerri to another townhouse in the complex. I didn't want to, because I was comfortable in the old place and was getting stuck with a smaller room in the new one. But all the others were leaving, and I had no one to ask to room with me. So I just went with Kerri. Again, she was never home, and I didn't like the three new girls we lived with. They were partiers. They drank a lot and played loud music and brought lots of strange guys home. One time, some guy stole all the food out of our house. The others thought it was funny, because the guy was fat and stole our food. I was terrified. We were lucky he only went after food. Another time a roommate's drunk one-night-stand got lost and crawled into my bed with me. I awoke to him touching me and screamed my head off. Since I was deaf, it was a bad idea to lock my door—what if someone had to tell me there was a fire or something? Again, my roommates thought it was funny. I hated living with them.

Kerri and my brother broke up around the time our lease was up. I wanted out of that place but didn't know where I could go or how to find new roommates. But Kerri still wanted to live with me. We were kind of friends by this time. We found a nice two-room house in a residential area. I was really happy there. I was more independent at that time than any other time in my life. I rode my bike all over town to grocery shop and go to appointments. I found you just had to plan grocery shopping carefully so you'd be able to get it all home on a bike. Sometimes, I had to go back and forth, but that was okay. It was summer; I didn't have a job, and I had just graduated from college, so I had time to waste.

Ilana Hermes

Physically, I became a woman when I was only ten years old. [That can happen at an earlier age to children with hydrocephalus because of pressure on the pituitary gland.] One teacher I had told my parents they must have me "sterilized." They refused.

While I was still only a young teen at the school for the blind, I met a guy whom I thought was cute. He finished school shortly after I got there but remained in the area to study at a college in Worcester, so we continued to see each other. The hostel mother and every adult who worked at the youth hostel where I boarded liked him and would let me go out with him any time I wanted. But a teacher at school warned that he was too old for me. I didn't know how old he was; I thought he was three years older than me. Then his parents came down to talk to my parents because of the real age difference—seven years! That's a lot for a teenage girl. But by that time, I was already caught in his web. We continued dating for a few more years.

When I was busy studying and a month away from my final exam, I got sick and needed a new shunt. I got sick on a Sunday, and my parents couldn't get hold of my neurosurgeon. So the general practitioner told us to go to the hospital to see a different neurosurgeon. It took five days, CT scans, an MRI, and a lumbar puncture before the neurosurgeon performed emergency surgery to keep me alive—all because the public hospital didn't want to give out my scan records, due to a conflict with my parents' private medical care.

My boyfriend wanted to buy me a ticket to visit with him at his home, but I told him I couldn't because I had just had surgery and was not allowed to travel. He got upset and came to see me. He wanted to book me in at a lodge with him; I refused that idea outright. So he asked where I wanted to go for the day. I said Kirstenbosch—I like that place. There I broke the relationship. He wanted to get engaged when I turned twenty-one. I wasn't ready to think about that kind of commitment yet, especially with all the health issues I had to deal with at the time. I was twenty when we broke up.

I had been bored in school and was happy when I graduated. After I finished twelfth grade, I wanted to study massage therapy, but the first massage training school I visited turned me away. They said I had to be twenty-three years old to study massage. I believe they rejected me not because of my age but because they did not know how to work with and accommodate a disabled person.

Mark Gasaway

I graduated from high school in 1973. I was supposed to graduate in 1972 but after becoming sick with encephalitis in the third grade and having to return to the third grade, I went on to graduate with the class of 1973. It was an honor for me to do this, as I attended high school without sign language interpreters or any real services for the disabled. It was also a huge challenge for me, but I was successful in my endeavor to succeed.

Upon graduating from high school, I worked part-time for my mother, who ran a day care center from home. I helped her with about ten or more children for three years. I did a lot of different things but mostly entertained the children by playing with them, making them laugh.

In the fall of 1976, I enrolled at a rehabilitation center about two hours from home and went there to see what I could do for a career. While there, I studied mechanical drafting. I also started learning sign language at this center, teaching myself to sign from a sign language book and talking with several deaf students at the center. I was there for ten months, leaving to attend Delgado College in New Orleans from summer 1976 to spring 1977. I left Delgado after one year and entered Georgia College, where I did not fare too well. I then applied to Gallaudet University in Washington, D.C., and began there in summer 1978, graduating in 1982 with a B.A. in social work.

Upon graduating from Gallaudet, I worked as a counselor at Camp Greentop, a summer camp for disabled children and young adults in Maryland. In the summer of 1983, again I was a camp counselor at a camp known as Camp Greenbrier in West Virginia. This camp was for hearing and sighted children and young adults, but there were some hard of hearing kids there, also.

With the summer camps behind me, it was time to find a steady job and settle down. I got a job working as a health services technician at a facility for the mentally challenged in middle Georgia. I worked at that job for two and a half years before leaving to move to Atlanta. I moved to Atlanta in 1986 after getting married the year before.

During the years after high school, I lived in a small house on my parents' land and was responsible for homemaking, cooking, and shaping my own way of life. Then when I went to work for the hospital, I moved into a small apartment on site at the hospital.

I would say there were some difficult and challenging times, but, hey, they were just growing-up issues and trying to understand more about all the "adult" issues of life! You can say that what I felt in the transition from high school to whatever lay beyond was a series of thoughts where I was trying to learn about all the things my parents and siblings went through when they were just out of high school. Of course, being deaf-blind makes a challenge more appealing, and it made me more determined to get out there and succeed!

The challenges and difficulties were not that much different than when I was a kid. Then, I faced each challenge as a part of my life, although I knew I was seen as different because I could not hear or see well. So what? I still had my own life to live and wanted to live it in the way I felt would be easier for me to deal with my limitations.

Melanie Bond

I was sexually enlightened at the age of sixteen when I lost my virginity to a deaf guy who would later become my first husband. Needless to say, my parents were in an uproar once they had found out what I had done. My father grounded me for five long weeks and ordered my mother and the rest of the family to not speak to me or have anything to do with me at all. In short, I was totally shunned by them, and I felt lonely and miserable with no one to talk to. This was one of the most hurtful experiences of my life. When I made a plea to talk with my father so that we could work things out, he ignored me. When my mother begged him to speak with me so that we could end this hateful charade, he became angry and violent with me. Besides spewing every filthy epithet at me, calling me a slut and my boyfriend a puke right up in my face, he also shook me so hard that one of my hearing aid batteries flew out. At that point, I walked out the door and never looked back.

A few days later, my mom found me and begged me to return home. I agreed to do so, knowing that school would soon be letting out for the summer. Shortly after I turned seventeen, I left home for good, knowing that my parents could not call the cops on me and force me to return home. In a sense, you could say that I had grown up pretty fast.

In January of 1975, my deaf fiancé and I were married. I was eighteen years old at the time. We lived in a duplex and then later moved into a home of our own.

Scott Stoffel

When I finished high school, everyone in my family just said, "Time for college." I had hated every minute of high school and was not at all enthused about this idea. My family lived in a small town in Connecticut at the time. There were no busses anywhere near our house, and since I couldn't drive, getting a job didn't seem plausible. So college was basically my only choice.

While I did have a girlfriend my last two years of high school, I did not have a single male friend at the school I attended. My self-esteem was low, and I was overly wary of being betrayed by guys pretending to be friendly because this had happened to me so many times as a kid. I just avoided groups of guys altogether, which retarded my social development significantly. That said, I wasn't up to living in a dorm, so I found a college that was close enough to home for someone in the family to drive me back and forth.

I didn't interact much with other students at college and even lost touch with my high school girlfriend. I just didn't know what to say or do to make friends. These were young adults, so I figured they were more mature than high school kids, but that was partly why I felt intimidated; I knew I was immature for my age. Just knowing that didn't mean I could will the problem away, either. I really didn't know how to interact with my peers. Between classes, I'd walk around outside and hear some guys talking about their cars or motorcycles, things I would never have. Then I'd overhear some young women discussing driving to the beach or a ski resort with their boyfriends and knew I'd be quite a fool to ask a valid girl out. I was inadequate and of no value to these legitimate human beings, so I just kept my distance.

My family's advice was redundant: "Smile. Act normal. Your poor sister has it *ten times* worse!" Life was bad across the board and getting worse. I started wondering more and more if there was a point to it.

I guess my parents sensed that I was coming unglued upstairs. After I dropped out of college, they whisked me off to Chattanooga,

Tennessee, to help my nondisabled older brother manage a computer software store. We found me an apartment within walking distance of the store, so transportation wasn't a problem. My job was to greet customers and show them where we kept the type of software they were interested in (this was back in the 1980s when the Apple II, Commodore 64, and Atari 800 were still around). The setup wasn't bad. It might have worked out all right. The trouble was that my weird neurological disability wasn't content to leave things as they were. After working at the store for a few months, I started having major problems understanding what customers said. A visit with an audiologist determined my hearing had deteriorated big-time, leaving me with almost no discriminatory hearing by the time I turned nineteen.

The reality came home in full when an Avon saleswoman came into the store, and I mistakenly thought she was a customer. I found out from someone else that she was asking me about what cologne I liked, while I misunderstood and thought she wanted Commodore software.

To add to my rapidly mounting distress, a really scary thing happened at the store one afternoon. My brother had an infant son at the time. His wife brought the baby to the store and put him in his car seat right in the doorway to the back room of the store. I saw him there but misjudged how tall the car seat was (I have poor depth perception) and tripped over him. He went flying and hit his head pretty hard on the floor. It turned out he was all right, but it rattled me at the time.

To my dying day, I won't understand why they put the kid there in the doorway, knowing that I was legally blind. I have often felt like people did things to deliberately exploit my disabilities. I have no other logical explanation for things like this.

I had no friends to talk to and was just going insane inside my head. My brother and his wife acted like my hearing loss was something I faked and were entirely unsympathetic. Finally, I just decided there was nothing in life for me and wanted it to be over with. In a sort of daze, I ran out into a highway without looking, hoping I'd get run down. When I heard the screech of tires (a sufficiently loud noise), instinct made me jump. My back foot hit the side of the truck as it skidded to a halt right where I'd been a second ago. The driver's window came down, and I'm sure a volcano of vulgarities came out. I realized I could have caused other people to get hurt and was so ashamed that

I just ran home and locked myself in my apartment. I never told my brother about it.

Becoming deaf on top of being legally blind and having other physical problems was something I just wasn't prepared to deal with or accept. I had enough residual hearing to communicate with difficulty in quiet, one-on-one settings, but that was all. I lost television and movies, which had been my main sources of entertainment until that point—I didn't have enough vision to read captions. I lost music. Since I couldn't communicate effectively, I could neither date nor even interact with family anymore. Hearing aids didn't work because of the discrimination loss, but that was my fault, according to my family. I didn't try hard enough, you see.

I felt like I'd been buried alive. With no effective communication mode or any real direction in life, I retreated to my parents' house and lived on books. They were all I had for years.

Wendy Williams

This next phase in my life was a really difficult one to connect with. Upon graduation from high school at the age of twenty, my grades were too low to consider college. I felt discouraged and at a loss about what to do. My parents suggested going to a small Christian boarding school to attend grade thirteen, which was the equivalent of a first year of regular college.

It was my first time away from home, and my world came crashing down on me. I could not cope with the flashbacks of my abused childhood, to the point where they disrupted my studies. I ended up failing. My parents kindly agreed to let me give grade thirteen another try, but I still couldn't pass. What was I to do next?

I worked for a few months as a nanny for two small children whose mother was on an extended medical leave. By the fall of that year, I was back home, pondering my uncertain future and feeling like such a failure. My mother saw an ad for a job at a group home for mentally challenged people. I refused to go, but she was adamant I was not going to stay at home and do nothing. So I felt I was forced to try the job. I well remember being so scared of the residents on my first day. The staff training me saw my fear and said I needed to give this job at least three months. I did not want to be a quitter—and what else was I going to do?—so I stayed put. In time, I came to know the residents and became fond of them. I developed lifelong friendships with some of the staff. I was thrilled to have a social circle at last, and I used to go on fun outings with them. I became maid of honor for one friend at her wedding.

One friend noticed my tendency to bump into people and to keep going. She brought it to my attention and suggested I look at their expressions when I crashed into them. I was taken aback to see surprised and/or angry reactions. After that, I allowed my friend to grab my arm and help me get around. Another friend encouraged me to see the eye doctor to ask about my vision. I remember sitting in his office so scared and asking him if I was going blind. His response was, "Yes." The news was so terrifying that I blocked it out, forgetting about it, until I was given a more explanatory diagnosis years later.

In a year, I became supervisor of one cottage at the group home. For the first two years, we were required to take the group home's classes, and while the classmates were few, I was happy to have top marks and to be acknowledged at both years' graduations with a beautiful bouquet of red roses. By my fourth year there, a new boss encouraged us younger staff to enroll in the Special Care Counseling program at a local community college. I was frightened about moving onto a new venture because of my poor educational past, yet I was burned out in my job, and I was in need of a change.

4
Degeneration

Only a small percentage of deaf-blind people are born with absolutely no vision and hearing. Many suffer from degenerative disorders, such as Usher's syndrome, that cause progressive loss of one or both senses. The effects of aging can also exacerbate sensory disabilities. Such progressive losses can happen quickly or be very gradual.

One of the most difficult challenges that confront many deaf-blind individuals is coping with declining sensory abilities. This is both a physical and psychological dilemma that profoundly alters one's life. Losing the ability to drive a car, no longer being able to hear on a telephone, or having to give up a career are just a few examples of how degenerative sensory disorders can cause turmoil, while more subtle things, such as increased difficulty with social interaction, can also be devastating. In fact, some will argue that it's better never to have had an ability than to have it for a while and then lose it forever. This is debatable, of course, but it serves as insight into the mental torment brought on by sensory degeneration.

I asked my contributors to discuss what they felt and how they coped when their abilities declined, not just to describe the physical changes themselves. There are a lot of strong emotions here, and they aren't happy ones. This is strictly about reality and the effect of extreme adversity on the human spirit; I made no attempt to falsely lighten anything.

Angela C. Orlando

I was thirteen when I first started losing my hearing. The doctors said I had Usher's syndrome. They believed I would lose all my hearing and vision before I reached adulthood. But at first, I only had to deal with my hearing loss. I did, in fact, become profoundly deaf by the time I was sixteen. We hoped the doctors were wrong about the Usher's syndrome. We tried to ignore the first signs of RP. But I think I really knew what was going on; the signs were there. I tripped over the dogs when they slept on the floor. I bumped into chairs that were pulled out and bumped into kids in the hallway at school. And I couldn't see in the dark; this was particularly obvious during marching band when we marched at night in areas with poor lighting.

When I was sixteen, I had cochlear implant surgery. This was back when it was still experimental for children to get implants, so insurance wouldn't pay for it. A rehabilitation worker from the state stepped in. She told my parents her office would pay on the condition that I had my eyes examined to confirm that I had RP. My parents refused. They knew I was dealing with so much already; they didn't want to add blindness into the mix until I was ready for it.

My parents had a rule for me: Because my brother, who had RP, had been in five car accidents in five years before he finally gave up driving, my parents insisted I would have to have my eyes checked before I could start driving. Keep in mind that people with RP could pass the visual exam for a driver's license back then, because a person's field of vision wasn't tested, just visual acuity. At first, I wasn't ready to deal with having my eyes checked, so I didn't begin driving right after turning sixteen. But by the time I was seventeen years old, all my friends were driving, so I wanted to drive, too. Finally, I agreed to the vision test. As expected, they found RP, so I never got to drive. That's how I got the official diagnosis for my RP. It was unpleasant news but not devastating, because I kind of already knew.

The hardest part about my vision loss was that almost no one knew about it. When I stumbled over things, my friends just thought I was clumsy. Kids thought I was ignoring them whenever I walked right past as if they weren't there. Nobody seemed to realize I just didn't have any peripheral vision. It was so embarrassing when I bumped into things. No one understood, and I didn't know how to tell them.

Marching band was the hardest part. I couldn't see in the dark. I couldn't get around when the lighting was poor. I struggled so hard to stay with my squad. People grabbed me, pushed me, and pulled me all over the place. I was so stressed and hated every minute of marching band.

I also had trouble socializing with friends as the night blindness got worse. It was hard for me to get to and from cars at night. If we walked along a street, I had to go very slow. This annoyed the other kids. One time at a party, we all walked to a local park in the pitch dark. I couldn't see anything at all and had a breakdown. I cried, and a friend had to lead me by the arm back to the house. No one really knew what was going on with me. Even I had a hard time understanding that the rest of the kids could see in these situations.

My night blindness made its presence known in my junior year of high school during a marching band performance. Every year, we did a special "Script Kent" in which the band would seem to spell out "Kent" in cursive writing. It was very popular with the crowd. But we performed this in the dark with glow sticks on our feet. This was my absolute most dreaded part of marching band. In order to get through it, I would hold onto the person in front of me and just follow along, until the lights came back on. It was embarrassing to do this, but I had no choice.

But then something amazing happened in my sophomore year: I could see during the "Script Kent" maneuver. I guess maybe it was an unusually bright night—I don't know why I could see all right that night. The experience gave me false confidence that led to a major embarrassment.

When the marching band performed "Script Kent" again the following year, I let go of the person in front of me, thinking I could see well enough to manage on my own. I had marched down the "K" for a few minutes before realizing this was way too easy. Finally, I stopped and braced myself to be hit by the people behind me. Nothing happened. I turned around and could only see the glow sticks worn by the band, as they marched along in the dark in a different direction. I was beyond horrified. I was mortified. I wanted to run off the field and hide. But it was pitch black—all I could see were the glow sticks behind me. Finally, I ran up to the band, jumped between two glowing feet and grabbed the person in front of me and held on for dear life, until the lights came on. I had no idea who I was holding onto, and I can only imagine what the people thought of me jumping in between them.

When the lights came on, I was relieved and amazed to see I had grabbed onto a friend. But my story was out. Everyone wanted to know what happened. How did I get lost in the dark? So I finally explained about my RP. Amazingly, I found myself laughing at the whole thing, too. It relieved the stress of trying to hide the problem.

Marching band in my senior year was much easier. If it got too dark, I left the field during practice. If it was too hard to march back to the bus after an away game, I walked behind the band at my own pace. If I needed help getting around, I just asked. People now understood and were willing to help me.

I underwent cochlear implant (CI) surgery on one ear when I was sixteen, a few months after I was diagnosed with RP. For the next twelve years, I did more or less okay. I considered myself to be hard of hearing with low vision. I could see well enough. I could read normal print. I just had no peripheral vision and trouble with night blindness. I used the sounds I heard with my CI combined with visual cues and lip-reading to understand speech. This worked well enough for me, and I was able to function in the hearing world okay. I used a TTY for the phone and closed captions with the television. I had trouble in noisy situations or in the dark but coped with it relatively well.

By the time I was twenty-eight, I had moved to Maryland and gotten married. I also had a son who was six months old when my new problems became evident. At first, it was hard to realize that something major was happening. I was having trouble seeing, but my doctor thought it was from a very bad cataract in my good eye. I even had cataract surgery but that didn't help at all. My new hearing difficulties were explained away, as well. I had just changed to a new CI audiologist, and it seemed like she was having trouble figuring out my needs. I actually remember saying that my speech processor seemed to be losing its map [i.e., programming]. We had to turn up the power a few notches. But what was really happening was that my auditory nerve was under attack and slowly deteriorating. Same with my optic nerve.

I began having issues with my feet, too. It started as numbness and severe pain in my toes and slowly spread all the way up my legs. Then it went into my finger tips and up my arms. I lost all use and feeling in my feet, legs, and hands. I couldn't walk at all. I couldn't feed or dress myself. I was in horrible pain. It was like pins and needles but much worse.

All this happened over a six-week period. In the end, I was totally deaf and blind and unable to control my body at all. And no one knew what was going on. At first, they told me it was "just nerves" and I would be fine after my cataract surgery. My father-in-law, who was my primary care physician, diagnosed me with postpartum depression and hysterical blindness. It both insulted and scared me to know he thought it was all in my mind.

They finally put me in the hospital about eight weeks after the onset of my problems. I had lost about twenty-five pounds in one month and my mother-in-law thought I was going to die. She pushed her husband into getting me into a hospital. There I was diagnosed—incorrectly—with a virus that attacks the nerves. I spent only eight days in the hospital and was then sent home, where my family had to deal with my very serious disabilities.

I was told by different doctors that my problems were only temporary and I would regain all function with time.

Six months after being released from the hospital I had a vision checkup. My doctor was surprised to see that my optic nerve looked pale. She took some special pictures that confirmed that blood was no longer being pumped into the nerve. There was so much optic damage that my eyes literally shut down.

My husband took me out to the car where he said, "You are blind now and forever." That's how I learned the news. It was a devastating blow. In an instant, I lost all will to live. I felt I had been through so much, and this was asking too much of me. I had a son, who was now a year old, though I believed he would be better off without me. I thought my husband should marry someone else and give Daniel a "real" mother. But, ultimately, I just couldn't leave him. I was his mother, and one way or another I had to *be* his mother. So my love for my son gave me the strength to go on, find peace in the world, and accept my disabilities.

Eventually, I did begin to heal a little. I am still totally blind, but my hearing returned to where it had been with the CI. Since I am now unable to read lips, I can no longer understand speech and must rely on tactile sign language. My CI does give me environmental sounds, which helps a lot to keep me in touch with the world around me.

After a year, my hands returned to normal, which was a real blessing. My hands are now the most important part of my body. My legs have partially healed. I have regained strength and some ability to walk. But I still don't have feeling in my feet and must wear leg braces. I have serious trouble with balance. I use a forearm crutch for stability and attend five hours of physical therapy per week to try to improve my ability to walk independently.

Christy L. Reid

Both my vision and hearing losses have worsened over the years. I don't remember anyone telling me that my optic nerve damage would get worse as I got older. And when my hearing loss became noticeable, no one predicted I would become profoundly deaf.

As a legally blind child, life was challenging enough, but I managed to lead a fairly normal life. I could hear; I had many friends; I was involved in sports; I enjoyed music and liked to record songs on my tape recorder. Then as an adolescent, my hearing started to go. It was like listening to a radio that constantly went off tune and grew dimmer and dimmer. My social life dwindled down to a few friends who knew finger spelling and some sign language. I just sort of felt lost, not being able to understand the conversations around me, so I ended up getting lost in a book. My family did their best to try to help, but it's hard to involve someone whose hearing was unreliable 100 percent of the time.

How did my disabilities affect me mentally? The hearing loss was harder to accept. But maybe because it happened gradually, from the time I was nine to when I was about sixteen, I had time to try to learn how to deal with it. When I entered public high school as a sophomore, I began to work with a deaf education teacher who introduced me to sign language. There was one other student in Poplar Bluff High School who was deaf and was fluent in sign language. I hung out with her a lot and began using sign language as a means of communication. I began building a small network of friends who were interested in learning finger spelling and signing. I even tried out for the high school cheerleading squad; the judges said I had a great voice, but my jumps weren't so great. There was another student who was pretty good at signing. She invited me to join her Girl Scouts troop, and I got to go camping and joined in other activities. But none of the other girls signed, and I depended on my friend for interpreting help.

I was a typical teenaged girl who dreamed of going out on dates. But there weren't any guys who were willing to ask a deaf-blind girl out. Finally, in my junior year, I was asked out to a basketball homecoming game and then to the dance. He was a boy two years younger than me, and at first, I was excited about getting dressed up and going out on a date. But as the night progressed, I learned his interests were physical, and I wasn't interested. I didn't go out with him again.

My family was always supportive and tried what they could to help me as my hearing loss became a serious problem. My parents always encouraged me to try to do things for myself, and my mom was very patient in showing me how to do things I didn't understand. For instance, she drew a picture with a black marker of the clasp on a necklace, showing me how to fasten a necklace myself. I liked to cook. Mom encouraged me to make desserts and dishes for the family.

My dad, a former captain in the National Guard, was tough and enjoyed challenging adventures. I used to go jogging with him. He tried to teach me to water ski, though I was never any good at it. Our family took up an interest in going on all-day tubing trips on a lovely river in the Missouri Ozarks. During one tubing trip, we stopped at a cliff where people were climbing up and jumping into the river. I wanted to try it, and with the help of Dad and my younger brother, I slowly climbed the cliff. Dad climbed a little above me, showing me handholds, while my brother climbed below me, putting my feet on toeholds.

As I got older, and especially after my third son was born, my balance deteriorated. Then in 2006, when I was forty-two years old, I experienced an odd numbness and tingling sensation in my feet and lower legs. I thought the problem was caused by my shoes. I went to a quality sports store and told the saleslady about the numb feeling. She said that was a common problem and usually meant that the person's shoes were too short. I bought a pricey pair of quality walking shoes and thought that would be the end of the weird feeling. But the numbness persisted, and it felt as though I was wearing a pair of tight knee socks.

In 2007, I went to see a neurologist. I was considering a second CI, and the surgeon who performed the implant surgeries wanted me to be examined by a neurologist to find out whether or not my balance problem was related to my first CI. It turned out that my balance problem had nothing to do with my CI. After the neurologist examined me and performed several tests, including a most uncomfortable and scary electrical shock test on my lower legs and feet, he determined that I suffered from nerve damage (neuropathy) in my feet and calves. He linked my optic atrophy, auditory nerve damage, and nerve damage in my feet and called it polyneuropathy. This is a general term referring to nerve damage. I left it there; it was enough for me to know that the numb feeling in my feet was not caused by my shoes.

The polyneuropathy could get worse and could affect a different part of my body. A year after the diagnosis, I made an appointment with a local chiropractic care doctor. I had been told that chiropractic care could help improve my balance, but never followed up on the suggestion. After visiting the chiropractor almost regularly for a year and a half, my balance has noticeably improved. I can stand in the middle of a room without support and without feeling disoriented for longer and longer periods of time. I can walk briskly without support in familiar areas. This is amazing to me, because before chiropractic care, I usually had to trail the walls in my own house and had to almost always touch something for support.

Ilana Hermes

My disabilities started with me being born with congenital hydrocephalus. As a result of this condition, some parts of my brain did not develop fully. However, because I received early intervention (i.e., physiotherapy, occupational therapy, and speech therapy) from about one year of age until I was thirteen, I did not notice the progression and severity of my disabilities until I reached adulthood. At that point, I had to start doing things I never had to do at school, and it made me more aware of my limitations. It suddenly felt like my ability to cope with my blindness—the fact that I couldn't walk as fast as others or do sports activities independently—was no longer good enough. I realized how much the early intervention had helped me cope when I was young. But I no longer receive those therapy sessions as an adult.

The question remains: do I need to resume these treatments to help me throughout my whole life? Was having them as a child enough? I think I could benefit from continued therapy. But, then again, I have pride and feel that, if I can learn to manage doing therapy by myself, I will understand my strengths and weaknesses and will be able to work around the progression of my physical disabilities.

My eyesight has long been gone, and I have no hearing without my cochlear implants, so I shall say these two sensory losses are "stable."

However, my implants have given me enough hearing to communicate, and they make it possible for me to interact with people. My hearing is not perfect with the implants, but I dearly love what they've given me.

When a longtime friend of mine moved with her parents to nearly within walking distance from where I live, she contacted me about visiting her. I told her that my mom was not home, so I couldn't get to her house. I would have gone to see her by myself, but I am no longer able to walk that far and need someone to drive me. So she said she'd come and visit me. She, to this day, has never come to visit me. Maybe she just doesn't understand my physical limitations now. It's not that I'm lazy or not trying; it's something I have to live with and deal with every day. That experience made me not trust people when they say they're coming to visit or going to take me somewhere. When someone says they will come and visit or pick me up to go somewhere, I wait, with the feeling in my heart that they won't come, and when they do, it feels like a big surprise.

All my life, my family has been very supportive. After my school years, I met new friends from church, and they are very supportive and accepting of my disabilities.

Judy Kahl

For years, I thought my hearing loss—discovered at age seven—was my only disability. Wearing hearing aids truly allowed me to live a pretty normal life and with little difficulty. As technology improved, my parents would get me the new, improved, stronger hearing aids, and I did well, especially with my natural ability to lip-read.

It was a shock to be diagnosed with RP at the age of twenty-five. I never had visual problems, nor did I have any family members with eye problems. The doctor asked me if I ever had problems with night vision, and I responded that I had difficulties in movie theaters, but so did everyone else. I had no clue that I would be diagnosed with a horrific disease that could rob me of my sight. Life had been wonderful at the time, as I was newly married with a beautiful baby girl, and then a routine eye exam told me the terrible news that I may one day be blind. I was just destroyed emotionally and truly did not know what to do.

My husband and family were very supportive. We tried to get information about RP, but all we could learn was that it is sometimes hereditary, progresses sometimes quickly and sometimes very slowly, and there is no known treatment or cure. That was it!

I always thought the hearing loss was my only disability, and to have two disabilities was unthinkable. I did not know anyone with two disabilities, especially two very important senses needed to function in life. Needless to say, I did not know that the two disabilities had one name, Usher's syndrome, nor did I know that I could become deaf as well as blind.

I always thought that my hearing aids would keep me in the hearing world, and I just prayed that my sight would not get worse. It was a "hope and pray" style of coping, and I tried never to dwell on it. My biggest coping skill was to keep very busy, so I would not have time to think about the scary possibility of my future. I can tell you, however, that it was always in the back of my mind, and it was the "dark cloud" that would even make the sunniest day sad, if I didn't fight it.

Whenever there was a visit to the doctor's or a vision-related incident, or I had a feeling that my sight was worse, it would trigger a twenty-four-hour crying spell. Those were my one-night pity parties. This was disease, and no one knew how or what to say to make me feel better. It was just my life to deal with this as best I could.

Two years ago, at the age of 61, I hit bottom. It was time for social security benefits, and they asked if I had a disability. Well, I had to prove that I was legally blind and severely hearing impaired, which meant I had to give them current hearing and vision reports. It was at this time that I realized my hearing had deteriorated to only 4 percent in one ear and 7 percent in the other. With hearing aids, I was lucky to get 15 percent of sounds and conversation. I realized that reading lips was getting me by, but with my eyesight deteriorating and my last remaining central vision being attacked by the disease, I was in serious trouble.

It was then that we checked into seeing if I was a CI candidate. I was, and I had both ears done within fourteen months. I am happily back in the hearing world and hearing better than I've heard in years—or maybe ever heard in my life. It is good. I have had people tell me that they don't see the strain in my face now that I hear better, and it does help me on a daily basis so much. I almost feel that I've eliminated one disability, and life is a bit easier with not having to read lips to hear. It's a true blessing for me.

Now, if we could just find a cure for vision loss . . . and we're working on that. Again, my coping skills have me keeping busy; I am working with the Foundation Fighting Blindness (FFB) to raise funds for research.

Mark Gasaway

I know that my disabilities have changed over time. I once had some residual hearing, but no more, and my vision has decreased to such a point that I can only see clearly about two feet in front of my eyes. I can still make out large objects more than two feet away, but these objects appear blurry. My peripheral vision has decreased, and I cannot really rely on it much. The nerves in my eyes are affected by nystagmus (involuntary movements of the eyeballs). When my eyeballs move because of nystagmus, it is hard for me to focus clearly on almost anything. I have to wait for my eyeballs to calm down.

This explanation of my vision is not due to a progressive affect but, rather, to the change in the structure of my eyes, perhaps because of age and eyestrain. My hearing, on the other hand, has just completely faded away.

Another area that was affected by the encephalitis is my coordination. My balance has been affected a lot and gives me a lot of trouble at times. Part of this can be traced to a spinal disc problem in my lower back and a knee injury. I love to walk and exercise outdoors and used to run road races. I still can run and enter a race now and then, but the training is not like it used to be. The hearing and vision losses have been with me so long that I have practically taken them as they have come. The balance issue bugs me at times and makes me feel like I have not worked hard enough to control it.

I did not quit working because of the disabilities but chose to go back to school and was not happy with the job I had at the time. I did well in school and am now trying to establish a program to help other deaf-blind folks. I have not lost friends due to the disabilities, as that has not been an issue. As for driving, I never had the opportunity to learn to drive.

My vision and hearing losses are not a big deal. What really frustrates me is my balance issues because I can look like a foolish drunk when it gets bad. The balance can be good one minute, and all of a sudden, I lose the good balance and my legs get tangled up. I can walk at a fast pace much better than I can at a slow pace. That is how I am able to control running, because I do better when my legs and feet work faster than at a slow pace. Because of the faster pace where I can control my balance, I like to say that my feet have a mind of their own.

My family reacted quite well to my problems and tried to support me in ways they felt were best for them without trying to control my actions or my reasons for doing what I wanted to do in my life. My friends at that time did the same but gradually have not been in touch with me very much. Both family and friends understand what I go through, for the most part. However, there are times my family does not understand, and family members do not really know what it feels like to be in the situation I am in with them when it comes to communication.

The communication issue is a problem because my family does not sign well, and they may feel that it is not important to communicate with me like they do with my siblings and extended family. I feel left alone, and that is not how it should be. To deal with it, I ask the family to answer me when I ask questions, and they attempt to do so but not always. Writing is their main method of communicating with me.

Melanie Bond

It is my personal belief that when I became pregnant with my first daughter I lost a significant amount of vision. My vision seemed to deteriorate at an accelerated rate during the pregnancy, despite others saying there is no connection between being pregnant and having RP. My dad pleaded with me not to have another child, because he was concerned that I might lose more vision. I simply told him that I was going to lose my vision sooner or later whether or not I had other children. As it turned out, I ended up having another daughter, and when I remarried, I had a son. I have no regrets having given birth to my three children.

At my current age (fifty-three), I am surprised that I still have "good vision days" when I can see things clearly outside, when the sun's shining and the sky's clear. I am able to see well enough to read at a lower magnification level. Then there are other days when my vision is hazy, and I have to rely on my hands to find my way around inside my home.

When I was pregnant with my son at the age of thirty-six, I surrendered my driver's license. I felt a keen sense of loss, since I had been fiercely independent for so long. However, I took it all in stride, knowing that I had a husband who was willing to chauffeur me to wherever I wanted or needed to go. Then there was the thought that I could never forgive myself if I injured or killed someone while I was driving a car. That would have destroyed me. So if it's one or the other, I'd much rather give up driving to save a life or two. I don't really have a right to complain about not driving, because I got at least twenty years of driving under my belt, and that's good enough for me!

My family was very supportive of me. My parents didn't coddle us when my siblings and I were growing up. We didn't live in a fantasy world where everything's supposed to be perfect. What we do have is an imperfect world where there are supposed to be problems—problems that beg for solutions and answers to help improve the quality of life for all who suffer from any type of disability. As far as I'm concerned, that includes the whole world. I'm glad my parents and siblings didn't cry or fuss or feel bad about my being deaf-blind. I believe in holding my head up and retaining my dignity. Sometimes, a friend or one of my siblings may tend to be patronizing, feeling that they know what's best for me. Uh-uh, I won't stand for that! Though I hear many deaf-blind people on the Internet stating that they'd like to throw a pity party for themselves, I just laugh at it. It's not a bad idea to make fun of ourselves from time to time!

On the other hand, that deaf guy that I married? Instead of being supportive of me once we found out I had RP and was now carrying the proud name Usher's syndrome Type 2, he broke down and cried—not for me but for himself. He went through all the stages of grief—the grieving, the anger, the bargaining—but, somehow, he missed the acceptance stage. His anger was inexcusable. He accused me for having hidden the truth from him and that he had been a sucker for ever having married me in the first place. He wanted nothing to do with me. The whole irony is that we had been married for more than six years before our first daughter was born and before

I found out that I had RP. But one thing that I have learned about deaf people is this: They all fear the possibility of going blind. I can understand that fear. When you're deaf, you have to depend almost exclusively on your vision. Most people can get by with the loss of one of the five senses. But to lose what most people would consider the most important two senses? To many, that would be unthinkable. That is, unless you've experienced deaf-blindness yourself. Then you begin to appreciate all the other senses that you do have, the heightened senses of touch, taste, and smell.

This is what my first husband feared above all: that my deaf-blindness might be contagious. And from that point on, any love or affection that he may have had for me died, because he simply couldn't handle my going blind himself. But I still had me, and I went on to raise my two daughters. In 1988, I married a sweet Canadian guy who was fully supportive of me and who willingly helped me to raise my family. I must say that I'm very glad that this special man, and my three children treat me as if I were a completely normal person. It's great to be accepted for who you are, and with that comes a sense of contentment.

I never went through the grieving process myself when I first learned that I was losing my vision. I think my ex-husband cried enough for both of us. In a way, I think I was the stronger one. And for my children, I was determined to be the best deaf-blind person that I could be.

Patricia Clark

Both my disabilities became worse over the years. Deafness was severe by the age of twenty-one, and finding employment was a problem. As my friends married, my social life dwindled. The number of bachelors dropped, too. I could hear only a few people on the telephone, and there were no fax machines or personal computers in the 1960s, let alone a telephone relay service. Within a few years, the telephone was beyond me. Few people understood how much this affected my life. I was never invited to any social occasions at all after that. Trying to get involved in social things through another person caused endless trouble—and still does.

The loss of music was a blow to my spirit. Music had kept me going through a difficult adolescence at home and had never failed to lift me above the trials of life. But as my hearing declined, the music I once loved faded away.

Reading was my other consolation. My vision didn't deteriorate as rapidly as my hearing, so I was able to continue reading for some years. But the vision gradually got worse and made this increasingly more difficult over time, until I couldn't read normal print anymore.

I did find employment but only ever had one very good job that I enjoyed and where I felt accepted. That was as a programmer at International Computers Limited (ICL), which was then the British answer to IBM. One day the manager called me in and expressed concern that my poor hearing was causing problems for the customers that visited our offices constantly. After three years there, I decided to take a hiatus and go to England. I was hoping to find a cure for my disabilities there and return to my job later on. Unfortunately, I was not able to get the job back when I returned to New Zealand.

Although I did not know it in my early adult years, the keratoglobus in both of my eyes was getting worse. While the vision in my left eye was good for a time, the right eye had been legally blind since birth; I could only see movement and light with it. In 1979, the cornea ruptured, and I suffered four years of pain as blisters formed in the right eye and I became virtually blind, as the other eye went in sympathy. During this time, my distress was so obvious that most people, including family, avoided me. When I was clearly in pain with my eyes streaming, they'd just walk out of the room. I saw many eye specialists and finally found one who believed he could cover the eye in such a way that the pain would be relieved. The procedure was called a Gunderson flap operation.

During these years, the effect on my life was severe. I spent much time lying in a darkened room. As I lived alone, normal household tasks were almost impossible. I had to give up driving. I existed from day to day. I probably suffered from depression, but it didn't occur to me to seek help. The dreadful struggle of those years pushed me to the brink of total despair.

The Gunderson flap operation freed me from pain, but soon after this, I became unemployable. I lived on an Invalid Benefit, which was far from generous, but I was free from a job where the boss was antagonistic, where work was withheld, and I was never invited to any social events. I had been forced to work in such a toxic environment in order to survive, and I was glad to be free of it.

I am now living in a retirement village with no hearing at all and facing imminent total blindness. The residents are, of course, elderly and can't be bothered with writing notes to communicate with me. I have a good home helper who does housework weekly and takes me shopping. She knows the manual alphabet (i.e., finger spelling). I have a Braille display on my home computer but am finding it hard to get training for use of the Internet. My current worry is whether I can manage my small household without sight, since the last of my vision is fading away. The village will provide a hot meal daily, but the cost is quite high.

I also have spinal arthritis and can't stand up for long. I use a walker to get around the house. Heart disease is another health issue, and it means that I get tired easily. But the isolation of being deaf-blind is the most acute of all these problems.

Scott Stoffel

Since my disorder is undiagnosed, I never had any warnings about what was going to deteriorate next. My vision supposedly went through rapid decline when I was four and then stabilized at about 20/400, although I have no memory of normal vision. The nerves controlling my fingers also declined during that time period, leaving me with limited use of my hands.

Those problems were all I noticed or understood about my disability until I was eighteen. No one ever told me I could lose more abilities. I just assumed my vision and hands were my only significant problems. When my hearing went through rapid decline at eighteen, it took me totally by surprise and left me shell-shocked. I tried regular hearing aids and later tried programmable aids, but neither restored my ability to discriminate speech. They magnified environmental sounds, but that actually made it more difficult to separate speech from background noise. Members of my family insisted it was my fault the aids didn't work—I wasn't trying hard enough. It got to be so frustrating that I just quit wearing them altogether. I retained enough hearing to talk to one person at a time in a very quiet setting for about nine more years, but the residual hearing eventually faded to the point where I had no speech understanding left at all. With my poor vision, I couldn't read lips or even sign language. Interaction with people and the world was a nightmare I preferred to avoid most of the time. Despair became overwhelming.

For years after the sudden hearing loss, I drifted aimlessly, searching for a place in the world for me. My life was lonely, and it never seemed like any of the people I knew understood what I was going through. I put myself in some bad situations out of desperation for companionship. Wine became a frequent refuge. I thought I was going to go mad if something didn't change, but I just didn't know what to do or where to go.

Then my bizarre disability played another joke on me. I developed numb spots on my feet and legs. This problem was a lot easier to deal with than the catastrophic hearing loss, but it was, if you'll pardon the pun, unnerving, all the same. I went to a neurologist, who did what every neurologist I ever saw did—he shrugged. Thanks, Doc, very helpful and well worth the wasted time and money.

My next decision was to accept that I was a deaf-blind person and needed some way to communicate. A good job or social life were impossible without an effective mode of communication. I talked to a state vocational rehabilitation counselor in Connecticut about it. She said the best place for a deaf-blind person to get rehab services was the Helen Keller National Center (HKNC) in New York. So I resolved to go there and try to start my life over again.

Tactile sign language seemed to be the answer to my communication woes. While it was anything but easy to read sign language by feeling the signer's hands, it was still better than trying to read real-time dialogue typed on a computer screen with my limited vision or using a dry-erase board. After spending over a year learning to read tactile sign language at HKNC, I decided to take another crack at college.

My first stint in college had been a total disaster, but I realized that a degree was necessary in order to get a good job in a field that was accessible to me. I enrolled at Hofstra University and moved to Hempstead, New York, to within a few blocks of the campus in January of 1997. I could walk to classes and had the benefit of some familiar interpreters from HKNC. And I was highly motivated to succeed this time around.

For one thing, I owed it to my new wife, whom I had met at HKNC. For another, I wanted to prove to myself I wasn't a worthless freak. My grades were good, and I began to think a career in computer programming was a realistic goal.

Then my practical joker of a disorder struck again.

No sooner had I started a full-time courseload after only going to college part-time for a year and a half than I started experiencing difficulty with balance and walking. I went to a neurologist, who shrugged and told me to have an MRI done on my brain. I did the test, but the doctor said he couldn't find anything. I always knew it was a vacuum up there.

So I started walking with a cane to avoid falling down, as well as to give the public a reason for why I appeared to be incessantly drunk as I stumbled around the campus. The development did little to improve my self-esteem and made the trek to and from the campus a laborious journey. Any ideas I had entertained about trying to get involved in some type of sport were out the window. I was back to being the one-man freak show.

As a wild-ass guess, I would say the numbness in my feet and legs was a precursor to the walking problem that manifested itself a few years later. I threw that theory at a neurologist once. He shrugged.

My disabilities stabilized for a few years, giving me a chance to finish college. I transferred to Temple University in Pennsylvania in the fall of 1998. After three more years of lethal effort, I emerged with a Bachelor of Science in Engineering for Electrical and Computer Engineering with top honors and got a job doing Systems Engineering for the Federal Aviation Administration (FAA) in Washington, DC. I was actually dumb enough to believe that the hellish struggles were finally behind me and that I'd get to live happily ever after. It takes a BSE with honors to be that intellectually challenged. The so-called Stoffel's syndrome had more jokes in store.

I had never been an ace at reading tactile sign language. I had limited use of my thumbs and the lower joints of the fingers, so it was difficult to close my hand over an interpreter's in order to "read" what was being said in a meeting or training session at work. But when I suddenly lost several more nerves in my hands shortly after joining the FAA, I found myself desperately trying to survive those meetings and training sessions. I lost both some feeling and several movements, leaving me unable to pick up much of anything through tactile sign language at real-time speed. I had to revert back to using typed interpreting. Abruptly, all that hard work at HKNC was meaningless.

What's going to go next? No way to know. All I can do is try not to think about it.

Tonilyn Todd Wisner

In November of 1995, I was diagnosed with a rare inner-ear disorder known as Meniere's disease. The cause was unknown, and there's no cure. It causes "Meniere's attacks," which are vertigo attacks with chills, nausea, vomiting, and seizure-like activity that can last for days. It can also cause deafness, balance distortion, double vision, oscillopsia ("jumping vision"), light sensitivity, tinnitus, and a few other things.

My hearing slowly got worse from Meniere's disease after 1998. By 2002, it stabilized, but I couldn't understand much speech with my hearing aid anymore and relied mostly on lip-reading. In March of 2005, I had a severe attack of vertigo that never stopped. I felt as if I was spinning all the time with no relief. For the first year, I could barely walk with a walker and, at times, couldn't at all because I was so dizzy. During the second year of the vertigo problem, I was still mostly bedridden but could get around my house by using walls, furniture, and a cane. I used a wheelchair when I had doctor appointments or went out anywhere. During this time, I was also suffering from Tullio phenomenon, which is a condition in which loud sounds make you dizzy—even your own voice. Mine was so severe that even the lowest sound made me dizzier. Not only couldn't I wear my hearing aid, but I also had to wear an earplug. Although my hearing had stopped getting worse, I could barely hear anything with my ear plugged and relied completely on lip-reading. It was during that first year of vertigo when I started having problems with my vision, but it's all so complicated and related to different causes, so I'll talk about my hearing first.

You might be wondering why I was not treated for so long. Well, none of the specialists I went to had any idea what was wrong with me. I started going to a training hospital, and for about five months, I was told that they couldn't help me—come back in one month. I did my own research and felt that I might have had a superior canal dehiscence, a hole in one of the balance canals of the inner ear, but no one would listen to me (déjà vu!). In late 2005, I was told that I would finally see the head of the ENT department, another neurotologist. But a few days before that appointment, hurricane Katrina hit us. All neurotologists (most specialists in all fields, actually) lost their jobs and/or homes in the surrounding area and left the state. So for a long time, I was left with no help and no hope.

In early 2006, the specialist whom I had planned to see started commuting from his new office in Pittsburgh to Baton Rouge one day a month. I got in to see him, and he told me that I had a superior canal dehiscence, just as I had been suggesting to the other doctors for a year (why doesn't anyone ever listen to me?). He scheduled surgery to repair the dehiscence a few months later. But a week before the date, I got a call saying that they had lost the budget from the state for a neurology department at the hospital, and I had to have a neurosurgeon assisting my neurotologist; therefore, I couldn't have the surgery. You can imagine how upset and hopeless I felt. After almost two years of thinking my life was over and I'd never be helped, I had a diagnosis and a prognosis for full recovery and then was basically told, "Oh, sorry, we can help you, but we won't." The person we spoke to even said, "Well, it's not like its life-threatening!" No, I had no life to speak of to be threatened at that point in time.

In March of 2007, I was at my ailing grandmother's house with my mom, when I got a call from my husband (then fiancé), Keith. A doctor whom I had seen at the beginning of my illness in Lafayette was at the hospital in Baton Rouge, saw my chart, and learned that my surgery had been cancelled. He was so upset that I had not been helped yet that he called on a Monday and said that his internship there was ending on Friday and that I *would* have my surgery on Wednesday, no matter what he had to do. He wanted me to get to Baton Rouge immediately to do pre-op! It turned out there was another approach that could be taken to repair the dehiscence that did not require a neurosurgeon. More risks were involved, but it was my only hope at that point. This doctor, Dr. Justin Tenney, is now a practicing neurotologist in different cities in Louisiana and is my biggest advocate.

I had the surgery, and it was a success. But there was one complication: I woke up completely deaf.

Now I need to back up for a moment and talk about my vision. Keep in mind that all this started eight months after the constant vertigo began and while I was going through that fight to figure out what was wrong with me as far as the vertigo went. I was nearsighted with glasses, but there had never been a sign that I'd lose my vision. In November of 2005, I started seeing flashes of light that weren't real and a little blurriness. I saw my ophthalmologist but she could find no problems. The ear doctors said it wasn't connected to the vertigo. I had an MRI and spinal tap to rule out muscular sclerosis (MS). By the end of December, I had blind spots in my central vision, everything was a blur, and I could no longer read regular print. In January of 2006, I was having trouble reading large print and knew I had to do something.

In less than three months, I taught myself both Grade I and Grade II Braille and started reading Braille books. It was around April that I learned of the Hadley School for the Blind and took many courses through the mail to hone my Braille skills, among other subjects. It wasn't until sometime in 2006 that my eye doctor could see small macular holes in both eyes. But they were so small that I should have been able to see clearly in all but a pinpoint spot in my visual field. There was no evidence of why I was blind—by the time she found this, I was legally blind and no longer reading any print. With most of the specialists having left the state (ones who took Medicaid), there was only one doctor I could see, a retina specialist. He could not find any reason for my blindness either. Neither doctor had ever seen macular holes like mine and said it was not macular degeneration—or at least any kind they had seen before. They also said it was probably genetic and that I needed to see a neuro-ophthalmologist for testing. I saw one who agreed with the other two specialists but could not give me a diagnosis. He said I needed genetic testing, but the closest facility that did these tests was in Houston, Texas. Louisiana Medicaid refused my request to go there. So I have been on my own ever since, teaching myself to deal with my diminishing vision.

Losing my hearing was hard, but it was something I could live with. I have never been afraid of being deaf, maybe because I grew up hard of hearing. But I have always hated not being able to see what was around me. I've always had my back to a wall, and blindness was one of my biggest fears. Accepting and dealing with blindness has been very hard for me. But the hardest thing is becoming both deaf and blind, because it takes away what kept me from fearing deafness—my ability to read lips and my love of visual ASL. I can no longer drive, so that took away a lot of my independence. I can't make any calls on my own, can't participate effectively in conversations much of the time because I don't know when people are talking or what is being said. My world has become an isolated and often lonely one.

The hearing loss didn't affect me mentally. It was the vertigo that was hard to handle, but I could still read and watch TV, and that kept me occupied. But after about a year, when it looked like there would never be any help for the vertigo and my life would be spent in bed, I became very depressed. As I started losing vision, communication became much harder, and TV was no longer an option. My ENT gave me antidepressants. The medication helped a bit, but not completely. I tried not to let it show, but I was a total mess inside. I was terrified. And the more vision I lost the worse that became. But I busied myself with learning Braille, my classes from Hadley, teaching myself to use a cane and fighting my state for assistance.

I joke that I am going through the grieving process backward because now, three years after the vision loss started, each additional loss brings anger, resentment, and depression. People say I am so strong for doing the things I do, but what else can I do but keep going and try my best?

When my Meniere's disease got so bad that I couldn't go places or be around people for long, my friends just kind of forgot about me. That was very painful, but that was when I learned who my true friends were.

My family was always supportive of me, but they never really understood my limitations. They still don't seem to understand the degree of my vision loss. But I can't say that they aren't supportive; it's just that they don't really "get it." I guess you really can't understand it, unless you're going through it yourself.

My husband (then fiancé) had a very hard time accepting my deafblindness. He has a language-learning disability that makes it hard for him to spell, so writing into my hand or using tactile finger spelling is very frustrating for him. I was—and still am—very slow, receptively, at both of these modes, so it puts blocks in our communication.

I realize the sudden, unexpected deaf-blindness has been very hard on those close to me and not just on me. I'm thankful for those who have stuck by me through it all. I've also met a lot of great people on the Internet, others who are deaf-blind, and they have been a great help in my struggle.

[Tonilyn is now totally blind, and vertigo continues to be a major problem for her.]

Wendy Williams

When my Usher's syndrome was diagnosed at the age of twenty-nine, my visual fields were 10 degrees with visual acuities of about 20/30 and 20/40, and my word discrimination with hearing aids was 96 percent. That was still pretty good, except for the narrow field of vision. Into my thirties and forties, my hearing remained stable, but my visual fields shrunk down to five degrees and continued to deteriorate. My visual acuities also declined. I began to experience close calls with vehicles coming toward me from the side. It frightened me; it was like a car just came out of nowhere and zoomed by very close to me.

In response to the trouble I had getting around on the streets, I applied to Seeing Eye in New Jersey. I was matched with a three-year-old golden retriever named Darby. The guide dog was a big help. I no longer felt afraid to cross a street.

At the age of forty-six, I discovered I had breast cancer with a fifty-fifty chance of survival. After surgery to remove the cancer, I felt something was different but couldn't put my finger on it. It seemed as if I was "removed" from everything around me. I could not focus on fine print. I kept looking at my bedroom closet door, thinking it was different, but how? Sometime later, it dawned on me that I could no longer see the fine wood-grain pattern on it. Also, sounds seemed hollow to me. I felt out of sorts and wished I could shake it off. After chemotherapy, speechreading became more difficult, as did hearing. I struggled to fill in the missing pieces of information.

Vision and hearing tests revealed fluctuations and then a gradual decline in my vision and hearing, starting with the right eye and right ear. At times, I had to strain so hard to make use of both my very limited vision and hearing just to figure out what was going on around me.

There were moments in which I found myself unable to take in any visual and auditory information, and if I was in an oral setting, I had no means of being able to receive input. I was terrified—how was I going to function on my own? If a person who once had good hearing views becoming deaf as devastating, then what description is applied to losing vision and hearing simultaneously? It was a living nightmare for me.

I received my first CI on the right side at age fifty, and it improved my ability to understand speech moderately. A few months later, cataract surgery on my right eye was a possibility, with the caution there was no guarantee of restoring any useable vision, due to the advanced stage of RP. I decided to opt for it, since I had nothing to lose. There was a slight improvement for a short period, and then I was seeing as if through a continuous smoky haze.

By the time I was about fifty-five years old, I had only light perception in both eyes and little hearing in the left ear. Thus I encountered great difficulty localizing traffic to make safe crossings with only the right cochlear implant and guide dog to rely on. I negotiated with a state traffic engineer for nineteen months to have vibrating traffic signals installed at busy intersections.

When I was given a second CI for my left ear, my ability to discriminate speech improved significantly. It made oral communication much easier.

In the midst of all these dramatic sensory changes, I had to make major adjustments on my own and implement adaptive skills previously acquired in blind rehab training. Instead of effectively navigating throughout my community with my guide dog, I found myself repeatedly getting lost and walking aimlessly, trying to get my bearings. I then had to limit my local travels to known routes. In addition to needing a speech screen-reader (voice output) to access my computer, I quickly progressed from regular print to large print to Braille for hardcopy reading. I was stressed and exhausted, particularly when I had to read technical books under pressure. I learned that planning ahead was important for my life to go smoothly. For example, I started labeling canned goods, so I opened a can of peas instead of a can of peaches for a tuna casserole. I had to depend on my sense of touch for most areas of daily living; it became very fatiguing and time-consuming to do the simplest of tasks. I found myself wishing there was a book of instructions to guide me in this journey, but I was left to figure out on my own how to accomplish household chores in different ways.

When I was working, my early morning routine went like this: I rushed through grooming my dog guide, Telly (this was after Darby), showering and dressing myself, feeding Telly, eating breakfast, and preparing lunch to go. Then I had to walk a mile in the scary darkness to my job. By the time we reached our destination, I'd arrive at my office exhausted, and the work day still loomed before me. I started leaving for work a bit earlier, so I'd have time to regroup prior to beginning my job activities. I had two jobs, really—being a psychologist and being a problem-solver. The problem-solver had to constantly try to find different ways to get the psychologist's duties accomplished. Of course, that didn't come with a paycheck, but it sure seemed like a job in itself. As my vision deteriorated, both tasks became harder. There were evenings when I crashed at home and wondered how much longer I could work.

I welcomed solitary moments to get breaks from the challenges of life, crashing during evenings and weekends. By the same token, I felt very lonely and wished for more loving support from relatives, friends, and coworkers, similar to when I had cancer. But I mostly was left to contend on my own.

5
Bad Medicine

To err is human, and doctors are as human as the rest of us. However, when a medical professional makes a mistake or fails to take a case seriously, the results can be disastrous.

Patients with multiple problems that can't readily be diagnosed can understandably be frustrating for doctors. Some doctors are content to slap dubious diagnoses on cases they can't figure out, while others wave a patient's unusual problems off as being purely psychological. Are these actions harmless? Not always, but you're not likely to hear about the cases when patients were hurt by them.

Many people with multiple sensory challenges fall into the "hard to diagnose" category and are common victims of misdiagnoses and inappropriate treatment.

Furthermore, some doctors—and even family members—fail to take the time to communicate medical issues with deaf-blind patients. The lack of communication can be damaging, both mentally and physically, yet few people seem to understand this.

The purpose of this chapter is not to launch attacks at particular medical professionals. Rather, it is to show how poor judgment, lack of concern, and inadequate communication on the part of any medical professional can profoundly affect a patient. In this chapter, you will experience things from the perspective of deaf-blind patients.

Angela C. Orlando

My older brother, Tony, was diagnosed with RP when he was twelve and I was seven. I wore glasses at the time and had 20/40 vision, so the doctors wondered if I had RP, too. They made me go to the Cleveland Clinic for lots of scary vision and eye exams. In the end, they said that maybe I was a carrier for the genetic disease without actually having the disorder. I never understood where they got that idea from or what it meant. And life went on. [A person can carry the genes that cause a genetic disorder without experiencing the symptoms.]

When I was thirteen, I began to lose my hearing. I was found to have a bilateral sensorineural hearing loss. My vision was the same, although I no longer wore my glasses. I had absolutely no symptoms of RP at that time. Still, the doctors looked at my hearing results and my brother's RP and diagnosed me with Usher's syndrome. The immediate effect of this was that my mother burst into tears right there in front of me, and I felt like my life was over.

I realize that in the mid-1980s, medical knowledge in the field of genetic disorders was lacking. Still, they really had no basis at the time to think I had Usher's syndrome. It made little sense, given that my brother had normal hearing.

They were right about one thing—I did eventually show symptoms of RP. This seemed to strengthen the diagnosis of Usher's syndrome, but my family was confused. How could I have Usher's and my brother only have RP? The two disorders are not carried on the same gene. Tony's hearing was actually better than normal, and he was a gifted musician.

For almost fifteen years, my diagnosis was Usher's syndrome, although we always had that little bit of doubt and wonder. Then my entire family donated blood to the Boys Town Usher's syndrome study. The results showed that I did not have a causal gene for Usher's and there was no Usher's gene in my family.

So then my diagnosis became "retinitis pigmentosa with hearing loss due to unknown origin." Again, a virus was suspected.

When my son was six months old, I began having trouble with weakness, fatigue, and numbness in my feet. My vision seemed to be worsening. My eye doctor attributed this to a very bad cataract in my good eye. I had cataract surgery, but she was wrong about the cause of the problem. My vision worsened rapidly until I became completely blind.

At the same time, my hearing was declining. I was seeing a new CI audiologist. She thought the problem was that she didn't know me well enough and thought she'd given me a map (programming of the CI processor) that wasn't quite right. So she had me come back in for some re-mapping. But she, too, was wrong, and my hearing faded until I was completely deaf, too.

Both these professionals meant well and really had no idea what they were dealing with. It's a shame I already had vision and hearing trouble that made it harder to realize there was a new and serious problem. If I'd had normal hearing and vision before this happened, the losses would have sent up immediate red flags.

My father-in-law, a family practice doctor, was treating my other symptoms. The fact that he was acting as my primary care physician is bad medicine in itself, I think. My husband and his father, Dr. Howard, didn't seem very concerned by my problems. They told me it was all in my mind and that I needed to pull myself together for the sake of the baby. At first, Dr. Howard thought I was just nervous about my upcoming cataract surgery. Then he diagnosed me with postpartum depression and hysterical blindness. He put me on a high dosage of antidepressants, and that was all the treatment I got.

Dr. Howard let me slowly deteriorate over the next six weeks. In the end, I was completely deaf-blind, could not communicate with people at all. I could not feel my hands, legs, or feet. I couldn't walk, dress, or feed myself. I lost twenty-five pounds in one month. What little food I managed to get down I would immediately throw back up. And I was in constant and horrible pain; it was like pins and needles but so much worse. Dr. Howard gave me a narcotic pain reliever, but even that didn't help.

Finally, he decided I might have a real problem and sent me to a neurologist friend of his, Dr. Gordon. I had a lot of tests done that showed severe neurological damage but did not pinpoint a cause. Dr. Gordon said I had some kind of virus. He told me to keep taking the pain pills and that my body would have to fight off the virus. And he sent me home.

It was my mother-in-law who finally got me into a hospital. She says she thought I was going to die and demanded her husband do something. Unfortunately, Dr. Howard and Dr. Gordon were still my primary doctors, even while I was in the hospital.

At the hospital, they did many different types of tests, including a horrible spinal tap. My obese husband forced me onto my side and practically laid on me to keep me still, while his sister held down my legs. No one made any attempt to let me know what was coming; they just treated me the way a veterinarian might treat a dog. I was so scared and kept struggling because they were so rough. I think they could have made some effort through gentle touch gestures, like letting me feel an empty syringe with no needle and then poking me in the back with a finger, to let me know what was basically going to happen. I still have nightmares about that incident.

They also did genetic tests, but no one ever followed up on that. My blood tests showed thyroid disease, but that, too, was ignored for many years.

Dr. Gordon diagnosed me with Guillain-Barre syndrome (GBS), a virus that attacks and damages nerves. So now I had a triple unrelated diagnosis of "GBS, RP, and hearing loss due to unknown causes." I thought I must be the unluckiest person in the world.

I had a very near disaster at the hospital. My parents came from Ohio to Maryland to visit me because someone had told them I was dying, although I didn't know that at the time. My ability to receive communication then was virtually nonexistent. All I knew was that my parents and husband took turns staying with me around the clock while I was in the hospital. But that wasn't the only thing I didn't know: Dr. Gordon and Dr. Howard ordered an MRI test one day to check for brain deterioration. You would think a family practice doctor and a neurologist of the twenty-first century would know that a person with a CI, which has a magnet attached to it, can't have an MRI done on the brain. But they ordered the test, and because I couldn't communicate, my husband gave consent for it and signed the papers for me. They had me on the table and were about to start, when my parents burst into the room. They had found the papers about the MRI with the consent signature in my room and came running to put a stop to it. Even then, the doctors didn't believe there was a problem and wanted to continue. Thankfully, my parents insisted they consult the hospital ENT, who promptly cancelled the test. Had the test proceeded, my implant could have been ripped right out of my head by the machine's magnetic field.

Although I wasn't really doing any better, Dr. Gordon sent me home after eight days in the hospital. He was quite content with the diagnosis of GBS and said it would take time for my nerves to heal. I was put on nerve pills and more pain medicine and sent home.

I didn't doubt the diagnosis of GBS, but there was one thing that didn't fit: Most people with GBS have lung damage and difficulty breathing.

They often end up on a heart-and-lung machine before they are positively diagnosed. Everyone said I was so lucky and credited Dr. Howard with his quick action in my case.

The next several months—even years—involved nothing at all; there was no treatment, follow-up, or tests. I took medicine and I waited. That's what Dr. Howard and Dr. Gordon wanted me to do. They kept saying, "It takes time for nerves to heal." I thought if I heard that one more time, I would scream.

I did begin to improve ever so slowly. I was put in a home physical therapy program for a few months, and they managed to get me kind of walking again, even though I still couldn't feel my feet. After six months, my hands healed enough that I could clumsily feed and dress myself. My hearing returned to where it was before the sudden deafness, with my CI functioning. The pain lessened very slowly and was still always present.

I saw my eye doctor three months after the hospitalization and again three months after that. Dr. Howard, Dr. Gordon and my eye doctor all believed I would see again. People with GBS usually regain their vision. It was such a shock to my eye doctor at the second checkup when she discovered that no blood was flowing into my optic nerve and my eyes had permanently shut down. The doctors decided the combination of RP and GBS had caused too much damage for my optic nerve, and that's why I was left permanently blind. I never saw that eye doctor again.

There were actually warning signs that something other than GBS was going on with my vision before this discovery. About four weeks before that checkup, during the time when my hands and hearing were showing improvement, I began seeing bright flashes of light in my eyes. It was like someone shooting a camera with a flash right in front of your face. My husband and his father said those flashes were good; it meant my vision was coming back. Actually, the opposite was true. If I had gotten to the eye doctor then, could they have saved my vision? I don't know. The idea haunts me.

The medical treatment I received over these next four years was bizarre and neglectful. You might even go so far as to say it was medical abuse.

I did not see my neurologist at all. Dr. Howard did not seem to think I needed regular checkups. I wasn't able to see my CI audiologist, either, for regular mapping. My husband didn't like to make the drive and felt my CI was useless since I couldn't understand speech anymore.

Once, I fell over something, and my husband just left me on the floor. My knee swelled up, so he finally helped me and called Dr. Howard. His dad came to the house with some medical supplies and drained it.

Another time, when I had some kind of vaginal sore, Dr. Howard checked it himself while I lay in bed. That made me feel very weird. But it was the closest thing to GYN care I was getting at the time.

When I was suffering from very severe constipation, Dr. Howard took me off my pain and nerve pills. I went cold turkey and felt horrible. When that didn't help the constipation problem, my husband told me to just "sit on the pot and squeeze some shit out." I would receive no other treatment for the constipation.

One winter we were having a family dinner at my in-laws' house. All of a sudden, my husband grabbed my arm and pulled it out of my sweat shirt. Then, while he held down both my arms, his father jabbed me with a needle. This is how I got my flu shot. No one bothered to even tell me what was going on until afterward, and both my husband and his mother knew how to sign into my hand by this time. The really shocking part is that someone with GBS isn't supposed to get a flu shot. It can bring back symptoms of the disease. But since I didn't even know the shot was coming, I couldn't tell them that. And Dr. Howard should have known that himself.

On May 21, 2005, I was bitten by a spider while playing outside with my son. I remember the date because it was the day before my son's fourth birthday. At his birthday party, I complained to my husband and his doctor dad that I was having pain in my leg and flashes of heat all the way down the leg. Dr. Howard said he'd look at it later, which he never did. I begged my husband to take me to the doctor's office to have the bite checked. I wrote emails to his mother, asking her to send Dr. Howard over. They did nothing.

Four months later I once again was having serious health problems. It seemed like I was having a relapse of the GBS. I was weak and fatigued. I was having trouble walking. I had to crawl up the stairs. I finally got Dr. Howard's attention, and he sent me to the lab for tests. The only thing that my blood showed was thyroid disease . . . again.

Dr. Howard sent me back to Dr. Gordon, who ran more tests. He said I still had severe peripheral nerve damage and altered my diagnosis to a recurrent form of GBS. He decided I needed try some type of experimental treatment.

All this time, I still had the heat flashes from that spider bite. I suggested the problem was from the bite, but the doctors dismissed that idea. Just in case, Dr. Howard put me on a round of antibiotics. And, miraculously, the problem was solved. The heat flashes stopped, and I regained strength and use of my legs. I was sure the problem was the spider bite and nothing more—it must have been badly infected after four months. But I'm just a lowly patient, so what do I know?

Dr. Gordon went ahead with his experimental treatment, known as intravenous immunoglobulin (IVIG). This is like a type of IV medicine to help the immune system. It is considered risky, because infusion can make the body sick. It was not normal treatment for a diagnosis of GBS, which is why it was considered experimental. Medicare wouldn't pay for it, but, luckily, since one monthly course of IVIG costs $30,000, my husband's insurance would cover it. I underwent eight months of IVIG treatments. I received infusion each month for five days in a row. The treatment would last about three hours each day. A nurse came to my house to administer the medicine and monitor my condition during infusion. The needle was left in my arm throughout the five days, but I was only hooked up to an IV bag during actual treatment.

The IVIG made me so sick. During six of the eight treatments, I developed an absolutely shattering headache, as well as dehydration and fever. I also had reactions to the needle in my arm and would be in utter pain by the end of each course. Other side effects included feeling very cold, shakiness, sore muscles, and weakness. They told me not to worry because it's normal for IVIG to bring about a "minor" recurrence of symptoms of the disorder. The funny thing is that my nurse kept thinking I had MS, instead of GBS. I wonder if my paperwork was even correct.

In August 2006, I left my husband and moved to Ohio to live with my parents. They were quick to take me to the Cleveland Clinic for treatment. They didn't want me to miss my next round of IVIG. After testing and examination, my new doctors were shocked that I was ever given IVIG as a treatment. When they got my medical records from Dr. Gordon, they found I was on an unusually high dose of IVIG, too.

My new doctors believed the type of nerve damage I have will not respond to IVIG. They immediately stopped all treatments. Not only that, they also threw out the diagnosis of GBS altogether. They weren't yet sure what I had, but they knew it wasn't GBS.

Unlike Dr. Gordon and Dr. Howard, the doctors at the Cleveland Clinic looked at all my symptoms together, hearing loss, vision loss, peripheral nerve damage—even the constipation and thyroid disease that Dr. Howard ignored were considered vital clues. And, thankfully, I was finally given treatment for those problems.

I have been seeing several doctors in multiple departments at the Clinic to try to find a reason for all my problems. They sent me to Dr. Narkovitch, a gifted genetic doctor known for taking genetic disorder cases that no one else can figure out. Dr. Narkovitch first believed that my brother and I both had a genetic disease known as mitochondrial cytopathy. He later had me tested for a rare genetic disorder called polyneuropathy, hearing loss, ataxia, retinitis pigmentosa, and cataract (PHARC), and I at last got a positive diagnosis. PHARC accounts for the vision loss, hearing loss, cataracts, and the polyneuropathy in my extremities.

Having a correct diagnosis makes it possible for me to have my son tested to see if he inherited the disorder or is a carrier of the gene.

Carol O'Connor

Back in 1997, I had to go into the hospital for an ear operation on my left ear. It was kind of like a skin graft to cover the big hole near my eardrum, as it was causing lots of bad ear infections. I was so desperate to get the infections stopped, but the tests went on for months before the doctors finally did something.

I was admitted into the ENT ward at Manchester [England] General Hospital. The hospital ward had an awful atmosphere that week. The other patients were all so damn ignorant, as I will never forget. I was shouting across the ward, but it appeared nobody was taking a damn slightest bit of notice. It was very frustrating. There weren't many nurses on that day. So I just sat there all day on the bed, bored to tears. When I pressed the button to go to the loo [toilet], nobody responded. Oh, I was all worked up. I just kept saying under my breath, "Where the bloody hell is the nurse?" But nobody would come and help this blind patient.

After a while, I was so desperate for a wee. So in the end, I had to grope for my cane, eventually found it, and felt for the sides of beds. Oh, I was so embarrassed, as I could feel everybody was staring at me. One woman just shouted, "It's up there!" I thought to myself, "How the hell do I know what you mean?" She was probably pointing; that's real useful for a blind person. Then she just shouted, "Hey, love, you're going the wrong way." Then she shouted, "No! Left a bit! No! More!" I was getting more and more frustrated. But I finally found the toilet without banging my head on the door. I just slammed the door and would've thought a nurse would have ran to me, but no.

So, anyway, when I came out of toilet, I tried to remember the way back to my bed, tapping other people's beds with my cane. Suddenly, it was silent. Oh, it felt terrible, but I eventually got there. But I can't believe there wasn't a single nurse there that could spare a minute to help me.

Later on in the evening, the trolley was coming into the ward. I could hear nurses talking now. My god, the noise in that ward! So I thought to myself, "Well, you lousy lot never spoke a word when I was struggling!" That hurt me quite a lot.

As I sat there on my bed, I heard this woman shout, "Come and get your tea, love." So, of course, not knowing who she was referring to, I just sat there. Later, after everybody had got their evening meals, I just shouted, "Where is my meal?" One staff nurse came over and shouted, "We told you earlier on. Why didn't you answer?" I told her I was totally blind. In the end, she brought my meal over. But she didn't even tell me what I had. Deep inside, I felt so bitter and isolated.

After that, I shouted for some tea. Nobody responded again. Oh, to hell with it! I tried to pour myself some orange juice I found inside a locker. I struggled, as it was a wide jug. I ended up spilling it. At this point, I thought to myself, "If I spill it, I might get some attention." But, no, I didn't. The woman in the next bed just said, "You're spilling that, love." So why didn't she—or anyone—try to help me? I realized I was fighting for survival on my own in that hospital.

Late at night, visitors' time, I was so excited to see my mum and two sisters and their kids. I told my mum what had happened, and she was so annoyed. The visiting time gave me a break, and I forgot about all the trouble earlier.

The next day they prepared me for my operation. This one nurse brought me two slices of toast. That was nice, but I thought you weren't supposed to eat before an operation. She said it was okay to eat, so I did. And guess what? I was feeling quite poorly after my operation. When I came back from the theatre [operating room], I was very sick in the stomach, had a shocking evening and night after that. And again, nobody bothered to help me.

The day after my operation the doctor came around and told me off. He said I was a silly girl for eating before the surgery. I told him it was the nurse on duty that morning who said I could eat. He said the staff nurse told him I asked for the tea and toast. Well, I was wasting my time, so I didn't argue.

The doctor told me to rest after he took the bandage off. I slept in the afternoon. They had pulled the curtains around my bed. When I woke up that evening, the meals had been served already. I hadn't eaten since the day before because of my stomach upset and was starving. So I asked a nurse if I could have a cup of tea. She said she'd bring me one later, but I never got it.

So when mum and my two brothers came at visiting time, I wasn't feeling good at all. Mum gave me a drink of orange juice. I was so relieved. But it was ages before I got my breakfast the next morning. Everybody on that ward got their breakfast before me.

Anyway, the day after that the doctor came around again, and to make matters worse, he told me the operation wasn't a success. I just broke down and cried and cried. He left, and not even a nurse came to me to comfort me. Oh, I felt very depressed. I just couldn't wait to get out of that place and go home.

My god, what a shocking bad atmosphere it was there.

Judy Kahl

Parents want to hear a doctor say that he or she can help their child's hearing. A doctor in New York City, who had helped a priest friend of our family, told my parents he could straighten out my eustachian tubes and that this would improve my hearing.

Needless to say, he was a "quack," for lack of a better word. He may have helped some people, but he just took my parents' money. There was no way he could help me. My hearing loss was nerve-related and was not fixable. I later found out the cause was Usher's syndrome Type II, but I think that doctor knew he couldn't improve my hearing all along and resent that he made us hope for nothing.

Melanie Bond

I can definitely recall one unfortunate incident that occurred when a doctor in Tucson attempted to use laser surgery on my eyes. At the time, I wanted my husband to accompany me while the procedure was being done. I had brought my FM system with me and was depending on my husband to relay any information from the doctor and/or nurse directly to me (by speaking into the microphone) so that I would know what to expect while the procedure was being done every step of the way. Unfortunately, I was not allowed to have my husband with me, even though I tried desperately to explain that it was my right to have him in the room with me. The nurse physically moved me to the seat where the laser machine was located. I started asking questions about the procedure and was shocked to learn that the nurse had grabbed my head to hold it still—I had been unaware that the laser treatment had already begun. If the doctor or nurse had said they were starting, I never heard it. I blurted out, "How could you start this procedure without informing me that you were ready to begin? How do I know you were aiming straight into my eyes if I was still moving around and talking?"

Needless to say, I was totally pissed off at the doctor. Once the doctor left the room, I told the nurse that they had both been wrong to deprive me of any means of communication and that I had every right to demand that my husband stay in the same room with me because he knows how to help me when I need his assistance. I thought about suing this doctor but felt it wasn't worth the time or hassle. As far as I was concerned, the damage had been done, and I was never going to go back to him again.

I totally rely on my husband and/or friends to relay information to me through my FM system when it is required. I do not understand most people's speech but am better able to understand my husband's speech because I've been with him for nearly twenty-two years now.

I had this procedure done on my worse eye. I don't know exactly what happened when I moved my head, but it sure scared me when I found out I'd moved during the surgery—only because the doctor hadn't bothered to communicate with me. The vision in the eye was unchanged following the surgery; there was no improvement that I could discern.

I also think there's a conspiracy in Arizona to hide the truth about valley fever (also called coccidioidomycosis, which is the second longest word in the dictionary). At least 95 percent of the population in Arizona might experience symptoms of a cold or the flu, not realizing that they have contracted valley fever. Those with a healthy immune system are able to fight off any lasting ill effects. However, the other 5 percent may be vulnerable to a valley fever attack that weakens their immune system. What happens is that there are cocci fungus spores in the air, and if you breathe them in, they will attack your lungs. And if you're not treated early, the cocci will disseminate to different organs throughout the body, causing one to feel weakened. That happened to me, most likely when I was out walking my leader dog on a windy day. Shortly after this, my body was covered from head to toe in the worst body rash I had ever had in my life. Then there was fluid in my lungs. At this point, my support service provider (SSP) took me to the ER at a Tucson Hospital, whereupon I was diagnosed as having pneumonia. I was given a ten-day supply of antibiotics. This brought about absolutely no improvement. I went back to the ER, and they prescribed a second round of antibiotics. Again, no improvement. The third time around, I wised up and asked the ER doctor, "Is there a possibility that I might have valley fever?" He assured me that I didn't have it. That turned out to be a lie. Once again, he prescribed a new round of antibiotics for me that did absolutely nothing for me, except weaken my immune system. Valley fever is a fungal disease, not a bacterial disease.

I sought a private doctor and asked her to test me for valley fever. Unfortunately, the lab messed that up, so the test had to be repeated. This time, I got a positive on the valley fever and was quickly given Diflucan, an antifungal drug.

Later, X-rays revealed two dark spots in my right lung, due to valley fever. The interesting thing about the cocci fungus is that it is considered lethal enough to be considered a deadly bioterrorist weapon. All I can say is that I'm glad that I am a valley fever survivor. I suffered a second episode of valley fever a couple years later and was put back on Diflucan.

Patricia Clark

The causes of my vision and hearing impairments were never really discussed—or at least not with me. Diagnoses were made, but they varied from one specialist to another.

When I was sixteen, I went to a clinic at the hospital. A form had to be signed. Then a doctor who happened to be there, but whom I didn't know, called me in with my mother and proceeded to make a lot of statements about my future. He said I must leave school and get an office job, so I could dig myself in for total deafness, which according to him, was not far off. My mother said I was not interested in doing office work but wanted a university education in music. He scoffed at this and told her that it would be a waste of money.

My mother was not a person to take this lying down. There was a dreadful shouting match, which the doctor won by default. My mother was reduced to tears—one of the very few times I saw her cry. I was so devastated that I spent the next two days in bed. My father knew someone on the elected hospital board and reported this incident. Nothing came of that, but my parents, as an act of defiance, bought me a much better piano than the old Joanna I was learning on. They could ill afford to do this, and I have the piano to this day. I am now totally deaf, but I can hear through the memories in my fingers.

The doctor was quite wrong about how quickly my hearing would deteriorate and how much I could accomplish. I spent twenty-five years employed as a computer programmer. I have a degree in music and two postgraduate degrees in psychology. I had many years of partial hearing and was not totally deaf until about the age of fifty.

When I was twenty-three, I travelled to England and worked there for two years. During this time, I was introduced to an ENT specialist. He said that he performed the "new" procedure of mobilization of the stapes and assured me that he could restore my hearing. [The stapes is a small bone in the middle ear, the innermost of the three small bones that transmit vibrations.] I was persuaded to have the surgery, and it was totally unsuccessful. The doctor came to the ward the next day, avoided looking straight at me, and said, "Your hearing will not improve." He then walked away. He had been so sure of success, or so he said, but I suspect I was a sacrificial lamb to the Great God of Science. After this, I had bad tinnitus in that ear, which I still have. My balance was also badly affected for a couple of months.

The worst aspect was the doctors' lack of concern for me as a person and their total rejection when they found they could do nothing for me. It seemed like they just wanted to get rid of me the moment it was clear something hadn't worked. They never made any effort to console me or consider how the failure affected me psychologically. It was just, "Well, this didn't work. Good-bye." I felt I had been conned and never really trusted a doctor ever again. I lost hope for the future. Professionals have no right to do this to anyone, and to a young person, it's particularly cruel.

Tonilyn Todd Wisner

My health problems have always seemed to be non-textbook and are either not diagnosed or have been misdiagnosed. I tell my doctors that they went to medical school for a challenge—and here I am! It's kind of a joke that I should be the final exam in some fields of medicine. If you can diagnose me, you pass. The first time I was misdiagnosed was when I was a kid and had a brain tumor. I got many inaccurate diagnoses before someone finally figured out what the real problem was. It started when my left eye began to "roam." An eye doctor gave me glasses and ignored me when I said they hurt my eyes. Then I started waking up with migraine headaches and vomiting every morning. I don't know how many "specialists" my parents took me to see, but it went on for months. I was told I had sinus problems, needed glasses—every doctor had a different diagnosis. Nothing they recommended helped, but the "specialists" knew what they were doing and weren't going to listen to me, even though I tried to tell them there was something more serious wrong with me. My symptoms got worse, while the treatments totally failed to help.

I eventually went back to my ENT, Dr. Norma Kearby, whom I had been seeing since I was six. She is the only reason I'm alive today. I went to her crying, ran into her arms, and told her that something was *really* wrong and no one would listen. She got me in to see a neurologist right away. I had a CAT scan and an electroencephalogram (it reads brainwaves). By the time we reached home afterward, the doctor had called and told my sister that I needed to come back to the hospital immediately. She had found the brain tumor—and it had to be removed as soon as possible. She told my parents that if it wasn't removed within a week, I would die.

Yet I had known there was something very seriously wrong for months before this. Why didn't any of those other doctors believe me?

Then when doctors finally removed the tumor, they did a lot of damage in the process. I was left with learning disabilities. Some cranial nerves were cut, such as the one that controls facial movements. Because of that, the left side of my face was permanently paralyzed.

When I started losing my hearing and getting dizzy spells many years after the brain tumor, I was referred to a neurologist. He did diagnose me with chronic migraines, which I'd had since I was twelve but had never been treated for. So I finally got some relief from those headaches. He said my dizziness could be migraine-related but referred me to an inner-ear specialist to be sure it wasn't something else. It took a year, but I did get a correct diagnosis of Meniere's disease. However, since then, I have had many other inner ear problems get worse, and these went undiagnosed or were misdiagnosed. The main problem was that I'd had a hole in the inner-ear canals that provide balance for at least two years, maybe longer, before it was identified. Initially, one doctor said a CAT scan showed the hole and the other doctor said it didn't. So it was forgotten about. Then a few years later, I was struck with vertigo that left me bedridden and didn't respond to any medication. For two years, I was like this, until the hole was officially found.

The surgery to repair the inner ear caused almost as much damage as it fixed. I lost the rest of my hearing. That is a possible side effect of the surgery, but I do feel that, if they had diagnosed me sooner and the hole had not become so big, my hearing might have been saved. I am still waiting for a diagnosis of my blindness. I've been losing my vision since late 2005, and no one has been able to help me or tell me why. I feel like

I have been dismissed by some doctors because I am "too complicated." I feel like someone should care enough to find the problem but that they just don't because it would take too much time. To date, I have had only two specialized tests, for one of which the results were lost, and no one bothered to redo the test.

Wendy Williams

After witnessing me narrowly miss being hit by a vehicle I neither saw nor heard at the age of four, my mother took me to the family doctor. She expressed her concern about my hearing. But the doctor told her the only problem was that I wasn't paying attention. My hearing was normal, according to that doctor. The doctor couldn't even tell that I'd learned to read lips to support my limited hearing.

It wasn't until four years later when my hearing loss was diagnosed. About the only accommodation I then was given was to sit at the front of the classroom in school. I continued to rely on speech-reading, since hearing aids were not recommended for me. I fell behind in language acquisition and academics in general, but the doctor didn't think a hearing aid was needed.

When I was seven, a needless tonsillectomy was performed by an ENT to "hopefully" improve my hearing. It didn't do a thing for my hearing loss. All it did was subject me to unnecessary fear and discomfort.

In my adolescence, the eye doctor told my parents and me that I had tunnel vision. This was to explain my increasing clumsiness. However, he failed to tell me I had RP, and that it involved night blindness and gradual shrinking of my peripheral fields. Thus, I continued plowing into everybody and everything, being embarrassed and injuring myself, since I did not receive the orientation and mobility (O&M) training to learn how to travel safely.

Medical staff denied my parents' repeated requests for me to receive speech therapy and to be enrolled in the deaf school. I mispronounced a lot of words and omitted the consonant sounds "s," "sh," and "ch" from words. But that didn't convince the staff that I needed speech help.

I remained a target of my frightened and frustrated mother's abuse, at least partly because the doctors refused address my problems.

I finally got my first set of hearing aids when I was eighteen, thanks to a hard of hearing camper's recommendation. I was happy that communication was easier, but I was sad for all the lost years of hearing and learning language.

When I was nineteen, an eye specialist shared with my parents that I had RP and that I likely would go blind. But the specialist advised them not to tell me this news. For the next ten years, I sustained more bruises and abrasions, as I tripped and stumbled and banged myself, feeling helpless and angry.

Finally, when I learned of the RP and Usher's syndrome at the age of twenty-nine, I experienced a huge sense of relief that there was a medical explanation. I then got the O&M training I had needed for so long and learned how to move safely. My parents' acknowledgment that they had known of this diagnosis a decade earlier triggered surprise and then anger in me. But they insisted it was the doctor's recommendation not to tell me about it.

When I was forty-six, I discovered a lump, and my doctor ordered a mammogram. She called me to tell me the result, saying she did not know what to say, other than to continue the monthly self-exams. When the lump began to hurt, I was back in my doctor's office. I recall her saying it looked disfigured and nothing more. I was puzzled at her seeming lack of concern. I requested a second opinion with the surgeon. A biopsy confirmed it was breast cancer. When I returned to the first doctor for a pre-op appointment, she said she was surprised it was cancerous. I was astounded by her response.

After surgery and chemotherapy, I requested my medical reports. The radiologist said that even if the mammogram did not detect a lump, a palpable lump should be further investigated. I was stunned. Female patients valued the expertise of this particular doctor. If this was the case, why did she not pursue an earlier, direct course of action for me? Was there a personality conflict between her and me? Was she prejudiced because of my disabilities and just hoped I would disappear? I may never know, but her conduct was inappropriate.

6
Rehabilitation

Rehabilitation services can help people with disabilities learn to cope with their challenges on a number of basic levels, including getting around ("orientation and mobility," or O&M), performing household chores, cooking, shopping, communication, attending school or college, and workplace adaptation. Such training and assistance can be invaluable in helping a person with multiple sensory disabilities adjust and find ways to get things done. Unfortunately, not everyone with a need can obtain rehab services, due to cost, locale, or lack of knowledge of the programs available. Others may have access to the services but decline to take advantage of them.

Even when rehabilitation services are available and used, the results are not always good. Few services are provided specifically for people who are deaf-blind, forcing such individuals to seek services from agencies specializing in either deaf or blind assistance, which do not consider the effect of the combination. And there is little, if any, specialized training for persons who have problems with the sense of touch or have motor difficulties in addition to hearing and vision losses.

This section is intended to give those involved in rehab programs a look at things from the perspective of the client with multiple disabilities. There are valuable insights here that can help service providers better understand and accommodate the unusual cases of people with multiple challenges.

Angela C. Orlando

My first experience with rehabilitation services came when I was sixteen and about to have cochlear implant surgery. I don't know exactly why the Bureau of Services for the Visually Impaired (BSVI) was interested in my case. I was only a sophomore in high school and didn't have career plans yet. But they worked with my older brother and found out about me. The counselor who worked with children met with me, my parents, and a few people from my school. BSVI offered to pay all the costs of my CI surgery if I would agree to have a vision test for RP. By this point, we were pretty sure I had RP, but there had been no confirmed diagnosis yet. My parents felt I wasn't yet ready to deal with that. They were shocked at the nerve of the BSVI counselor and literally told her to go to hell. And that was the end of rehab for awhile.

We tried again two years later when I was getting ready to graduate from high school. Now I did have the official diagnosis of RP, so BSVI was willing to work with me. They made me go through all sorts of visual tests to confirm my disability with their own approved doctors, as well as achievement and intelligence testing. The latter was done at a special center for the visually impaired. They did not take into consideration my hearing loss. I had trouble understanding the spoken questions and scored pretty low in some areas. My high school did the same tests in an accessible format for me, and I did much better.

The BSVI testers also wrote in their report that I had lower-back pains and was taking drugs. That's all they said about it. I was angry, because there was a reason for this. I had bruised my tailbone in an accident four days before and was still recovering. I had wanted to reschedule the appointment but was told by BVSI that if I did, they would not work on my case.

The BVSI counselor, armed with this faulty report, decided I might be a risk for rehabilitation services. She sent me to work with a psychologist for six weeks. I actually liked the psychologist, and our sessions were pretty good. She sent a report telling BSVI I could achieve in a career goal program and that there would be no risk in working with me.

So, finally, after all that, I was entered into a rehab program with the Bureau of Vocational Rehabilitation (BVR). But the fight wasn't over. They still had doubts about my ability to become a special education teacher—that was my career goal. They wanted me to go to a two-year school and become a teacher's aide. I refused. I told them I'd become a teacher with or without their help. They decided to stay on the case.

The first step would be to fund my college education at Kent State University. This hit a snag when the BSVI counselor missed a very important deadline with filing a paper. This meant they could not cover my first semester. But since it was her fault, she offered me a deal: She knew I had been saving money to buy a computer and suggested that BVR would buy me the computer, while I paid for my first semester with my saved money. This turned out to be a dream deal for me. They got me a huge system, plus a laser printer. I was happy about that one.

For the next five years, I went to school. I had no further contact with BVSI or BVR, except filling out a monthly form about my progress and sending copies of my grade reports. No one contacted me before graduation to talk about job opportunities and how to find work. I was doing that on my own but with little success.

I moved to Maryland three months after college graduation. I started working at the medical practice owned by my boyfriend's father, while I looked for a teaching position.

Ohio BSVI closed my case and marked it a success. And I had to start all over in Maryland, in the Maryland Division of Rehabilitation Services (DORS). I had to do the vision and hearing tests and the achievement and intelligence tests again. But this time, there was no trouble with the tests.

I was assigned to a counselor who didn't seem to understand why I was there. I had a job, he argued; I didn't need anything else. They wouldn't help me find a teaching job unless I was unemployed. I don't think he understood that RP made me legally blind and that I couldn't drive because of my disability. When I asked about transportation services he said, "What do you think we do here? Buy you a car?"

I gave up on getting help from DORS. I found a teaching job on my own. When that didn't work out so well, I found a new job, where I was happy. And then I got sick and became much more disabled. I suddenly lost all of my vision and most of what little hearing I had.

Once I was strong enough, we went back to DORS to talk about independent living and care-taking for the disabled. My counselor looked at me wide eyed and confused. He said, "There's nothing we can do to help someone as disabled as you." And he sent me away. We tried to help educate this man in the needs and rehabilitation of people who are deaf and blind. We sent him information and even tried to put him in contact with rehab teachers who worked with deaf-blind adults. He wasn't interested.

After a few years of nothing, I was transferred to a counselor who worked with people who are deaf. She had no experience with deaf-blindness but was willing to learn. She even attended deaf-blind camp in Maryland.

I was in the Assisted Living program. They got me some equipment, like a Braille note-taker, Braille TTY, home alert system, embosser, and a vibrating alarm clock. They provided equipment but no training. And I was unable to use most of this stuff.

Eventually, I was assigned an Independent Living teacher who came to my house. She did an assessment but wanted to wait to receive the kitchen gadgets that had been ordered through a grant before she did anything else. Those gadgets didn't arrive, and we never worked together again.

The one successful thing that came out of my time as a DORS consumer was being set up to work with a sign language teacher. Becky, an interpreter with a local school system near Baltimore, was very eager to teach me tactile sign language. She was very knowledgeable about working with people who are deaf-blind; she was involved with the deaf church in Baltimore and volunteered at all the deaf-blind socials and camp. We worked together twice a week for about eight months. She also took me to deaf socials and deaf-blind events, so I would have people to practice with and contact with other deaf and deaf-blind adults. And then I moved back to Ohio.

This time, BSVI set me up with a brand new BVR counselor—who had only been on the job for one month—because she knew sign language. But she never talked to me directly; she always used an interpreter.

We hit a major roadblock. I was trying to begin a new vocational goal. Despite my disabilities, I wanted to go back to work. I wanted to support myself and my son. I may be disabled but I am healthy and smart and able to function on the job with reasonable accommodations. But we never made it past the medical paperwork. My old doctor in Maryland sent back the forms, saying I was too disabled to work. My new doctor at the Cleveland Clinic wouldn't fill out the forms until he had a diagnosis. And since finding a diagnosis has been the hardest part in my medical case, that could take a very long time.

After six months of waiting, a representative from Ohio Deaf Blind Outreach suggested I switch to the Homemaker program for a few months. I could work on needed skills like independent living, communication skills, and technology setup and training, and begin mobility instruction. By the time I was finished with that work, the medical paperwork would be complete. It seemed like a good plan, but there was a flaw: The Homemaker counselor was an idiot who dragged my case along for eighteen months, with few services provided. I did get training in cooking and cleaning through a teacher from Deaf Blind Outreach. I did get a mobility teacher, but he was ineffective and didn't do anything. He let my physical therapists figure it all out and said he'd step in later. More and more time went on without my needs being addressed.

In May of 2008, I finally called a meeting with Ohio Deaf Blind Outreach, an HKNC regional representative, the Homemaker counselor, upper level BVR and BSVI representatives, and my physical therapist—she wanted to attend and is a great advocate. I demanded they place me back in BVR and address my vocational goals and other needs. I fired my mobility teacher and asked that a new one be appointed. I expressed my interest in attending training at HKNC in New York. It was agreed, and paperwork was quickly processed to get me into HKNC in the summer. My stay would be short, only four weeks, but it was all I could manage, since I am raising a child and need to be home for him.

My goals at HKNC were to receive assessment and begin training in vocational exploration, communication skills, mobility, and technology. HKNC was to get started and then Ohio BVR would take over from there. I feel I never really got out of the evaluation stage at HKNC. Most of my reports merely listed things I already knew about myself or skills I had already achieved before I arrived at HKNC.

There was good and bad at HKNC. I loved technology classes and felt we got off to a great start with me learning how to use a computer with Braille display. In vocational exploration, we came up with a career goal for me to become an online tutor or teacher. And I thought creative arts classes were awesome, even if that had nothing to do with my rehabilitation.

But there was a lot of wasted time at HKNC. Due to schedule confusion and constant changes, I was often left waiting for an instructor who never arrived. I asked that I not receive low vision classes, since I am totally blind, and that independent living be removed, since I had that locally already. But that was never done. They say that HKNC does whatever it is the student needs to succeed—the focus is on what works for the individual. But I didn't see that. My training seemed to center around making me fit into the plans and beliefs of the teachers. For example, I don't like using a Screen Braille Communicator. I have one but choose not to use it. We wasted so much time working on that machine. I didn't learn a thing and still don't like to use it.

Maybe if I had been there for a longer time I wouldn't be so upset and cynical about my training. But little things kept happening. There was a teacher who made me sit for four class periods while *she* worked on my resume. She never asked me a question or anything, just had me sit there for hours while she worked. That same teacher took me to the lunch line one day and just left me. Due to my balance problems and difficulty with my arms, I can't function on my own in that kind of situation. I didn't know how to follow the line, get food, or communicate with others to ask for help. It wouldn't matter because once we reached the end of the line, I couldn't walk to a table on my own, much less while carrying a tray of food.

The dorm was horrible for me. Because of my physical disability and total blindness, I have trouble getting around. They told me not to walk around on my own, because other students might bump into me and I could get hurt. It seems that many students don't use white canes, and there are accidents. I had three people slam into me at different times. The only thing that kept me upright was my sighted guide. I understood the restriction, but it made me 100-percent dependent on staff people, even for things I could do independently at home. I felt very institutionalized. I didn't like my roommate, but if I left my room, I was accosted by a sixty-five-year-old man who wanted a relationship. The staff tried to make it easier for me. I put up with it for a month but couldn't have done it for long-term.

I still felt mostly positive about my training at HKNC when I returned home. But two things happened since to sour my feelings about the whole experience.

First, I was asked to complete a survey on my time at HKNC. This survey arrived to me without directions. I began answering questions under the assumption that the survey would be confidential. Those kinds of things usually are. I named people in both positive and negative ways. I was critical about things I did not like, in hopes that they could be changed. It turns out that the survey was sent to all my instructors for everyone to read every word. I was so embarrassed. And the teacher I didn't like actually contacted me to talk about what I wrote on the survey. I just think the whole thing was unprofessional.

Second, although HKNC was quick to bill BSVI for my training, they were very slow to release my report. My local BVR counselor would not do anything, not even hold a planning meeting until she received the report. That report came out two months after I left HKNC and is full of inaccuracies and errors.

Mark Gasaway

As a child in the 1960s, I did not receive any services, in part because they were not available then. Perhaps the only services available were enrollment in the Georgia School for the Deaf (GSD) or another institution. I told my parents that I did not wish to attend GSD, but when I was in fifth grade, I agreed to attend a facility in the Atlanta area that would give me some training and help me understand how it was for people with disabilities because this facility was a place for the disabled to learn about life. I think I was there about three months or so. It was at this facility that I developed an understanding of people with disabilities.

I have never been a student or visitor of HKNC or Perkins School for the Blind. I went through high school on my own, and upon graduating from high school, I went after life. I did receive rehabilitation services from VR and attended the Georgia Rehabilitation Center in Warm Springs for ten months in 1976. Upon leaving the center, VR services paid for me to attend Delgado College in New Orleans (1976–1977) and then Gallaudet University in Washington, D.C. (1978–1982).

VR was also instrumental in helping me find a job with the IRS in 1987. I left the IRS in 1997 and entered school without VR help. I have been searching for part-time work since 2002 and have found nothing; VR has not been active, either because they are just so slow or because they are not interested.

The benefits of VR were the jobs they helped me get, the schools they sent me to, the other services they helped with. The odd thing is that now the whole system has changed, and they are not interested in helping you like before. Talking about rehab and especially VR really turns me off and is not a favorite subject of mine.

When I first got the rehab services, they really helped back then, but times have since changed. The help is not there without a darn fight. Having to fight for the services I need is stupid. However, I will continue fighting. I am not alone in how I feel about VR these days, as there are many people who have the same feelings. Just face it; VR stinks in the South!

One area in which I believe they have failed is in not trying hard enough to help us deaf-blind obtain equipment that will help us with job investigations and research. There is also a big void in having the proper counselors working with people who are deaf-blind: counselors who are able to communicate fluently and understand the scope of the dual disability. They simply do not understand the full scope of what deaf-blind means or how it affects the individual's ability to do a job, and how alternative approaches and adaptive technology can help deaf-blind people do a job well.

The one factor that really motivated me to seek rehab services was that I needed help with jobs. Unfortunately, things are not going well for me.

Melanie Bond

Through VR, I was placed with the Michigan Department of Treasury and worked there for nearly 19 years. In the spring of 1996, I attended the Kalamazoo Training School for the Blind for four weeks to learn some new blind skills that included Braille lessons, O&M training, adaptive kitchen skills, and health classes. Unfortunately, the Kazoo Training Center was more focused on talking books, talking computers, and other audio equipment that did not benefit me in any way, due to my hearing loss. In addition, I found myself totally alone in the evenings, not being able to participate in discussions with hearing-blind students that were usually held in the lounge or cafeteria. I ended up going to my room every night and was determined to memorize all the Braille Grade 2 contractions before I left the Kazoo Center. Through O&M, I was able to borrow an FM system and was surprised to learn how much it helped me in terms of understanding what was being said. The Michigan Commission for the Blind purchased a Comtek FM system for me.

The next rehab experience took place in 2001 at Leader Dogs for the Blind, where I underwent training for four weeks to receive my first leader dog, Hailey. Hailey was well trained for day and night traveling and was able to guide me around detours, go shopping, whatever. Hailey stayed with me for six years before I returned her to Leader Dogs for the Blind in 2007. She had some aggression issues, and the decision had been made to retire her to the family that raised her as a puppy.

When I lived in Tucson, Arizona, in 2004, I contacted the Arizona Deaf and Blind Division to look for work. At that time, I was given a brand new portable CCTV and Zoomtext (screen enlargement) software for my computer, but there was no job. I also attended classes for the blind at the Southern Arizona Association for the Visually Impaired (SAAVI). I received O&M training in Tucson—where I came perilously close to being hit by a car driver when he made a left turn on a green light and nearly clipped me in the crosswalk. Obviously, the driver hadn't been paying attention to me or my white cane. Fortunately for me, my O&M instructor yanked me back to the curb, barely saving me from injury.

In 2006, when we moved to Sierra Vista, an O&M instructor named Mimi did my O&M training. She was able to orient me to my new environment and the transit system. When she learned that my husband had lost the transmitter from my old FM system, which could not be replaced due to outdated technology, she obtained a new FM system for me through a private agency. She also ordered a vibrating alarm system for me, but when that showed up, we discovered it was defective. To this day, I still do not have a vibrating alarm system.

Also at this time, I filled out all the paperwork so that I could attend HKNC. My hope was to learn to be able to sign tactually and to improve my receptive skills.

When we moved back to Michigan in 2007, the counselor from the Deaf-Blind Unit at the Michigan Commission for the Blind asked me why I had moved back to Michigan when Michigan was totally broke. In other words, there was no money for services. I wanted to look for work, and they willingly paid a job agency to help me find work. But nothing panned out for me. In the end, they terminated the services of the job agency (who knew nothing about my deaf-blind issues), and that was the end of it.

The rehab services I received were far more than adequate. I couldn't believe my luck when I learned that the civil service exam process was being waived to allow employees with disabilities to be hired by the state, perhaps in an attempt to meet equal employment opportunity and affirmative action guidelines. In lieu of the civil service exam, our rehab counselors placed us into a variety of jobs on a six-month trial basis. If the employers were satisfied with our work and we passed the probationary period in a satisfactory manner, the state would hire us on a permanent basis. I was thrilled when my supervisor bypassed the six-month probationary period and went ahead to start the process of hiring me on a permanent basis. All I can say is that this was the best deal of my working career.

The VR offices in Sierra Vista, Arizona, and in Bay City, Michigan, decided to hire a private job agency to help me find work. Though I had explained my need for a job in Sierra Vista that did not involve having to interact with the public, they gave me two job leads that were absolutely worthless. First, it was suggested that I might want to apply for a job as a door greeter at Wal-Mart. I told them, "You've got to be kidding me!"

The second lead was a job that I jumped at. I was told that the Cochise Community College was looking for a teacher who could teach an ASL course. I was excited! But when I showed up for work, it turned out that there was a big misunderstanding. They weren't looking for an ASL instructor—they were looking for an ASL interpreter to interpret for a deaf student who was attending college! I was absolutely dumbfounded by the job agency's unprofessionalism. What's more, no matter how much I tried to explain what my deaf-blind needs were, the counselor at this job agency simply didn't get it.

Scott Stoffel

As a legally blind child, I received some assistance from the Maryland State Services for the Blind. This consisted mainly of tutors and large print textbooks for school. When my family moved to Connecticut in

1980, I received some strong reading glasses, so I didn't need the large print anymore, although I continued to use tutors through high school.

My parents claimed that they spoke with a rehab counselor about my problems in public schools and asked if they should put me in a school for handicapped children, as had been done with my older sister. The counselor told them not to do that, because the schools for the disabled had poor academic programs, so I'd learn more in regular school. My vision was the only disability taken into consideration at the time, although I had a mild hearing loss and limited use of my hands to deal with, also. These other problems didn't have a major impact on my ability to learn, but they had enormous effects on the social side of school. But the counselor wasn't concerned about the increasing social problems I had in regular schools. Academics was first, last, and only.

My school years were profoundly miserable. I have often wondered why rehab counselors completely ignore the social development of children with disabilities. They seem to think that life revolves strictly around grammar and math—and they are very wrong. I was always the "freak" kid at school, the kid with all the weird problems who didn't fit in with the norm. As a kid, I didn't really understand why I was so weird and inadequate; I just knew that I didn't belong and never would. But none of my rehab counselors cared about that in the least.

I also received some mobility training during my senior year of high school. That mostly involved learning how to use a white cane, but I never used the cane afterward, because I'd learned to get around all right with what vision I had. I just didn't like the funny looks people gave me when I used the cane. Some people would note that I was obviously looking at things in a store and ask why I had the "blind" cane. The public doesn't accept the concept of being legally blind: you are either blind or you can see fine, period. That was exasperating, and I just didn't like walking around with an advertisement that said I was "defective." Rehab counselors will invariably say that is stupid thinking, but that's because they never look at the social issues.

When I lost my hearing in 1987, my life completely caved in. I spent a few years in limbo before I finally made the decision to find a way to deal with the double whammy of being deaf and visually impaired. I ended up being referred to the HKNC in New York. I was told it was the best place to go for people who are deaf-blind. I'd never even heard the term "deaf-blind" before, much less met another person with the combination of vision and hearing loss—aside from my sister, that is. A visit to the center didn't get me excited about staying there for an extended period, either, but I knew I had to do *something*. This seemed to be my best option, so I signed up for a thirteen-week evaluation.

I was fortunate to be given an experienced case manager at HKNC who genuinely tried to help me pull my life together. If not for her, I probably would have left a long time before I actually did. Now, that's not to say I didn't like the other people involved in my training program there. I worked with some very dedicated people and even got to know some of them a little bit. But my other disabilities, particularly the hand problems, threw a monkey wrench into the equation of their "usual" training. The hands were supposed to become the eyes and ears of a deaf-blind client, but mine weren't terribly cooperative, and no one really knew how to get around that obstacle.

There were pros and cons to my experience there. I will discuss both.

The first thing that struck me at HKNC was the social subdivision among the clients there. The center typically had no more than forty adult clients at one time. We all lived together in a small dormitory next to the training facility. I discovered that "deaf-blind people" were not a single group but seemed to be split into three groups that did not interact well with one another. The first group was the "deaf" group. These were people who had been born profoundly deaf and depended on sign language as their primary communication mode. The second group was people who had some usable hearing for at least part of their lives and had developed oral communication skills. I fell into this "oral" category. And then there were some people with learning disabilities or such little exposure to society that they seemed like children in adult bodies.

I had the misfortune of arriving at the center at a time when there were very few oral clients. I quickly discovered that my lack of signing skill made it almost impossible to communicate with the deaf group. I had to use a dry-erase board for communication until I learned sign language, and not many people in the deaf group were keen on this mode. I was not inclined to be pushy with the board. It took a while before I was able to make any friends.

The third group of people I mentioned ranged from people with serious learning disabilities who were totally dependent on staff for daily life activities to adults that had been so sheltered by families or institutions that they still acted like children. There were people in their thirties who walked around with dolls or played with toys in the student lounge. Hey, they're people, too! Be sure to say that with vehemence when someone asks why they're grouped together with people with somewhat normal minds and social development. It wasn't that I had anything against those people, and I was glad they could get rehab services. The thing is: when I was lumped in with them, it sure seemed like society was trying to tell me something about where I ranked with respect to the glorious norm. It made me feel like I had to constantly prove I was a developed individual.

I remember watching a nineteen-year-old guy play with his toys in the student lounge one evening with his mom sitting nearby. He'd smile and giggle whenever one of the people on the dormitory staff pretended to be impressed with something he made with his connecting blocks. At first, I was appalled by this fellow. I kept thinking about how he would survive in the world when his parents could no longer take care of him. Did he even realize how little respect other adults had for him? He obviously didn't care about those issues. I started to wonder if it was better for a deaf-blind person to just be a child forever and never know what he or she was missing in life. His world was a simple world where simple things, like toys and candy, could make him happy. My world was a hopelessly complicated world of endless struggles where contentment was pure fantasy.

After I'd been there for a few months, more people in the oral category came in, and I was able to make some friends. It was an interesting learning experience for me to talk to other people with similar problems to my own. We had to use dry-erase boards or computers to communicate, but it was great just sharing with people who were going through some of the same struggles. It made me feel a little less freakish, although the problems I had with my hands prevented me from being good at sign language and never let me stop feeling "different" from the rest.

Training areas at HKNC included tactile (touch) sign language, Braille, independent living skills, mobility training, and job assessment. I was most interested in the last area, but the people in that department didn't seem to know what to do with someone like me. Despite my bad hands and total lack of interest in factory labor, they insisted I perform several assembly line simulations to assess my abilities in that type of work. I thought this was downright silly but did it, anyway. I didn't want to come across as obstinate. Of course, I did poorly, but they said my options for work were very limited without a college degree.

My case manager later intervened, putting a stop to these wasteful exercises and arranging a sort of internship for me as a copy editor at Publishers Clearing House. I had solid writing skills, so this work was more up my alley. I used a variety of magnifying glasses to get the editing tasks done and did well in terms of accuracy, although my speed was subpar.

I learned Braille fairly quickly, but my hands made it very difficult for me to read Braille, so I stuck with magnified print. I didn't have enough feeling in my fingertips to make Braille practical for me, but I gave it a shot.

The bad hands also hampered my ability to "feel" tactile sign language. While it was a tremendous lift for me to again be able to talk to people without needing a writing board, I had a lot of trouble understanding tactile sign at a rapid pace. I could converse fairly well with someone who signed into my left hand at a rate slower than normal speaking pace, but when I used an interpreter to try to follow someone speaking at a normal pace, it was very frustrating. The women that tried to help me learn to use tactile sign effectively were great people and really tried their best. Some of them even worked as interpreters for me when I started taking some college courses at nearby Hofstra University. Having a familiar interpreter is helpful. But I found out that no matter how hard I or they tried, I just couldn't read the signs fast enough to keep up with machine-gun-mouthed lecturers. I felt guilty about that failure, too, because they were trying so hard. So I pretended I understood more than I actually did. I would tell them things like, "I got 75 percent of that lecture," and then I'd up it to 80 percent a few weeks later to fabricate progress. But in truth, I could only pick up about 10–20 percent of those lectures, and the ability declined as fatigue set in during long classes. But I didn't want to hurt their feelings with all the effort they put forth to help me out, so I let them think it was working great and then desperately tried to learn all the class material from the textbooks.

When I realized a degree was the only way I could get a job in a field that was both accessible and of interest to me, Anne, my case manager, suggested I give Hofstra University a try. Hofstra was on the pricey side, but she helped me find some funding to get the ball rolling. I eventually transferred to Temple University and earned an engineering degree that led to my employment with the Federal Aviation Administration.

Tonilyn Todd Wisner

In the ten years that I have been deaf, two years completely without sound, I have never received any rehab. In the two years that I've been blind, I have not received any rehab. I have applied for it but was turned down until recently. I was promised tactile ASL lessons and mobility training, but there has been no follow-up, only unanswered emails.

I had to take it upon myself to learn tactile finger spelling, Braille, and use of a white cane. The state rehab services have yet to provide anything. It's very frustrating.

I also requested help with finding work and getting any necessary job training. The rehab counselor declared I am too disabled to work and refused to help me. I am very upset about this because I know I am capable of doing something.

Wendy Williams

My first rehabilitation training was at the age of seventeen. After medical staff had denied my parents' repeated requests for speech therapy, I was allowed to have one month of speech therapy at a camp for deaf and physically handicapped children and teens. It was my first exposure to deaf youth, who were encouraged to use speech and not sign. Behind closed doors, they taught me the British two-handed finger spelling. The speech therapist chose to work on "s," "sh," and "ch" sounds with me. She and the other camp staff were kind to me and respectful, and my self-esteem soared.

After being diagnosed with Usher's syndrome when I was twenty-nine, I received my first O&M training from a wonderful student-in-training and her supervisor at a rehabilitation agency. I learned to carry the cane for identification purposes during the day and to implement it at night. I was amazed how the heavy pedestrian traffic on a busy city street parted like the Red Sea.

Refresher O&M training was given to me a few more times in other states. Once, the instructor had a background in deaf-blindness, and I felt empathy from him when he took both the visual and auditory senses into account as I traveled.

At thirty-seven years of age, I was having close calls with vehicles coming from my left and right. In my application for a dog guide, I feared rejection because I had the added hearing disability on top of the standard visual loss. For the interview, the representative guided me to an intersection. He directed me to close my eyes and tell him every time it was safe to cross. I said a prayer, as I knew this was a most challenging task for me. I responded only when I heard no traffic whatsoever. He then told me to open my eyes and said I was 100-percent correct. I quietly blew a sigh of relief.

Throughout my training at the school, I tried to function as a visually impaired person and hide my hearing loss. It was stressful, as I feared losing my most precious new four-legged companion, Darby, as well as my safety. It was not until we both were on the plane ride home that I began to relax, though not altogether. I still had to prove to the school and to myself I could be a responsible handler. In the end, my loyal and devoted dog guide worked to his fifteenth year.

In my mid forties, I entered a National Foundation for the Blind (NFB) rehab program for two summers for Braille, technology, O&M, and independent living skills. Again, I felt I had to function as a person with good hearing, similar to the majority there when in group activities, such as the weekly all-school meetings. I pretended to hear when I could not understand the students who were soft-spoken or too far away. In classes, we were required to wear shades, and the instructors used my FM listening system. By learning to rely on my sense of touch, I became better skilled at reading Braille, cooking, etc. This experience prepared me for the time when I was to lose the rest of my residual vision, about seven years later. Using shades for O&M did give me confidence in walking about indoors and outside.

The blind instructor encouraged me to rely on my auditory sense, but I did not have enough hearing to pick up cues such as hearing drivers rev up their motors at intersections. One time I was waiting at a bus stop with the instructor and two other students. With my shades on, I heard a blur of sounds that I could not associate with specific sources. I asked the instructor if the bus was coming, and he replied, "No." I waited some more, and I repeated the question—silence. I whipped off my shades to find myself standing alone with my dog guide. Angry, I caught the next bus back to the school and met the instructor in his office to retrieve my FM transmitter. He ripped into me about all my failings since starting O&M with him. I knew it was his attempt to scare me into keeping my mouth shut. I pondered whether to tell my counselor, but by the time I saw her again, the experience was of little significance.

Socially, I felt lonely at the rehab center and yearned for the monthly weekends when I could return to my home to be with friends. I was scheduled to return for a third summer of further training, but I was diagnosed with cancer and never completed this training.

7
Education Part II: Adult Education

In chapter 2, the panelists discussed their primary and secondary schooling experiences. Adult education, which includes college, technical or business schools, and work training programs, differs significantly from early education, so it is covered here as a separate topic.

One notable difference between early and adult education is that challenged individuals must actively seek disability accommodations and advocate for themselves more. Parents or counselors may still be involved, but individuals must take charge and begin to steer their own ships, so to speak.

Finding direction and purpose in continued education is another issue. Many people with sensory disabilities struggle to figure out what they can do with their lives, what types of work they are physically capable of, and how they will live independently, in addition to finding ways to effectively participate in college and other forms of adult education. This goes far beyond the normal dilemma of discovering one's niche; it's a double challenge that can be quite daunting.

Angela C. Orlando

Pursuing special education at Kent State University was a breeze for me, academically. I had already learned how to teach myself from textbooks, so I was well prepared for what was expected of me in class. I had good study habits. I could write clearly and scored high on tests. I spent all my time outside of class doing homework and studying. The library and student center study lounge were my favorite places on campus.

At the start of each semester, I told my professors that I was hard of hearing. This never really caused much of a reaction from them. They'd say, "Okay," and pretty much forget about it. I sat up front and looked like I was paying attention. But, in truth, I had no idea what was being said and was usually daydreaming. Disabled Student Services (DSS) sent out notices to each of my professors, saying that a note-taker would be needed for the class. The professors were instructed to read this notice to the class, and interested people would call DSS. They made all the arrangements for me and paid for the note-taker. All the note-takers had to do was use special carbon-copy paper that I gave them in order to make two copies of their notes. Some note-takers were really good; some were awful. But I never complained.

I had a problem once with a professor teaching a summer computer workshop. This was at the College of Education, and he just happened to be the head of deaf education at Kent State. His assistants were all deaf ed grad students. I wasn't a deaf ed major and had never met him before this. When I told him I was hard of hearing and would need a note-taker, he said, "No, note-takers won't work for this class. You have to have an interpreter." I explained that I didn't know sign language; all I needed was information in writing. But he wouldn't allow it. After the first class, the professor contacted DSS and arranged for an ASL interpreter. They told me it was okay that I couldn't read sign. I was supposed to focus on his lips and lip-read the interpreter, but his hands distracted me and, besides, I couldn't read lips effectively without sound cues. I had no idea what he was mouthing because he was not speaking (just silently mouthing) and was always behind what the speaker was saying. So after awhile, I ignored the interpreter and focused on the actual speaker. This didn't work, either. The interpreter kept tapping me to get my attention, and the professor stopped in the middle of his lecture to tell me to focus on the interpreter. The interpreter got fed up after two days and stopped coming. That was a relief to me, but the professor told me if I returned on the fourth day without an interpreter, he would kick me out of the class. I was bewildered by this attitude from the man who was head of deaf education at the university. I returned the next day, anyway. Although he let me stay, he wouldn't allow me to have an independent role in our group project. Instead, he assigned two of us to do the work and told the group to ignore me. I ignored him and learned what I needed on my own.

One surprisingly successful year really motivated me and led to many more. I took on a triple special education major, focusing on multiple handicapped, orthopedically handicapped, and developmentally handicapped. I became a math tutor and then took a job doing direct care work at a residence for children with profound developmental disabilities. I graduated from Kent State summa cum laude with a GPA of 3.975. My college school career was pretty impressive, but I wasn't really happy. I did well in my classes but struggled in the field. My hearing loss made it hard for me to understand other teachers and adults, although I did okay in small groups with the children.

Because I couldn't drive, placement for field experience and student teaching was difficult. I had to be in a local Kent school so I could get there by bus. They ended up placing me mostly at Longcoy Elementary School, my own old elementary school. I really thought this was a good thing. It was located right by my parent's house, where I was still living much of the time. It seemed a perfect match, but now I can see the problem. Here I was, a brand new adult, trying to find my place in education, back at my old elementary school. Many of my old teachers still taught there. I felt like a kid again as soon as I walked in the door. And many of them treated me as a kid. During my first field experience, I was placed in a second-grade classroom with a woman whom I had known since I was very little. I was so intimidated by her, and she was rough on me. I did fine when I took the special education kids out in the hall for one-on-one work, but in the classroom I felt like an eight-year-old and couldn't seem to do anything right. She gave me a really bad evaluation.

I had two more field experience placements at that school. By the middle of the third one I realized that I was screwing it all up again. I really needed to pull myself together. So I made myself a behavior chart much like the ones we used with our students. I picked several behaviors I most needed to improve on and marked my progress each day when I got home. The results startled me. When it came to working with the students, I was doing quite well. I could initiate to help them or to act when they did certain things that were right or wrong. And I could do teaching tasks without being asked and focus on any student needs. But it was a little harder for me to initiate with the teachers. For example, I had to push myself to ask the teacher, "Is there anything I can do to help now?" or ask a specific question about a student or lesson or something related to education. But I could not, not ever, seem to ask questions about the teacher's personal life. Even a simple, "How was your weekend?" was beyond me at that time. I guess I thought I wasn't supposed to be personal with them because I was just this lowly college kid and they were the *teachers*. It's not how I wanted it to be, but it's how I seemed to feel at the time.

In the spring of 1997, I was getting ready to start my student teaching. I was to do two different eight-week placements. But as the semester start approached, I still hadn't heard about a placement. Finally, my coordinator called me, saying we were going to have a meeting at Longcoy to discuss a placement for me. Instead, I was in for a brutal emotional beating. The principal, two special education teachers I had worked with during field experience, and the student teacher coordinator, who happened to have been my old sixth-grade teacher but was now working at the University, got together to tell me why I couldn't be a teacher and why they wouldn't let me student teach at Longcoy. One of those special education teachers had been my role model since I was twelve. She was the reason I went into this field. And it broke my heart to have her tell me now, five months before graduation, why I couldn't ever teach these kids. At the end, I went home and cried for days.

The coordinator gave up my case. Someone else at Kent State picked it up and decided to try at a different school. A teacher agreed to take me, and I had a very good experience there. This was at a school I had never attended, and for the first time, I felt like a teacher. I wasn't equal to the real teachers in my mind, but I wasn't treated like a kid. I even managed to form relationships with the other adults at the school. It was a really positive experience and helped me find confidence in myself.

But I still had to do student teaching with a certain group of children, and that meant I had to go back to Longcoy. It was the only place I could get to where they taught these kids. The new coordinator contacted the principal and teachers again. I don't know how, but she got me in. The two teachers would later say that meeting was the fault of the coordinator (my old sixth-grade teacher), and they just followed her lead. I don't know exactly what happened. I'm just glad they gave me another chance. And things were really good this time. I think it's because I had finally found faith in myself and knew I could do this. I found success with the students, and that made it easier to deal with the adults. And luckily, in this placement, I didn't have to work with any of my old teachers. I was, however, extremely grateful when they told me, if I wanted, I could walk to my parents house and eat lunch there. I think the suggestion was just to be nice, but I jumped on it. I couldn't stand the idea of eating in the teachers' lounge with my old schoolteachers.

Now, twenty-two years after graduation, I find myself back at Kent State as a nondegree student. This pretty much means I'm doing the work but not for a grade or credit toward a program. I am taking ASL 1 right now and am enrolled to take ASL 2 in the spring. The class has been a real experience—or should I say an *experiment*. There has never been a totally deaf-blind student at Kent State before. So we are all trying to figure this out as we go along.

Kent State now has a very good Student Accessibility Services office. They fight really hard to make sure students with disabilities get all the accommodations and services they need. I have a whole "team" for my class. I use two tactile interpreters. Since tactile sign language is so exhausting and intense, it is normal for one deaf-blind person to have two interpreters. They rotate, so neither one gets too tired. I also have a note-taker who is fluent in ASL and understands what the professor is talking about. She uses the textbook, overheads, notes on the board, and professors' signing to make sure I am getting all the information that is presented to the other students.

However, we have had problems with access to information. The professor has not been very open to making sure I have all information ahead of time. He uses overheads and passes out handouts, but I never get copies that are accessible to the blind. That's why the special note-taker was finally brought in.

I have a copy of the textbook in electronic Braille that I can read on my Braille Note machine. But since it's a sign language class, so much is graphical. I can't view the pictures or do the activities on the accompanying DVD. It makes it harder for me to practice. The head of ASL Studies came up with the idea that I could work with student volunteers from ASL 5. Those students need six hours of interaction with someone from the deaf community. So I am working with two of these students who go over lessons with me and help me practice signs. That has been wonderful. I like the idea that we are helping each other. It's a mutually beneficial relationship.

People ask me a lot if I am actually a part of this class or if I'm just sitting on the sidelines. I am very much involved in the class.

The professor has made sure of that. He's a great teacher and very funny guy. He even teases me a lot, which is something I'm not used to. Normally, instructors would just ignore my existence. This professor even talks to me one-on-one himself rather than going through an interpreter.

Next semester, I will have a different instructor for ASL 2. As much as I like my current teacher, I am glad to be trying someone new. My current professor is very laid back. Whenever I have a problem, he just says "relax" or "we'll figure it out." It ends up being the job of the interpreter to figure these things out, which isn't right at all. And for no reason that makes sense, he never had me take the written part of the midterm. It would have been very easy to work that out, but he just let it slide. I need an instructor who will take this seriously and work on accommodations. I don't want to be excused from work.

Carol O'Connor

I left the Shawgrove Special School in Didsbury, Manchester, when I was sixteen years old. I went into an employment training center in a place called Denton. Oh boy, I loved it there! There were six of us who started that day.

First of all, we were all given a guided tour around the training center by Mr. Bacon, the trainer. It was a massive-big place. I first went into the hairdressing program, but I failed there, due to my limited sight. Then they put me in a typing program, but I wasn't happy with that, either. The typing gave me headaches and strained my eye.

In the end, they found the right thing for me: working in a sweets shop. Oh, I really loved it. I started packing lollipops in boxes to go to other shops. I packed all different sweets in different boxes. They saw that I was doing so well, so I stayed on for the six months of training. I went to training for six hours, five days a week.

After the six months was up, Mr. Bacon and all the staff and students had a meeting. We students got certificates for our good work. On the last day, the staff put a buffet up for us all as a leaving party.

After that, I got my first packing job in a factory, packing sweets. I loved it.

Christian S. Shinaberger

I started junior college right after graduating from Samohi High School. I didn't know where to transfer to at that point, and I decided to redo math, a subject I didn't do well in. At that point, I was still living at home. Santa Monica College was easy to get to by bus, and it was cheap. Hey, tuition at the time, in the late 1970s was $10 a semester—my books cost more than that! It had a good reputation as well. I really enjoyed it.

I started dating for real and had my first sexual relationship there.

My accommodations were note-takers and readers, and I still had access to a Braillist to do up notes for me. I had to find the note-takers and readers, but the secretary in the Office of Students with Disabilities was very helpful. In fact, she knew more about what was needed than the special ed counselor did. Most of the teachers were cooperative as well. For example, in my physics class, I located a physics book in Braille. It wasn't the one they were using, but I couldn't get the one in use Brailled in time. The teacher had this other book and told me which chapters and sections to read to cover the required material. Of course, the conversion tables were the same in introductory physics.

Most professors were good about getting exams in time for the Braillist, or the secretary got a reader for them, and the teachers were okay with me needing extra time. In some cases, like anatomy class, the professor gave me the directions while I had my hands on the cadavers.

I got my first job as a tutor for Human Biology 25, General Biology 3, Human Anatomy, and Physiology 3 at Santa Monica College. So I guess I was interacting pretty well with my hearing aids. I went on the Morro Bay campouts twice with college friends while there.

Then I learned that the University of California at San Diego (UCSD) had a physiology major. I went there for three years and got my B.A. in animal physiology with emphasis in human physiology. I lived in the dorms there for three years. I actually managed to have fun there, as well. I'm amazed, looking back, as those dorms were built like cell blocks with truly crappy acoustics, but the kids put up with me. I was a bit older than most, as I had transferred in from junior college. I brought a lot of units with me, as well, ranked as a senior by the end of my first year there. It was interesting for most of the freshmen: I was the first deaf-blind student they had ever seen up close. Surprisingly, most of them took it quite well. Most were helpful.

The UCSD Office of Students with Disabilities was very good. They got a mobility instructor right away to teach me how to get around campus. They also provided good on-campus transportation. They were good at getting readers and note-takers signed up, once I found them. I got a lot of readers in the dorm—when the students learned they could get paid better than minimum wage and work right on campus that helped a lot. Several told me that reading the material to someone else and discussing it helped them understand it better, too.

One of my organic chemistry professors found a tutor/note-taker for me, and he used to administer the exams to me in person. He was also provost of Revelle College. He let me use his high-quality molecule model to show him things like twist boat hexane rings, since I couldn't draw them. I could demonstrate I understood the structure of a molecule by making a representation with this model. Sadly, I had to give it back, but it came in handy for taking exams with him.

I also had to take one more year of Latin there. That professor even gave me his home number, and I could call him to discuss things. He always arranged to give me the exams in person.

After graduating from UCSD, I went to the UCLA School of Public Health to get my masters in epidemiology. I ultimately got my PhD there, as well. When I first started at UCLA, the School of Public Health was very cooperative, and the staff assistant was really great about taking care of paperwork and helping with picking classes and other things. Initially, the Office of Students with Disabilities was a disaster, and that was quite a letdown after UCSD. Then Kathy Molini, who used to be the secretary at Santa Monica Junior College, took over, and things really improved.

Generally, I got along with the students just fine. I usually could find a female student or two to take notes and work as readers. I also now had Versabraille II to use for note-taking and working with my first IBM PC full-time at home—I got to live at home while attending UCLA.

Christy L. Reid

The deaf education teacher working with me in high school encouraged me to apply to Gallaudet College, as it was called in 1982, which I did, and I was accepted. I entered Gallaudet in the fall of 1982, and it was an exhilarating experience.

Although I didn't use sign language as a means of communication at first, I quickly learned I could communicate with almost anybody I met on campus. I began college experience by participating with the New Signer's Program (NSP), which really helped me to understand sign language and start using ASL. I did not have an interpreter or class aide to help during NSP classes, but that didn't even occur to me; my vision was good enough back then to be able to understand when the signer was within a close range. Looking back, I realize that I probably got a lot of practice by interacting with my classmates and teacher on my own, and it helped me to understand different people's styles of signing.

Once school started, I tried out for the pom-pom team and was selected. I had always been active in dancing and gymnastics and had been a cheerleader while attending the Missouri School for the Blind. It was fun and exciting to dance with the other eleven girls during half-time at football and basketball games. It was also hard and sometimes frustrating, because I couldn't see or hear when it was time to start the dance. But our coach and my fellow teammates were supportive and tried to help work out these problems. When we lined up, ready to begin a dance, the girl near me would signal to me by swinging her pom-pom out on the side and I could feel the breeze and knew it was time to start.

After the excitement of my first year at Gallaudet wore off, my academic life became harder and took up most of my time. I would spend hours in the library using a CCTV to read and do homework. In my second year, a CCTV was set up in the basement of Carlin Hall, the dormitory building where I lived, which made it easier and more comfortable for me to study. Before my third year began, my parents purchased a CCTV for me to use and keep in my dorm room. Nonetheless, depending on a CCTV was slow, and I could only manage nine to twelve credit hours per semester. It took me seven years to earn a B.A. degree.

Although by the time I graduated in 1989 I was tired of school and desperately needed a change, I decided to apply for entry into

Gallaudet's graduate school and was accepted. I continued functioning by using a CCTV, and by that time, I had learned how to use a computer with a magnification program. Still, it was a struggle and strain on my eyes. Even though I thoroughly enjoyed graduate school—the professors were on a first-name basis with the students, and I learned a lot of very useful techniques and information in rehabilitation counseling—I finally decided to take a break from school and search for employment.

Throughout my years at Gallaudet, I was always provided with a class aide who interpreted the lectures and class discussions. While I was an undergraduate student, the class aide would sign close to my face so I could see the signs. As a legally blind student, I was excused from the art history requirement and instead took ceramics. In addition, the math department helped to set me up in an independent study program in algebra and geometry; I was more successful working at my own pace. As a psychology major, I was able to take social psychology and statistics in psychology in the independent study option and was very successful. As a graduate student, these same accommodations were offered; however, by that time, my vision had worsened, so the interpreters used tactile sign language with me. In addition, a classmate would volunteer to take notes for me, and the department secretary would type them and make enlarged copies for me.

The entire college experience was a time of growing more independent, which I feel prepared me for life after college. During my earlier years at Gallaudet, I attended several Gallaudet Association for the Deaf-Blind (GaDB) meetings and made friends with other students with visual and hearing loss. For the first time in my life, I identified myself as a deaf-blind person. Later, I joined a sorority, which became an important social outlet, too. The other sorority members were very helpful, taking turns to interpret at meetings and other events for me.

Ilana Hermes

The year after school, I studied reflexology and meridian therapy at the International School of Reflexology & Meridian Therapy. I had no vision in one eye and only motion perception in the other but had good hearing, except for persistent tinnitus. Before the study year started, I went to the lecturer and told her about my disabilities. The only accommodation I wanted was for her to read out loud whatever she wrote on the blackboard, so I could record everything with my Dictaphone. I contacted Tape Aids for the Blind to ask if they could have my textbook recorded on audiotape. I received it shortly after inquiring.

When the course started, it went well. I realized that I needed another student's assistance to see when the tape in my recorder needed to be changed. The lecturer, however, later forgot to read what she wrote on the blackboard. I thought that I had two choices: either give up or ask other students to make carbon copies of their notes that I could take home and have someone read to me, so I could write them in Braille. I chose the latter, and that worked out quite well.

I then decided to write my textbook into Braille by transcribing it from the audiotapes. However, the sound quality of the audio was not good, so I had anyone available read my print textbook, while I transcribed it in Braille.

When the practical lessons started, the lecturer showed me some techniques by using me as a model to demonstrate to the class. Later, she had my mom attend class to watch how the techniques were done so that my mom could help me practice at home. I had to do 200 practical hours before receiving my qualification. If I passed the theory exam but my 200 hours were not completed, I wouldn't receive my qualification until the hours were completed. My mom helped me learn the techniques so I could perform the practical experience hours.

I set a goal for that year, together with studying and doing my best, to transcribe the textbook into Braille for myself. In this way, I learned and had the book available for reference for myself in the future. But a month before the final exam, when I had only 50 practical hours left to perform, my shunt (for draining excess fluid from the brain) broke.

I woke up in the morning with a very severe headache and started vomiting. I had to have surgery to replace the shunt. But at the same time this was happening, I experienced another problem, not unusual for sufferers of hydrocephalus, although I don't know if the shunt failure triggered it: My immune system malfunctioned; the white blood cells started attacking healthy body tissue. The white blood cells destroyed my hearing nerves and left me totally deaf. It was a horrible experience and left me in a dark, silent world, not knowing what to do.

The shunt replacement and recovery took a while. When I was recovered enough to get around and do things again, I wanted to finish the reflexology training, but I couldn't hear to listen to the instructor or tapes anymore. My parents encouraged me not to give up, and I wanted to complete the course so badly, so I taught myself how to read lips by touching the speaker's face. I did not receive any formal training with this technique; I just started trying to do it with family and got better at it with practice. It helped that I knew how to speak and could feel my own face and lips while I spoke. When I resumed the course, I had to do the theory exam aurally, and it was quite a challenge to understand the spoken questions using my hands. Despite all the adversities, I kept going and finally earned my certificates. The help and encouragement I got from my parents played a major part in my success.

In 2003, after I had received my first cochlear implant, I went to study Marketing N4, Communication N4 and N5, Computer Practice N4 and N5, and Office Practice N4 at the Institute for the Blind, which is an hour's drive from my home. I boarded at the hostel but later went to rent a flat with a friend whom I met at church. Although all study materials accommodated my blindness, it was difficult to follow what was said in class with my CI. I also struggled to hear the audio screen-reader for the computer. However, I took this challenge and studied real hard after class on my own. I passed all subjects.

In 2004, I studied Swedish massage. I had a private lecturer who worked with me one-on-one. I had my theory notes in electronic format and had them transcribed into Braille. Since I have difficulty using my hands, she said that she adapted the technique for me. I asked her to teach me both the traditional technique and the adapted technique, and she showed me both. I had enough practical practice and felt quite comfortable in this new addition to my career.

At present, I run The Relax Centre, together with my parents, from home. We employ beauticians to do all the treatments that I can't do, such as nail coloring, due to my challenges.

Judy Kahl

I attended Youngstown University in Youngstown, Ohio, from 1962 and graduated in 1967. I received a bachelor's degree in elementary education with a minor in music.

My friend from high school and I commuted the first year. The campus was only a twenty-minute drive from home. I was a music major my first year, which was extremely difficult for me with my hearing loss. Not only were the courses tough, but it meant learning and practicing on different musical instruments. After my first year, I changed my major to elementary education, and music was my minor. That was better suited for me.

I did not have any resources available to me, other than talking to my professors to explain that I wore hearing aids and might have some difficulties with note-taking; however, I don't remember any "extra help" being offered to me. I did manage to make friends, and if I missed something, I would ask if I could read their notes for things I might have missed in class. It was always the extra time on my part to get the lesson or assignment right. I studied and worked hard to keep my grades above average.

The social part of college was not a problem at all. I joined a sorority, and I was elected to be a "sister" to a fraternity. When I made cheerleading at the end of my freshman year, I moved on campus. This was a fun time for me, and I enjoyed the independence. It was a daily struggle not to play every day and take care of my lessons.

I also worked part-time at the School of Business Administration. My job was to type and run off all tests for the professors. Whew, I could have been real popular, but I had to honor my job over receiving "instant popularity."

Up to this point, my hearing loss was my only disability. Although I had difficulty seeing in dark parking lots or movie theaters, I did not realize that I had night blindness, which was the beginning stage of RP. That diagnosis did not happen until the age of twenty-five.

Mark Gasaway

I was in training at the Georgia Rehab Center in Warm Springs before attending college for one year in New Orleans. I earned a B.A. in social work from Gallaudet University in Washington, D.C., in 1982 and an M.A. in organizational management from the University of Phoenix in Atlanta in 2005.

In between my time at Gallaudet University and University of Phoenix, I entered Georgia State University and took several courses toward a degree in deaf-blind education, but the program I was in was eliminated from the school's list of degrees, so I was unable to continue at Georgia State.

The kinds of accommodations I received from all the schools I attended were sign language interpreters, note-takers for some classes, and large-print materials. These accommodations were enough. At Gallaudet, I had special interpreters who relayed the professor's signed lectures for me, since I could not see the professor's signing with my limited vision. At the University of Phoenix, I had interpreters for both classes and team meetings.

I received all the major accommodations I needed. However, there were instances where the large print material was not available.

Most of the time, I was able to "fit in" and make friends with the help of the interpreters. At Gallaudet, I fit in nicely and was able to make friends very easily. I lived on campus in a dormitory and had no problems, not even with kids playing with the fire alarm system.

At the University of Phoenix, I used public transportation to get to classes from my home in Atlanta. Sometimes, I was able to get rides home from other students. No problems with that.

The education I received was more than beneficial. It helped me understand better the aspects of being disabled and different. I learned to become more open toward others' needs and accept who I actually am, a member of the disabled community and a member of the unique deaf-blind community.

Patricia Clark

When I left school at age eighteen, I was awaiting the results of an important state university entrance exam. I had done badly at school in the previous three years, due to deafness and bullying by the teachers. Nobody expected me to pass, so my joy was overwhelming when I did, in fact, pass by 1 percent. I was stunned. I was determined to get a university education, and in spite of the generally low opinion held of me, I still had a spark of faith in myself.

My family lived in a university city, so I was able to live at home. I wanted to study psychology and music in a double major for a B.A. At this point, I had a truly dreadful hearing aid that distorted sound.

Nobody told me how to get the best from it or even how to switch it off and on. The first-year classes were large; 130 students did first-year psych, but only 35 were doing first-year music. I turned the hearing aid on for lectures and off in the cafeteria. It was a steep learning curve with that rotten aid, and it caused me much anxiety.

I took to psychology like a duck to water. I took to music like a bird flying free. I loved student life. My musical education prior to this consisted of piano lessons from a suburban teacher who knew nothing outside of piano. Suddenly, I was writing music and listening to big-name composers I'd never heard of before. The first year was one of a sudden reversal from being dumb to being near the top of the class. I've had several reversals like that in my life since that time.

The second year was much harder academically and involved some evening lectures. My parents were having a very bad time with my father's chronic illness that resulted from World War II, and the marriage of my brother, whom they both leaned on. His absence left a huge hole in their lives. He was the referee in their marriage, and without him, they were constantly arguing. The atmosphere was awful at home, and I stayed away as much as possible, but this meant that I only had four hot meals a week. Breakfast was eaten at home, and I made sandwiches for lunch, but an evening meal in the cafeteria, although modest, was too expensive. My hearing aid broke down regularly, and it had to be fixed no matter what else went by the way, including food. Batteries had to be bought weekly and left a hole in my meager budget. I sold some textbooks to tide me over and gave piano lessons. I got jobs during the long vacation, but there was never enough money. My mother worked to keep the household going. There was never any question of financial support from my parents; they didn't have any money, either.

At the end of that year, I was exhausted mentally and physically. It taught me a useful lesson: You *must* look after yourself and eat properly. I had to find ways of making more money.

In spite of all this, I got good grades, and I was taught to think. My mind expanded. I still regard this as one of the best things that happened to me. Social life was quite good, too, although one boyfriend I really liked said plainly that, although I was a nice girl, he would never marry me. Later in life, a couple of other men said the same thing, and I assume this was because I was deaf-blind.

The third student year was also hard work academically but less difficult financially. Transistor hearing aids became available and made a big difference to me (this was in 1957). The sound was better, and running costs were much lower. My hearing got worse, but the new hearing aid made it possible for me to hear enough in lectures to get by.

I still loved my studies, but three years of hard grinding was enough. I graduated and started looking for employment. What made those three years so happy was that I was doing something I believed in, and I was successful at it.

Scott Stoffel

I started college immediately after high school—mainly because I didn't know what other options existed. I opted for a local school, so I could continue living at home.

The University of Central Connecticut offered all the things you expect from a university, but I found out two things when I enrolled there: First of all, the State Vocational Rehabilitation agency that had provided me with tutors and assistive technology throughout primary and secondary school informed me that they would not provide any support for me in college unless I moved away from home. Second, the school's disability resource center didn't have much to offer, either. I was accustomed to having tutors go over lessons with me and help me get all the stuff I missed from the board and other visual aids, so this was a major change. I decided to just take two courses the first semester and see if I could manage with just hearing lectures and reading the textbooks. I didn't choose a major and had no real goal in college. My motivation was infinitesimal.

I took trigonometry and freshman English. Coming out of high school, I had very poor grammar skills but was pretty good with vocabulary. And I had done well with high school trig my senior year, so what the heck. I spoke to each professor about my limited vision, but neither seemed very interested. To make matters worse, both were obsessed with writing on the board, which I couldn't see at all. Oh, yeah, they let me sit in the front row, but that was meaningless. Come midterm, I was doing terrible in both classes.

My parents hired my last high school tutor to help me pass the English course, although she had no direct contact with the professor and could only review assignments and textbook lessons. I just tried to sweat the trig out by studying the textbook. I got my grades out of the failing zone but still ended up with very discouraging "D" scores at the end of the semester.

I didn't make any friends, either. I felt like a weirdo among "normal" young adults and just kept my distance. I dropped out of college and thought about suicide.

I guess my family was worried about my mental health. My father set me up with a job at a family-owned computer store in Chattanooga, Tennessee, and I found an apartment within walking distance. It might have worked out, except that I lost most of my hearing six months later.

At this point, I think I reached the sewers under Hell and was still digging. I spent a few years going back and forth between chasing hopeless whims and wanting to end the wretched story. I made one actual attempt at self-destruction but was "saved" by instinct one second before a speeding truck would have hit me. The only good things that came out of this chapter of my life were that I taught myself how to write and learned the Basic programming language from a reference manual with a lot of trial and error. Call it "home-alone schooling."

For whatever reason, I decided to regroup in 1994 and find a way to deal with deafness on top of my old problems. A stay at the HKNC in New York got me to thinking I should try college again. I started "round two" at Hofstra University, mainly because it was near HKNC. I wasn't even sure what to major in—I loved creative writing, but a career in computer science seemed more practical. So I took classes in both categories. The disability resources at Hofstra were okay, but I got most of my help through my HKNC counselor and several outstanding professors.

I used tactile sign language interpreters in classes, but it was extremely hard to keep up with lecturers for two hours nonstop. Some of the interpreters were instructors I'd worked with at HKNC and was accustomed to, which made it a little easier. But the long lectures wore me out and became increasingly frustrating as my hand got tired. I could only "read" signs with my left hand, due to insufficient motion and sensitivity in the right. So I worked out some one-on-one sessions with professors willing to accommodate. One professor communicated with me by typing slowly in large font on a computer.

For two years, I really gave college my all. I had to split the time between classes and teaching part-time at HKNC. Couple that with the fact that I read about one-fifth as fast as a person with 20/20 vision, and you can guess how much time I had left after academics and work. A good night's sleep became a thing of the past. And I actually chose that time to get married! Go ahead and raise your brows—logic has never played a role in my life. But I needed motivation and someone to fill the social void. I was back to my old habit of avoiding social contact with "peers" at the university. All I did there was work on academics. One difference now was that I had a goal: I wanted the college degree so I could get a job with a solid pay.

I really pursued the academics this time around. In fact, I even found out I could get high grades, provided I gave up my spare time to class work. I did, promising the wife it was only a temporary circumstance that would mean good things for us later. Endure now; be happy later—that was my motto. It might have worked out all right, except that I ran out of money to pay for school.

My HKNC counselor had been confident I would have no trouble getting scholarships for deaf or blind students after I turned in some good grades at Hofstra. But she was quite mistaken about that. The deaf community slammed the door in my face, because I wasn't born deaf. Basically, I was told to seek a place of solitude and do something that normally requires a partner of the opposite sex. The blind community had a few scholarships I was technically eligible for, but the award committees preferred younger people, especially women. I ended up with zero between the two. Wow, I'd never realized what a worthless freak I really was! People never ran out of reasons to reject me. Student loans and credit cards got me through 58 credits and into debt.

Strike two.

I remember going home after withdrawing from Hofstra and talking to myself in the bathroom mirror: "There's the Ultimate Loser." I'd failed again, for all practical purposes, and it really hurt. I still didn't have a degree, still couldn't get a good job.

The idea of giving up—*again*—after all that time and effort was a tough pill to swallow. So I looked into less expensive universities and cheaper areas to live in than Long Island. I found out that state VR services provided different amounts of tuition support for different areas of study (I qualified for VR support because I no longer lived with my parents). All of this led me to Temple University in Philadelphia six months later and a major in engineering. I'd been thinking about robotics engineering ever since doing a term paper for a computer science class on artificial intelligence, so the change in direction wasn't as drastic as it may sound.

I found the disability resources at Temple were excellent, and some help from dedicated faculty made the engineering pursuit possible for me. Sticking to my academics-only approach, which included full-time summer courseloads, I made it to my bachelor's degree in three more years of nonstop school. The director of the disability resource center at Temple helped me pick up a few small scholarships, as did the head of the Electrical and Computer Engineering department. That financial aid, combined with the higher amount I got from the state VR for the engineering major, carried me to the finish line without a cent left in the tank.

It was an academic success. I finished at the top of my class, magna cum laude. I received a few honors group memberships. My senior project (a sort of "giant" Braille computer display to help people who had trouble reading small Braille) drew some media attention.

But I never escaped being me. I accepted an induction into the Golden Key National Honors Society and decided to attend the ceremonies and reception. It was time to get involved with something and meet some people. I had a tactile interpreter sitting with me to summarize what was said. Now, I realized interpreters could be distracting to others, so I intentionally positioned us at the outer end of the row of seats. But no sooner had she started signing into my left hand than all the people in the row just behind us grimaced and moved elsewhere. Despite a crowded house, the row remained conspicuously empty the entire time. Ah, there's nothing like being a part—in my case, a hemorrhoid. Then my interpreter needed to leave after the ceremony. I contemplated the reception for a few minutes. Let's see . . . here was a room full of bright, young human beings chattering away the evening. And over here was a thirty-something worthless freak with no way to interact. Reality-check time. Forgoing the preposterous notion of mingling, I left the legitimate people to their fun and went back to my own world.

My disabilities continued to get worse; my marriage was ailing, and my social life was dead and buried. Nobody could understand why

I wasn't happy on graduation day. I only attended the graduation ceremony because it shocked so many people that I didn't have any desire to go. Why should I? I'd been nominated to be the student speaker—it was something to do, at least—but the board of trustees had a reason to reject me, too: they didn't want an engineering student. Well, at least this time around, I only needed to change majors, instead of gender, age, or auditory ability at birth.

I went anyway and sat there with 5,000 graduating students. I didn't know a single one of them personally. Was I a part of something? If I was, it sure didn't feel like it. I felt more like a sideshow at graduation. I guess I was a sideshow, really—the first deaf-blind engineering graduate ever to come from Temple. Come see the amazing Mr. Weird. He even talks!

To save the marriage, I had to find a good job in a hurry after graduation. I made use of the Federal Workforce Recruitment Program while at Temple and got an opportunity in systems engineering with the Federal Aviation Administration (FAA). I qualified for a job as a general engineer because of my dual major (electrical and computer engineering). And since it was with the Feds, there were sufficient disability resources for me to get by on. So I jumped, moved down to Washington, D.C., and started working three months after earning my B.S.E.

Tonilyn Todd Wisner

As an adult, I received my associate's degree. When I started working on my degree, I had not yet been diagnosed with Meniere's disease. My vision was fine, and my right ear was working perfectly. My main problem at that point was the hearing loss in my left ear that was caused by the brain tumor I had removed when I was a kid.

It was during midterm exams of my first year at Delgado Community College in New Orleans that I began losing hearing and getting mild dizzy spells. It was actually during one exam that I had my first vertigo spell. After that, my hearing quickly deteriorated.

I saw the special needs counselor, and she provided me with an FM loop system. The professor wore a lapel microphone, and I had a remote unit and an earpiece to listen to lectures. I still had a hard time, because I couldn't use my lip-reading ability from a distance. But it was the best we could do, and it helped me complete my degree. I had one professor for three classes who hated the mike and refused to wear it, until the special needs counselor spoke with him. But I could tell that he resented having to wear it. Oh well.

My biggest problem was my French class. I couldn't read lips in French. And trying to understand movies in French was very hard. My professor really worked with me, though, providing transcripts of the movies and lecture information in writing.

After I graduated, I became very ill with the Meniere's disease and could no longer live alone. I moved to Lafayette to stay with my dad and attend classes at the University of Louisiana in pursuit of a bachelor's degree in Computer Science. I had a note-taker for each class, simply another student who agreed to take their notes on special carbon paper that provided me with a carbon copy of their notes. However, I attended one class and then was sick in bed with vertigo for three days. That was when I knew I would not be able to continue with college. My vision deteriorated, and I began having trouble with balance and more frequent vertigo.

The only education I've had since becoming deaf-blind are classes I took through the Hadley School for the Blind. My state VR service has said I am unemployable and will not help me with training or finding a job.

Wendy Williams

I graduated from high school with low but passing grades, and thus I entered the workforce, instead of immediately pursuing a college degree. In my heart, I hoped to pursue my childhood dream of college sometime in the future.

In my fourth year of working at a group home, our supervisor encouraged four of us younger staff to enter the Special Care Counseling program at a local community college. I experienced mixed feelings about leaving familiar territory, yet I was burned out from the seven-day work week with its demanding physical labor. I was nervous as to whether I could succeed in school. I found myself in a program of twenty students with supportive teachers. At first, my studies were a challenge, as I struggled to relearn to concentrate on the lectures and my books. I required little in the way of accommodations, having enough vision and hearing to get by, and graduated in the top of the class.

Since I had done well at the community college level, I decided to tackle undergraduate university to major in psychology in a large city. Here, I was in auditorium-size classes and had difficulty hearing the professors and taking notes. I contacted the university's Liaison Officer for Disabled Students, who was useless. Someone connected me to a professor who was head of the deaf school. He managed to obtain an FM listening system through Easter Seals. This device enabled me to hear the professors, provided they were willing to use the clip-on microphone; a few refused. Still, I could not keep up with the speed of note-taking. A couple of students kindly loaned me their notes, but they left much to be desired.

I asked the professors to reserve a front seat for me. Some did; some did not. In the latter cases, I found myself lined up outside the classroom doors and rushing in with the crowd to compete for a front seat. At times, I physically claimed a front seat (e.g., put my books on the desk), and other students still wiggled their way into the seat. Sometimes, I had to settle for a desk further back in the room.

Tests based on lectures given within a large, noisy classroom were challenging. I barely passed.

Finally, prior to the start of my senior year, I was directed to meet with a new liaison officer. She spoke to all my professors and told them they must wear my FM system's microphone, provide quality lecture notes, reserve a front seat for me, and give me unlimited testing time in a quiet setting. While I appreciated the assistance of the Liaison Officer, I was too burned out from the stresses of the previous college years to regroup and better my grades. But I was able to finish and earned my bachelor's degree.

The professor who secured the FM system for me suggested I apply for graduate school at Gallaudet University. I questioned my chances of being accepted with my mediocre grades but decided to apply. I explained the reason for the discrepancies between my undergraduate school performance and my community college grades to the professors there, and they seemed to understand. I became a School Psychology student with the understanding we would progress one step at a time because the professors were not sure how my declining vision and hearing in combination would affect my ability to complete the program.

Upon entering the cafeteria for the first time, I heard clapping hands and looked in the direction of the students that had clapped. The students stopped clapping when I looked. Later, it was explained to me the hardcore deaf group was screening me. Because I reacted as a "hearing" person, I would not be welcomed into their circle.

We were required to take sign language classes and become fluent in that mode of communication. I worked hard to see the signs of the professor and other students in the introductory sign class, resulting in eye strain and headaches. The professor then agreed to arrange one-on-one sign classes for me with a deaf tutor using tactile signs. Initially, it took some adjusting for me to feel comfortable with hand contact with a stranger. The intense concentration needed to "read" the tactile signs and recall their associated messages drained me mentally and physically. With practice, tactile communication became easier and faster.

In the other classes, the wonderful professors willingly wore the FM microphone and provided note-takers, plus a tutor to assist me in learning the school psychology assessment tools. Much of my non-class time was devoted to the heavy reading and homework that were a part of the graduate studies.

Because of my life experience and interest, I started focusing on people who are deaf-blind. I completed my practicum and internship at a school for the blind with deaf-blind students.

As I walked across the stage with my cane to receive my diploma at the graduation ceremony, I was speechless at the standing ovation I unexpectedly received. My roommate told me it sent shivers up and down her spine to witness this round of applause for me. In both community college and graduate school, I had great classmates, resulting in long-term friendships. In undergraduate studies, I was blessed with a few special friends, though for the most part, I was lonely. That ovation really surprised me.

A former colleague and I lived in a boardinghouse, an apartment, and YWCA (Young Women's Christian Association), while attending the community college. I resided in dorms in undergraduate and graduate universities. I preferred the quiet and relaxing setting of an apartment to those settings that demanded sharing public facilities. The alarm systems at Gallaudet were hypersensitive, waking us up and sending us outdoors most nights.

Learning in undergraduate school, with its mostly inadequate accommodations, was of little value to my education. I benefited greatly from the educational programs provided by the community college and graduate university, both positively preparing me for my career as a school psychologist.

8
Careers

One of the greatest challenges for people who are deaf-blind is identifying feasible careers and then finding and maintaining actual jobs in those areas. Sensory disabilities throw multiple monkey wrenches into this equation. While VR services and good accommodations can help pave the way for a productive career, obtaining the ideal situation is far easier said than done.

I asked the contributors to discuss their experiences with jobs and careers, to describe the jobs they've had and talk about workplace accommodations, transportation issues, satisfaction with their jobs, and social interaction with colleagues. One should keep in mind that being deaf-blind makes doing most tasks more difficult than they would be for a person with normal senses, and many of these people experienced further deterioration of their abilities while already working. It is not surprising that these accounts frequently speak of struggling and frustration. Perhaps if employers and other workers had a better understanding from the perspective of a deaf-blind worker, the work experience could be happier and more productive for all concerned.

Angela C. Orlando

Ever since I can remember, I wanted to be a teacher. I used to play "school" with my friends or by myself. I'd be the teacher and my stuffed animals would be the students. I loved having workbook pages to play with and even made up my own grading book for my special "students."

When I was in sixth grade, the school started a program for children with mental retardation and developmental disabilities. These were kids with autism or Down syndrome and other conditions that left them physically and mentally disabled. I became a volunteer in this classroom because it was "cool" to get out of class. But I found I loved working with this group, and I wanted to have a class just like this. So my career goals were strongly in place by the time I was twelve.

After graduation from college, I began sending out my resume and applications, but there was just nothing available in the area. I went on a dozen interviews, but the jobs weren't right, or I had the wrong certification, or they just didn't hire me for whatever reason.

Finally, I decided to move to Maryland, where my boyfriend lived. The schools in that area were desperate for teachers. There was a lot of teacher turnover and new special education departments. Both the Washington, D.C., school district and Prince George's County were desperate for teachers and would hire people who weren't even certified. But I didn't realize how poor and unmanaged those districts were.

I got my first teaching position as a special education teacher at Clinton Grove Elementary School in Maryland. The school was 80 percent minority students, and the mission was to educate the black male children in a certain way. The school was lacking in resources. The library barely had any decent books in it. And teachers had to provide all their own materials. I spent most of my paycheck buying paper and pencils and other things for the classroom. I even had to provide my own copy paper for worksheets.

I wanted to teach children with mental retardation, but I ended up in a class for children with learning disabilities and behavior problems. In Kent, Ohio, these kids would have been included and taught in a regular classroom. But at Clinton Grove, children were still in self-contained classrooms. My class was the "younger" students. This was a strange mix of first and fourth graders—there were no kids in second or third grade in special education at this school. I had to prepare two sets of lessons and have two separate classes going on at the same time. This created so much background noise and confusion. It made it hard for me to be in control of the class.

I don't think anyone at that school even knew about my visual impairment. I didn't tell them. But they knew I was hard of hearing. At first, it seemed like a dream setting when I learned the principal had a background in deaf education. I thought I would get support from her. It didn't happen.

I was struggling to hear and understand the students over all the noise in that double classroom. I couldn't pick up on when the kids cussed or when they said inappropriate things. They knew it, too, and took advantage of it.

One time, we were talking about resources and jobs. I asked the students to name some jobs. One boy said "hooker," but I didn't pick up on it. Another time, two of the kids started saying "whatever" or "don't know" when they were reading aloud and didn't know a word. I missed that, too. I found these things out later from my assistant.

I went to the principal for help with this. She merely told me if I was handling the class right I wouldn't have this problem. She seemed to totally dismiss how the noise of the classroom was distracting for someone with a hearing disability. When trying to explain, she'd cut me off and say, "I have thirty-three years' experience in deaf education. I think I know better than you."

The worst part of the class was my assistant. She was new to the school, too, but she had been a teaching assistant for fifteen years at another school. The principal kept telling me I needed to follow the assistant's lead and learn from her experience. But what I saw in that classroom shocked and upset me. Ellen was nasty and mean. I saw her pull a kid all the way across the room by his leg. She told students to "shut up." A few of the kids had fine motor skill problems and were in occupational therapy; she would make fun of them and call them babies when they had trouble doing certain art tasks.

I had no idea what to do. On one hand, the principal was telling me this assistant was so great. On the other, I'm seeing abuse. I had never been in such a situation before.

Ellen also hated me. I have no idea why. She frequently told me I was the worst teacher she ever worked with. She made sure to explain that it had nothing to do with my disability. It wasn't discrimination; I just totally sucked as a teacher.

By February, my whole life was falling apart. I hated getting up each day to go to work. I couldn't eat and had lost twenty pounds. My new marriage was unraveling. My husband told me I had to pick the job or him.

The final straw was the principal's wishy-washy excuse for not providing support. One day, she'd be telling me she understood I was overwhelmed and needed help. The next day she'd be yelling at me and threatening to fire me. She never gave me a chance to explain what was really going on in the classroom. And she wasn't giving me the support the district office said she had to—not because of my disability, but because I was a new teacher. My major evaluation was approaching, and everything was still out of control. I was so worn out. I could have informed the district I still had not been given the training or services they had said I was to get. I could have tried to blame the principal for not following through. But I was just too tired, couldn't take it anymore.

One of my worst students actually began to thrive in the classroom around Christmastime. With him under control, the whole class was a lot calmer. But all of a sudden, around Valentine's Day, the boy had a complete reversal. The whole class was in chaos and the principal told me to solve it or be fired. I certainly tried, but nothing was working.

One day after school, the principal and Ellen were talking casually about the problem. The principal mentioned in an offhand manner that she had known the boy would have trouble because he had been taken out of his foster home and put back in the care of his mother. She had known this for weeks and never thought to tell me. That was it for me. The next day I went into her office and resigned.

So here I had become a statistic—just another teacher who didn't make it through the first year. I was ashamed and depressed but also very relieved to be out of that place.

It took me several months to recover from the whole nightmarish teaching experience. Then I applied for a tutoring position at Sylvan Learning Center. It was part-time, and I only expected it to be temporary work. I told the directors right up front about my disabilities when they interviewed me. I didn't even expect to get the job, but I did.

Strangely enough, I loved this job, and I was really good at it. It wasn't the area I had dreamed of, but it was still satisfying. I was teaching three students at a time on their individual programs in academic reading, elementary math, beginning reading, study skills, and writing. The students worked hard. There was a great token reward system in place that really motivated the students. I had to focus only on teaching, and I liked that part. I also liked not having to bring home mountains of paperwork each day. There were no lesson plans to be written or papers to grade.

I was instructed by the directors to tell the students of my hearing impairment and explain how best to talk to me and get my attention. This wasn't a problem. There was a lot of background noise while other teachers taught kids, but they gave me a table as far away from others as possible and in the quietest spot. When all else failed, the students wrote down what they wanted to say, so I could read it.

I had cataract surgery less than a week after starting at Sylvan. There was no hiding my vision loss this time. My whole face was bruised from complications of the surgery, and I lost significant sight in my good eye. I began using a magnifier at times to help me read small print. The directors didn't mind, though. In fact, one of them gave me a full-page magnifying plate to try out.

I was good at this job, and the students really liked me. More and more students requested me as their teacher. The directors saw I could do other types of work and began giving me extra hours. I started administrational tasks and other work, like testing, writing up programs, and getting materials ready for new students. They were training me to become an assistant education director.

I got along well with the other teachers. They saw me as a link to the directors. They would consult me about problems with certain students or confusion with programs. Sometimes, they would leave me notes, and I would approach the directors on their behalf and make sure things got done. Eventually, the directors allowed me to make such decisions on my own, and I was more in control of the work students were doing. I knew the programs and knew the students, so I was able to make the best recommendations.

Then I became pregnant. I continued to work up until the very day I went into labor. I was on maternity leave for two months after that. And then I came back to an utter shock—the entire management staff that had hired me was gone. They had all been replaced. The new management knew nothing about me or the work I was doing or how to deal with my disability.

From the very start, I had problems with Holly, the new center director. She was rude and crude and very stubborn. She seemed to be on a vendetta to get rid of anyone and everyone from the old management. She immediately cut my hours in half and reduced the work I was doing. She suddenly decided I wasn't capable of teaching and wouldn't assign me any students. She cut my hours even further, saying there wasn't enough work to do. But I saw on the schedule she was interviewing and training other teachers to do my jobs. Holly refused to work with me in regard to my disabilities. She would constantly talk to me from across the room. I had to run up to her and have her repeat things, and she hated that. She said I couldn't tell students about my hearing impairment, because it would cause them to misbehave and upset the parents. She always left chairs out and boxes on the floor that I would trip over. And then she'd complain I was a hazard. She blamed me for things I didn't do. I did things the way I was trained, and that would be wrong. She'd blame me for things other people did, even when I could prove it wasn't me. And sometimes she'd tell me to do something and then tell me a week later I was doing it wrong.

I had an outstanding evaluation from the year before, but I got a horrible evaluation from Holly. It was hard to believe the two evaluations were about the same person. They were so different.

I wasn't going to give in this time. I clearly recognized discrimination and was ready to fight. I kept records. I made notes of everything I did and had my own statistics of how fast or slow I worked. I made copies of the schedule that showed she was training others to do my job. I kept all the stupid notes she gave me about what she wanted me to do each day—they all had smiley faces she drew at the bottom—I hated that! I kept a pencil in the bathroom and a piece of paper in my pocket. Anytime something happened, I would go to the bathroom and document it immediately. I had this whole file of notes and info all ready for a lawsuit.

Finally, Holly decided I had to go so badly she was willing to pay for it. She put me on paid leave until I provided documentation from my doctor about what accommodations I needed. I didn't get any, of course. I had already been using the accommodations I needed until she came in and took them away. Now she wanted a doctor to tell her what was reasonable.

Unfortunately, it was at this time when I became really sick and lost all my residual hearing, vision, and ability to walk. I was too sick to work and too sick to fight. I knew they would just point out how badly disabled I'd become, and I'd have no chance in court. I know my disability hadn't affected my work at all, but being this sick would make it impossible to prove that.

One of the other directors called my house when I missed the deadline to provide the paperwork. My mother-in-law explained about my illness. They sent me flowers. That was the end of my teaching career.

I sort of got my revenge, though. About six months later, my husband went to Sylvan to get documentation of my employment for Social Security. He discovered, once again, that they had an entirely new management staff. Both directors had been fired. They didn't even last a full year.

Maybe I'm crazy or just plain stubborn, but I am working toward teaching once again. I just can't give up on it. Teaching is my life. It's all I ever wanted to do. Now I am going to try for a position as an online teacher or tutor. Maybe that approach will be more successful for someone with my disabilities. We will see.

Christy L. Reid

I have worked in several jobs from the time I was a senior in high school until my last job as a deaf-blind specialist in a new state project in Mississippi. As a psychology major in college and later a student in vocational rehabilitation, most of my work experiences involved working with deaf and deaf-blind people in the rehabilitation field.

Even my first paying job when I was a senior in high school involved working with disabled people. I was hired as a helper in the local community college cafeteria. My duties were cleaning the tables, pouring coffee for customers, and helping out in general. My boss was a blind man, and his girlfriend, who also worked there, was a visually impaired woman. I taught my boss and his girlfriend the manual alphabet, so we could communicate more efficiently. They were eager to learn, and soon, we could carry on interesting discussions when there weren't customers to wait on. It was a fun job, and the money I earned made me feel grown-up.

I received similar accommodations in all my job experiences, depending on my visual needs. In all the jobs, I received interpreting assistance, from either a coworker volunteer or by a hired interpreter. The interpreters used tactile sign language with me and helped me during staff meetings, training workshops, communicating with parents of the consumers I worked with, and assisting in community outreach projects I was involved with. My vision was good enough for me to use a CCTV and magnification technology when I worked for a program in Baltimore for deaf-blind adults with mental disabilities—my first full-time job.

The Missouri Rehabilitation Services for the Blind (RSB) purchased a magnification system for me to use on the job. I was still receiving support from RSB and was in the process of getting set up in the new job in Baltimore. The magnification program was installed and set up on the agency's office computer, and I used it to write daily progress reports on the consumers I worked with, as well as quarterly and annual reports. A CCTV was available for me to use to fill out forms and read paper materials related to my job.

When I first moved to Baltimore, an O&M teacher was provided by the Maryland Services for the Blind, part of the transition from Missouri, to teach me the route from my apartment to my workplace using the subway and bus. The O&M teacher also taught me how to travel to a nearby shopping mall and to the Inner Harbor, as well.

I enjoyed being independent and using public transportation to a limited extent. The only problem I experienced was working with consumers with behavioral problems. I learned how to professionally handle behavioral problems, but when the behavior got out of control and I didn't see the behavior disruption, I was at a disadvantage. I never got hurt on the job, but I felt nervous being around the consumers known to have violent outbursts.

Several years later after I had learned Braille and made the switch from magnification to Braille technology, I worked full-time as a deaf-blind specialist in a new statewide project in Mississippi. It was a good, professional job with room to grow. The state of Mississippi purchased a fantastic computer system for me to use at work, complete with an 80-cell Braille display, a Braille embosser with embossing software, and a scanner with text-to-Braille software. The Missouri RSB funded training for me to learn to use all this new equipment and also paid for interpreting services for me during the first three months of employment. I was once again receiving services from RSB, and they assisted with the transition to Mississippi. The program where I was working eventually hired a staff interpreter who helped me with phone calls, interpreted in staff meetings and training workshops, and helped me communicate with parents of consumers, as well as being available to interpret for deaf-blind consumers in the program. Part of my job was to teach staff ASL and communication techniques with deaf-blind people. Many of the staff learned finger spelling, and some staff made good progress learning ASL.

I seldom had communication difficulty with my coworkers and occasionally would visit with friends from work on weekends.

I did not receive O&M services to learn the route to my workplace; it was not necessary. The job was located in Tupelo, Mississippi, a small town, and I used a taxi to take me to work and back home. I only had to give the driver a note with the workplace address printed on it and assumed that he would drive me to work without problems. Most drivers didn't have any trouble and didn't try to talk to me, once they understood I couldn't hear. But a few times, a driver would get confused about having a deaf-blind passenger in the backseat who sat silently gazing out the window. One morning when I was in a cab heading toward work, I didn't realize the driver was trying to talk to me. When we got to the parking lot and after I found the correct door leading into where I worked, I met one of my coworkers who said a cab driver had just called and said he would be arriving with a non-English speaking woman—me.

I didn't stay long enough in any of my jobs to advance my position. But while I worked as a deaf-blind specialist in Mississippi, my supervisor conducted routine work performance evaluations, and I received equal evaluation. I received good scores and an outstanding score for community outreach services. If I had stayed longer, I may have had the opportunity to grow and advance in the deaf-blind project. But, unfortunately (as far as my professional life is concerned), I could not stay on in Mississippi. I had a three-year-old son who had just been diagnosed with optic atrophy and had shown signs of inner-ear hearing loss. Hence, my husband, Bill, and I felt that we needed to live where our son would receive good services as a legally blind and, possibly, hearing-impaired child.

The only discrimination I encountered in my work experiences was when I worked at the Illinois School for the Deaf (ISD) in a summer vocational workshop for deaf youth. I learned about the job while attending a job fair at Gallaudet University, where I met Peter Seiler, who was superintendent of ISD at that time. I was interested in the description of the job, and Dr. Seiler wanted to give me the experience. Having previous experience with deaf-blind people, Dr. Seiler wanted to be sure I received adequate accommodations during my stay at ISD and arranged for two full-time interpreters to assist me on the job. My duties in the summer workshop were to tutor deaf students in the classroom in vocational concepts and to supervise a few students at their assigned worksites. In spite of Dr. Seiler's preliminary arrangements, when I arrived at ISD to begin my job, I sensed that other deaf staff and deaf students were uncertain about having a deaf-blind person in their midst and how to interact with me. I especially felt their doubt in my abilities when we went on a weekend trip to visit a guest farm. There was a sack swing attached to a huge tree. Staff and students formed a large circle around the swing and one by one each person took a turn sitting on the swing and being swung in a big, fast circle. I wanted a turn, too. I wanted to have fun, too. But I was told it was too dangerous for me. I knew if I wanted to join in the fun, I would have to step forward and insist on having a turn with the swing. Finally, I was allowed to climb up on the sack swing and, at first, was pushed tentatively around the circle of people. Then I was pushed higher and faster, and it was wonderful flying through the air! After that, the deaf people seemed to feel more at ease with me, and I was able to participate more fully. For example, later that night while we were visiting the farm, some of the deaf staff, including me, went to a nearby bar for drinks. I felt very pleased that they kept my beer glass equally full, a sign of acceptance.

Ilana Hermes

My first job was as a receptionist at a hairdresser shop. That didn't work out so well and only lasted two months.

Then I worked for four years testing Braille machines. Problems with my shunt caused me severe headaches, so I sometimes had to stop working and lay down for a while.

I had my certificate in reflexology but was not able to find a related job. A few years later, I decided to study Swedish massage. I had trouble using my hands, so my instructor modified the techniques a little bit to help me. It worked out well, and I soon became quite comfortable with the techniques.

After some practice work, I started working with my parents at our own home business, The Relax Centre. Because of my frequent and severe headaches, it helps a lot to be able to go to my room and lie down when I need to. Working at our home makes things easier and less stressful for me, and it eliminates the issue of transportation to the workplace.

Now that I have bilateral CIs, I am able to understand speech fairly well. I can communicate with our customers and have gotten to know some of them. Things can seem so normal that the customers sometimes forget I am blind. One time, I did massage on a woman's feet, and she asked me to paint her toenails afterward. I had to remind her, "I'm Ilana. I can't see to do that. But I can paint your whole foot." My mother or an employee handles the pedicure duties at our business. I thought this was funny.

Some of our customers assume I am deaf and trying to read their lips when I have trouble understanding them. I just tell them that I can't see their lips; I'm just trying to concentrate on hearing what they're saying with my implants.

Judy Kahl

After college graduation, I was fortunate to receive a teaching position in Wyandotte, Michigan, as a second-grade teacher. At this time, I was only dealing with a hearing loss, but with the aid of two hearing aids, I did quite well. I did read lips and rarely missed anything, except in noisy situations or some phone conversations. I always worked overtime *not* to miss something, but it became second nature. Sometimes, it was difficult for me to understand messages over the loudspeaker, but I would just ask another teacher or student, if necessary. It didn't happen often, so it was okay. I do remember always doing the very best I could, and this would make me anxious, anticipating some situations. This took a great deal of energy and was exhausting at times.

Socials were always tough, as that meant lots of noise, and hearing just one voice was hard. I would just try to pick the quietest location, and reading lips helped a lot.

I loved teaching but resigned at the end of the school year, because my boyfriend, Joe, proposed to me. We got married that August.

We lived in Germany for a year and a half, until Joe finished his four-year term with the U.S. Army. Our daughter was born in September of 1968, and this was when I was diagnosed with RP. Life was so wonderful, and to learn at the age of 25 that I had a disease that could rob me of my vision was devastating and frightening. I thought the hearing was my disability and to have two disabilities just didn't seem fair. It was a very hard time, and so little information was available to me. I was told that there was no cure or prevention but that it was progressive. There was no way of telling me how long I would have my sight, and that was it. Just terrifying! Now, what was I to do? Twenty-five years old, married to a wonderful man, beautiful daughter, and I may go blind one day—that was my dilemma.

I had to figure out a way to cope with this. Trying to learn to live a normal life with normal people and surroundings with dual disabilities . . . it meant a life full of struggles lay ahead for me. But I was determined to make the best of it and not give up the good things I had in my life. What other choice do we have?

Mark Gasaway

Because I graduated from Gallaudet University with a B.A. in social work, I initially and naturally pursued a career in that field. I love offering a helping hand or knowledge when necessary. A lot of times people may need assistance with something, but they will not admit they need that assistance. In social work courses, we were taught to be prepared to assist those who needed help while at the same time letting the person know they should strive to achieve some personal goals.

So with that philosophy, I got a job working with deaf mentally challenged individuals at a facility for mentally challenged people. I worked there for two and half years before deciding I had had enough.

I left the facility and got a job working for the IRS in Atlanta. Yes, the IRS was different from my major field of study, but I was not having any luck pursuing a social work–related career in the Atlanta area, perhaps due to not being able to drive or some other aspect that the general public has a hard time understanding.

At both jobs, the main type of accommodation I received was sign language interpreters. At the IRS, I needed a CCTV for reading, but it was not provided to me when originally requested. This delay made me feel unimportant and burned out. By the time the CCTV was finally approved—after a good two years—I was ready to leave. But I stayed on and worked at the IRS ten long and unhappy years.

Being a friendly person, I interacted with coworkers quite well and had no problem with those I interacted with a lot. However, coworkers

I did not interact with much were those who did not try to communicate with me. I interacted with the deaf coworkers first and foremost.

There was one deaf woman who enjoyed picking on me for her insane reasons. She was bossy and became angry with me on more than one occasion, even going as far as to try to start a big argument while the unit manager was away on vacation. She even physically pushed me. She got fired, in part for her temper toward me and in part because she was missing so much work time. I never liked being around her and could see she had problems from the time I met her.

Prejudice against me because of my disabilities? I am sure there was, but I am not the kind of person who wants to sit down and discuss how someone feels about me. However, the example above about the deaf woman who enjoyed picking on me was a good example of someone being prejudiced. I never asked her, but other coworkers told me how she would spew things about how much she disliked me. Her reasons were not my problem. There may have been others who were prejudiced toward me but did not show it or talk about it.

At the facility for the mentally challenged, my disabilities blended right in. I was assigned a caseload of five mentally challenged adults, two who could be very mean. They were a challenge to work with, but they showed improvement after I started working with them.

No advancements happened for me at the IRS, even though I had a college degree, and that was another reason for becoming burned out fast. In my opinion, the IRS rarely promotes people who are disabled.

Did I fit in at the jobs? At the IRS, not really, no. The work atmosphere was not a very friendly atmosphere toward someone with a hearing and vision loss, even though I worked with a few other deaf individuals. At the facility for people with mental challenges, I fit in much better. One reason for this may have been because I had disabilities and could share my knowledge and experience with others who worked in that field.

Melanie Bond

My family and my school counselors had never encouraged me to pursue a college education or a career or vocation. One of my strongest aptitudes was writing. I grew up writing in my diaries and journals. Not only did I develop better writing skills, but writing was good therapy for me, too.

I never intentionally set out to pursue a journalism or writing career, but when the Michigan Department of Treasury hired me on as a file clerk, little did I know that it would lead me to a career in writing procedural documentation that included procedures, policies, bulletins, charts, job outlines, form instructions, organization charts, purpose and objectives, decision tables and system flowcharts. I did all the graphics work myself, using templates and rulers. I was also involved in editing and proofing the *Treasury Ledger,* a monthly newsletter that went out to all 1,800 Treasury employees. Though it took many years, I eventually worked my way up through the ranks to achieve my goal of becoming a departmental analyst.

I have to say that I had it really good when it came to getting the accommodations I needed at work. My supervisors were the best! I made my office so comfortable that it was like "my home away from home!" Air circulation inside the Treasury building wasn't great. Because I suffered from respiratory problems, I asked for and received an oscillating fan. When my work area was moved next to a tall window, the glare from the window bothered my eyes. I asked for dark tinting on the window to help cut down the glare, and I got it. When the overhead office lights started to bother my eyes (I could actually feel pain in my eyes from the intense glare of fluorescent lights), I asked to have the lights directly over my desk turned off, and I asked for a small full-spectrum lamp on my desk, even though there were fluorescent tube lights under my shelves.

I noted that in another area of the department the lighting was more subdued. In this case, the lighting was aimed toward the ceiling, casting a soft glow over the work area (indirect lighting). I requested that for our work area, too, but that idea got vetoed quickly. Win some, lose a few.

When I went to the Kalamazoo Training Center for the Blind for four weeks, I used two weeks of my annual leave time, and the department willingly paid for the other two weeks so that I wouldn't have to take a loss in pay. That was great! My supervisors suggested an ergonomic chair for me, and I willingly accepted their offer. It did much to relieve the strain in my lower back.

At the time I was first hired, I was driving myself back and forth to work. My working hours were from 8:00 AM to 5:00 PM. However, when we switched to Daylight Savings Time, I found myself facing either dark mornings or twilight evenings going to and from work, which made it hard for me to see. I asked if I could change my working hours to 8:15 to 4:45 with a half-hour lunch break so that I could still have a bit of daylight left to get to work and back home safely. Fortunately, driving to work was a straight shot and only took me about five minutes. Shortly after Harvey and I were married, I never had to worry about driving myself to work, because he willingly took over the driving for me.

I got along very well with everyone and especially with my supervisors.

When my supervisor hired in a new temporary worker, I was stunned to find out that this worker was the stutterer that I had known back in elementary school! She became my best friend. My supervisors loved her, too, and wanted to hire her on as a permanent employee. Unfortunately, the department let all the temporary workers go because of tough economic times. But speaking for myself, I pretty much got along with everyone, and everyone was kind to me at work, but I was not close to anyone.

I did not feel any prejudice against me for my disabilities, even when it became known that I was also losing my vision, in addition to already being deaf. I did notice a few coworkers looking the other way when I began using a white cane. It was somewhat hurtful, but overall, I was pleased that I was treated so well by everyone.

The only work-related "social scene" that I engaged in was when my supervisors and coworkers would go out to lunch together on special occasions. I enjoyed eating good food—no question about that! But I did have a hard time following the conversations that went on around me. My supervisors were very generous with me. They would recommend a dish for me, and I'd try it out. We also had parties at the office where we would each bring in a dish to pass—everyone loved my hot Oven Omelet, and it was usually gone before lunchtime. Sometimes, my coworkers would gather around the coffee machine and chat, but I wasn't really into that.

I volunteered to serve on the Affirmative Action and Equal Employment Opportunity board, the 504 board, and the State Handicappers Association for Public Employees (SHAPE) board, which included state workers with all kinds of disabilities. It was quite an interesting group! I was the editor of the SHAPE newsletter, and I served as VP for one year. At all the meetings, an interpreter was provided for me. I was also a board member of the Center for Independent Living in Lansing for one year.

But toward the end of my employment with the Department of Treasury, I did feel somewhat discriminated against when my request for a Windows-based personal computer was denied. It left me no choice but to retire earlier than I had anticipated because I needed a computer that could run a more powerful screen-magnification program.

I worked harder than anyone to prove that my disabilities did not hinder my job performance in any way. The fact that I had a hearing loss and a visual impairment did not deter me from doing my job in a competent manner. I was able to stay focused on my work, and, fortunately, there were few interruptions from coworkers when I worked. When the Department of Treasury first came out with the Employee of the Month award, guess who my supervisors nominated for this award? Me! (Brag, brag!) In acknowledgment for my having gone above and beyond my normal duties, I received a $50 check and a short interview and a photo shot with the State Treasurer.

Patricia Clark

So much negative stuff was thrown at me during my adolescence that I was very frightened about employment. My dear old mother said to me a thousand times, "*You* can't do *that*." She also told me that I'd have to get a job in a back room somewhere, so I wouldn't have contact with other workers or with the public.

Armed with a B.A., I wanted to earn some money to travel. I put aside career hopes for a while and got a dreary job in the public service. My boss had his hands all over me. He was forty-five, and I was twenty-one, so when I went to the union, they said that if I made a formal complaint of sexual harassment, I would lose my job, not him. And that is what happened. He also went around saying he had to work with this ghastly deaf girl.

I then went to London, where I had office jobs for two years. On my return to New Zealand, I tried hard to find a career opening. This proved impossible, and after being unemployed for months, I again took a dreary public service job. After three years, my employer bought a mainframe computer and invited staff to train as computer programmers. I applied and was chosen, without the faintest idea of what it was about. There were nine in the class, and the teacher was truly dreadful.

He had personality problems. He was so merciless that, after a few weeks, only four were left standing. The rest had given up. He never missed an opportunity to humiliate me for my disabilities.

By this time, I was hooked on computers and was lucky enough to get a job with the multinational British company International Computers Ltd. I spent three excellent years there, until the manager called me in and said, unless I got "fixed up," there was no job for me.

Again, I went to London, and in 1970, programmers were in demand. After two years getting good experience, I returned to New Zealand and set out to find a job. Once again, I was in the public service, and it was hell on earth. The manager crucified me for my disabilities, denied me training or meaningful work, let alone promotion, and I was rarely included in social activities. I spent seventeen years in this toxic environment simply for the pay packet. Efforts to find something better got me nowhere, and I had a mortgage to pay. Early retirement was a blessed relief.

You may say that the public service *did* employ me when nobody else would. I'd reply that it's a bad situation when a person with good qualifications and experience, who is hard-working and keen to please, can't get a reasonable job. It's better to have people with disabilities employed in work they are trained to do than have them on state assistance. The atmosphere in that place was so bad I'll never get over it.

Scott Stoffel

When I finished high school, I had no clear direction for a career. After an unsuccessful semester in college, I worked at a family-owned computer store for a year. It was during that time I became deaf on top of being legally blind. The hearing loss forced me to resign, as my job had been to talk with customers. The family didn't make me give up working there; I chose to because I knew I was dead weight and hurting the business.

The next few years of my life were murky. During those aimless years, I only had part-time jobs, such as delivering papers. I tried to sell a science fiction novel but couldn't get a break with a serious publisher. I hated being broke all the time, and I hated the way people looked down at me for not having a job.

After a stint in rehab at the HKNC, I gave college a second go. While I was in school, I did some part-time teaching work at HKNC and did a summer work experience as a copy editor at Publishers Clearing House. But those jobs wouldn't pay the bill for full time at Hofstra University, so I transferred to Temple University and relocated to eastern Pennsylvania.

My then-wife worked for the three years I was at Temple, so I could focus on school full time, including summer courses. I did a little student work there to pick up a few bucks but did not have a regular job. Financially, we barely managed to make ends meet, and Sandra passionately hated her jobs. She was ready for a divorce at the start of my senior year. I was devastated and asked her to wait until I finished the college ordeal and see what kind of job I could get.

I tried to sell a fantasy novel but was again spurned by all the major publishers. I ended up with a meaningless small press contract.

I applied to the Federal Workforce Recruitment Program in my senior year. The program helps students with disabilities find jobs with federal agencies. It was through this program that I landed an interview with the FAA and was given a position as a general engineer within the Systems Engineering department.

Life certainly changed a lot when I got that job. I went from living on pennies to earning an upper-middle-class income. We moved into a nice apartment in Arlington, Virginia, where we had easy access to stores and restaurants. Sandra quit working and became a compulsive gambler.

My office was located in Washington, D.C. I used the Metro subway system to get from Arlington to D.C. and then rode an FAA shuttle from the main headquarters building to my office. I sometimes got a ride home from a thoughtful colleague. There were only two different trains on the subway track I used, but the only way I could tell them apart was to stand close to the electronic sign and try to get my wavering vision to discern whether the train coming started with a "B" or a "Y" (for "Blue Line" and "Yellow Line"). I couldn't read the whole name. Unfortunately, my vision sometimes played jokes on me, or the sign would be inoperative, and I'd get on the wrong train. I could figure out whether I was on the right train or not pretty fast: The train I wanted would soon come above ground and cross over the Potomac River, while the other train came up and went into Arlington National Cemetery. So I knew I had it wrong every time I ended up in the graveyard. In that case, I got off and backtracked to the Pentagon terminal and tried again. On one unlucky occasion, I ended up on the wrong train three times and was over an hour late by the time mercy let me make it to work.

I had less trouble with the FAA shuttle bus, once the drivers got to know me. But I did get on the wrong shuttle a few times. Once, I ended up taking a thirty-minute ride to who knows where. It's loads of fun when two shuttles look about the same, and you can't hear to ask the driver questions.

My supervisors at FAA were very good about providing accommodations. My first boss had a CCTV, a large computer screen, and a large-print TTY in my work area the first week I was there. I later got Zoomtext (a screen-enlargement program) for my PC. A coworker gave me a large dry-erase board to hang on the wall for people to write messages on. Another coworker frequently assisted me when I had to go to other buildings.

FAA shared a sign language interpreter office with all of the Department of Transportation (DOT). When I first began work, the interpreter service was very reliable. They had several interpreters with tactile experience who worked with me frequently for meetings. It is particularly helpful to have the same interpreters when you use tactile, because it can take time to get to know a new interpreter's style. I was never great at reading sign with my hands, due to my nerve disorder, so working with a familiar interpreter was a big help. Once I got used to these folks, we did pretty well.

But my luck changed a few years later when DOT decided to hire a new interpreting contractor. The new service was less organized than the first one and had very few interpreters with tactile experience. They frequently had to bring in interpreters from outside to work with me, which meant I rarely got the same one twice. I found myself constantly having to adjust to new styles, and that only made it harder for me to keep up with meetings. On top of that, there were a number of occasions when no interpreter showed up at all, leaving me to sit there at the conference table like a complete idiot. But the important thing was that DOT saved money on the new service.

To add to my woes, FAA decided to reorganize. If you've never been through reorganization before, it's kind of like swallowing a live grenade. Upper and middle management throw the employees and frontline managers into a blender and congratulate themselves for drastically "improving" the agency. I got plucked from System Architecture, an area I was just starting to feel comfortable with and thought I was contributing to, and bounced around a few makeshift work groups with mile-long names, until I ended up being assigned to the Safety Engineering work group. Never mind that I had no training or experience with Safety, and never mind that the only available training was in the form of all-day lectures—I could do tactile sign with a familiar interpreter for an hour at most.

I'm not the type to whine, so I gave Safety my best shot. I received some very rudimentary training from a contractor that was part of our group and read all available materials on the subject. But the big punch in the puss with Safety was that the primary function of a safety engineer was to attend meetings of other work groups and provide safety support. Oh, great! Communication was my top shortcoming, and they gave me a job where communication was a prime requisite.

At home, Sandra's gambling got totally out of control. She applied for every credit card she could get her hands on and blew every cent on Internet casino websites. Despite my six-figure salary, we couldn't cover all the finance charges and sank hopelessly into debt.

Maybe it was the trans-lethal stress of the whole situation that caused my neurological disorder to act up. The nerves in my hands got worse at this time. I lost the ability to move several finger muscles, and the sensitivity of the skin became duller. Reading tactile sign rapidly became harder—even with familiar people. It got to where I couldn't even follow a short meeting through an interpreter. I discussed the problem with my supervisor and DOT's Disability Resource Center representatives and decided to switch from interpreters to CART (computer-assisted real-time captioning). They hired a contractor to come to my meetings with a special computer and type what people said in large print. My vision was not good enough to read at sufficient speed to keep up with meetings, though.

When the CART didn't work, my boss told me he was willing to try something else. I have to give him credit for that. I know working with me was the strangest thing he ever did, but he stood by me until the end. The trouble was that there were no other feasible options. I no longer had a real-time communication mode that was fast enough to facilitate effective participation in meetings.

In an act of desperation, I underwent cochlear implant surgery in 2006. The normally three-hour surgery took eight hours, supposedly because of equipment failure during the operation—Stoffel's syndrome rides again! But it would have been worth it if the implant had given me some speech reception. It didn't, and I think I left my mind on the operating table.

My career entered an endless loop: I needed faster real-time communication; I had no effective real-time mode. I took up drinking to deal with the dilemma. After work, I'd go home, grab a bottle of whisky and guzzle until I passed out. Sleep was the only relief from the nightmare.

Sandra didn't like the boozing but continued to gamble my earnings down the drain. People at my office kept prompting me to find an answer to the communication issue. A problem without solution is a sure catalyst for insanity.

As the pressure to find a solution that didn't exist built up, my sanity decayed like a watermelon in a desert. My boss suggested several times that I see a shrink. I failed to see how Prozac was going to solve my communication problems, but it bothered me that my mental breakdown was starting to show. I became concerned about my job security on top of everything else. Ultimately, I filed for bankruptcy and then applied for early retirement due to disability. I was approved, and my career was over and out after eight years.

The people I worked with were polite and respectful toward me, although I never really felt accepted. I kept a word processor open on my computer at all times with a large font, so people could come in and talk to me by typing. But there were only a few people willing to do that on their own initiative. I could tell most people who were "forced" to come in and talk to me—out of work-related need or because of pressure by a supervisor—wouldn't have been less comfortable if they'd been sitting on nails. I tried to be friendly and funny, but I just couldn't alter reality. Freaks are freaks, and valid people don't want to be around one.

During my first year, I volunteered to teach a lunchtime "extracurricular" class in basic sign language. Back then, FAA required employees to attend a few workshops each year that had something to do with social diversity, and my class fell into that category. I ended up with a group of about sixteen. We met for five sessions that included learning the manual alphabet, how to curse in ASL, and a little bit about interacting with deaf-blind people. Things seemed to go pretty well, but when it was over, no one wanted to sign to me. A few people "showed" me something in finger spelling but pulled back every time I tried to touch their hands. I explained—again—that my vision was insufficient to read finger spelling; I needed to touch their hands and feel it. That idea apparently appalled them. Soon, everyone gave up on sign altogether. I liked to think I wasn't the ugliest person on earth, but maybe I was wrong.

I attended a few office socials during my first few years. I was determined to make some friends and stop being the "creature in the corner." I was allowed to request interpreters for in-house socials. But talking through an interpreter always seemed to make conversations awkward and impersonal. I ended up spending most of my time just talking to the interpreters. Group conversations are particularly difficult to follow through an interpreter, and I was never fast enough to keep up. I realized fitting in was a lost cause and quit going to the socials after a while.

There was a small deaf community at DOT, and a deaf guy was hired by Systems Engineering not too long after I started there. But I had as much trouble communicating with deaf as with hearing people. With my useless hands, I couldn't make many of the hand shapes used in sign language. So while I could understand the deaf folks, they couldn't understand me.

While I was in System Architecture, I was promoted twice. I got to know the NAS (National Airspace System) Architecture quite well and was comfortable working with the database. But after the hell-spawned reorganization, I never found a niche again.

When I finally threw in the towel, it was very difficult. I'd made it to a Level 13 federal employee. One more promotion would have put me in management. But there was no possibility of getting that promotion in Safety, since I could not perform the expected meeting support duties and was thus unable to get good performance reviews anymore.

Tonilyn Todd Wisner

During my senior year in high school, I worked as a teacher at a child development center. I continued to do that during the summer. I still had good vision then and one good ear.

At the end of high school, I saw a guidance counselor, because even though I was an "A" student, I had to spend all my after-school time studying and still quickly forgot things. I was afraid to start at a university, because I knew it would be harder than high school. I was tested and found to have severe learning disabilities. So it was recommended that I start on a part-time course load. In the fall of 1988, I started college at the University of Southwest Louisiana, which is now called U of L. I majored in teaching, but because of my memory problems, I was afraid of not making a good teacher.

I also worked as a bartender and a front desk manager. I wound up quitting college and going back to work as a teacher and also drove the school bus. I did that for a year, and then my friend and neighbor asked me to be a nanny to her three-year-old and three-month-old, so she could go back to work. I did that for about three years and then decided to become a Certified Nursing Assistant. I got my certification but injured my back on the job, and that ended my career.

I then decided to go into computers. I started a program at Delgado Community College in New Orleans. By this time, I was confident that I could handle school, and I took on a full 18 credit hours. My studies included different aspects of computers, French, Spanish, and ASL. I also worked part-time running the college's language lab, tutoring French, Spanish, German, and ASL and was also a teacher assistant. I had a second job as a physical therapy aid, as well. During my first year, I lost most of my hearing in my right (only hearing) ear from an unknown cause. I couldn't get a hearing aid and started using an FM loop system provided by the college. The FM loop system was an amplification device that had a microphone that the professor wore, while I wore a receiver with an earpiece and a volume control. This helped in my computer classes, but my French and Spanish classes were more difficult, since I could only read lips in English.

When I went back to college, I also worked as a receptionist and physical therapist technician. As I lost my hearing and balance, I was unable to walk with patients and unable to book appointments made by phone. But my boss and coworkers were really great during this difficult time for me. My boss actually hired someone to take over the phones for me so I could keep working there as a receptionist.

When my vertigo got really bad and I could no longer communicate well, my boss created a job for me: I wrote a computer program to create a database of all patients for the ten years they had been open.

Everything was in paper files, so I came up with a numbering system and different search methods in the program, in which they could find exactly where any patient's chart was. I also was unable to walk to work anymore, even though I only needed to walk about four blocks, so my boss and coworkers took turns getting me to and from work. That project took a few months to complete, and by the time I was finished, I was too sick to keep working.

I could read lips, so communication was not that hard. Also, two of my coworkers were learning ASL, so they could sign a little.

At the end of the year, I had a vertigo attack that lasted about thirty minutes. I saw a neurotologist, an inner ear specialist. For months, I suffered constant dizziness and vertigo that lasted one to two days at a time. My doctor encouraged me to quit school and work and go on Social Security. But I was determined to complete my associate degree. And in July of 1996, I graduated with a 4.0 GPA with a degree in Computer Information Systems. I had minors in French, ASL, and mathematics. During the graduation ceremony, I made it across the stage with a walker and the help of a good friend who also interpreted the ceremony for me. I also never quit either job.

I attended one more day at college to begin working toward my bachelor degree in computers. But after that one day, I was sick in bed and was ultimately forced to stop working and go on full SSI.

Wendy Williams

When I was a child, I wanted to be a child psychologist, to be there for struggling kids—there had been no one there for me. I would have liked to have been a doctor, but with my limited vision and hearing, I thought it was impossible.

My first employment was at a group home in a village, per my mother's insistence and against my will, since my high school grades were too low for postsecondary education. I did not know what I wanted to do. Up to this point, I did part-time work as a caterer's assistant and a nanny. Much to my dismay, I was hired on the spot at the group home.

I moved into a room in a staff house and hardly slept a wink, dreading my first day. I was initially assigned to a section in which there were fifteen children, teens, and women with a wide range of cognitive abilities.

A staffer had been assigned to show me the duties on day one. She could see the fear in my face and told me to give it at least three months. I did not want to be a quitter, so I took her wise words of advice seriously. For the next several days, I continued to work in that section. It was difficult physical labor, doing basic attendant responsibilities single-handedly (e.g., feeding, bathing, dressing, cleaning, training, entertaining, etc.). I was constantly on the move and on my feet for eight hours a day, except for the fifteen-minute coffee break and thirty-minute meal time.

I then worked in other sections and cottages of the group home, working all shifts. After a year, I was promoted to Section Head of the first section I had worked in, supervising staff and being responsible for the maintenance of that section, in addition to the basic attendant tasks.

I became attached to the residents and developed friendships with some of the staff. I was treated with respect by the administration and my colleagues, not at all perceived as a disabled person. I did not know there were such things as disability accommodations back then, but there was little I would have needed. I removed the hearing aids connected to my glasses to talk on the phone. I tended to trip on residents sitting on the floor, if I had to move quickly in an emergency, but was able to get around safely for the most part.

After four years of intense physical work, I was burned out. It was at this point an administrator encouraged us younger staffers to attend community college to become educators with the hope we would return to mainly instruct residents.

Upon completing community college, undergraduate university, and graduate school, I sought employment as a school psychologist. I sent more than seventy resumes, and I was open about my disabilities, as well as my abilities. I had two interviews and was hired by one school down south. My duties mainly consisted of psychological testing and counseling. Again, I felt the staff respected me. I did not need accommodations at this point, although my social contacts were limited to a few people that worked at the same school.

Then a new supervisor was hired. He asked me out for a date, and I declined. When there was a major budget shortfall later, the decision was made to let me go, even though I was not the newest staffer in the department. There was no union and no ADA, so I had no means of contesting this layoff.

After two years at that school, I found myself conducting a second job search. I was hired at another school up north that contracted me out to a different school in the area. My responsibilities were similar to the previous school, plus behavior management. All went well professionally and personally for the first decade. After my battle with cancer, I began to lose the rest of both my residual vision and hearing simultaneously. I requested hearing accommodations for meetings, as it was increasingly difficult for me to speech-read and hear in those settings. The administrators put me through a series of stressful meetings across a number of months to discuss accommodations and job duties. One peer accompanied me to the later meetings for note-taking. This colleague was appalled and confirmed to me my impressions of the meetings—that the administrators used badgering, harassment, and intimidation.

I connected with a union representative to ask about obtaining accommodations. She stated accommodations should be provided within a short time period, and that if the meetings continued, she would be in communication with the administrators. Suddenly, the administrators brought the accommodation meetings to a halt, saying they would provide a loop system for meetings.

The next struggle was getting colleagues to speak into the loop mike so I could hear them. Some administrators were diligent in expecting the staff to talk into the mike when I brought it to their attention. Others were not. A friend kindly paid for the services of an expensive ADA attorney to inquire into the status of accommodations in my work site. She said the provision of the loop system was considered "reasonable," even if some colleagues chose not to use the mike.

After that, print became more difficult for me to read. I requested a scanner to copy text into the computer, so its speech screen-reader could read the material to me. The media staff, with the approval of the administrator, furnished a CCTV for text that could not be scanned. It was a challenge putting the large print into my very small visual fields.

During this time, I lost hearing in my right ear and then in my left ear, requiring bilateral, sequential cochlear implants. In the meantime, my reading medium changed from large print to Braille. Thanks to the kindness and patience of the media staff, materials were provided in Braille or via the computer, as well as a reader.

I remember having to read technical books, which were harder than pleasure books. I had to read fast, and out of sheer exhaustion, I would collapse with my head and arms on the desk. In time, I read technical books better and was not so tired.

The early morning routine prior to work involved waking up to a Braille clock, grooming, dressing, eating breakfast, preparing lunch to go, and it was followed by a mile walk with my dog guide in the very scary predawn darkness. I arrived at work exhausted. I sat in my office chair, needing a few extra minutes to regroup before the start of the work day. I felt as if I had two jobs—one being a psychologist, the other being a problem-solver, constantly trying to find different ways to get the same duties completed.

The school changed administrations, and the new one was unsupportive and targeted a few of us staff, wearing us down, devaluing us. I was wiped out; it took so much energy to meet demands, to make changes and to deal with the taunting, let alone the adaptations to my deaf-blindness. My employer had to cut a number of positions, including mine. I applied to the contracted school for the new psychologist position opening, but the administration decided not to hire me. My employer was supportive and agreed to put me on disability status.

It is very sad indeed when increasing deaf-blindness and the subsequent need for accommodations are paralleled with increasing disrespect from the workforce.

9
Daily Life

While homemaking and running errands involve things most people take for granted, such routine activities can be a lot more complicated for people who are deaf-blind. A hearing-sighted person can pick up the phone and call a plumber when the kitchen sink leaks or hop in the car when it's time for an appointment with the family doctor. But how would you handle these things if you had multiple sensory disabilities?

Some deaf-blind people are fortunate enough to have someone to help them with their daily activities, but many do not, and all have to rely on themselves sometimes. Even the most mundane tasks can create significant stress for people who are deaf-blind and require far more effort and problem-solving thought.

Here, the contributors talk about how they approach managing their homes and tending to errands.

Angela C. Orlando

Homemaking is a topic that makes me want to cringe. I've seen professionals and non-deaf-blind people talk about homemaking as an indicator of success. Barbara Walters marveled over how incredible a certain deaf-blind man was, simply because he could cook a meal.

Well, guess what? I don't like to cook, and I don't like to clean. It has nothing to do with ability and success. I'm just not interested. I'm never going to be. Yes, I can do it. I've lived in an apartment with other young women. I lived in an apartment with a man. I lived in a house with my husband and son. I took care of my home. I just didn't like doing it. It has nothing to do with my disabilities. It's just who I am. Some people like to do chores and some don't.

I live with my parents now. It's their home. My dad does the yard work and home repairs. My mother does most of the cooking and cleaning. My job is to care for my son, keep our rooms clean, and put away laundry. It works for me.

I've had training in cooking and cleaning. I have many kitchen gadgets to help me. For example, I have a George Foreman grill, microwave cooker for rice and pasta, and a microwave gadget that hard-boils eggs. I have Braille measuring cups, tongs for the toaster, other utensils, and long-armed oven mitts. People who are deaf-blind can use many of the same items that blind people use. We just need to avoid the "talking" ones.

I have Braille labels on food and cleaning items. These labels have both Braille and print. That way, my parents can put the labels on while putting away groceries. I rely heavily on these labels to identify what I need. Sure, I can use my sense of touch and smell. But there are some items I just don't want to sniff.

I have an electric sweeper. It works on both hard floors and carpets. I don't have to worry about sweeping messes into a dustpan. It goes right into the machine. I just remove the bag when it gets full.

I don't cook and clean as much as I should. But I *can*. I've got the skills. I just lack the desire. Someday, my parents won't be around to help me as much. That's when I'll have to do more of this on my own.

My parents drive me to appointments or shopping. They'll take me wherever I need to go. They also help a great deal in getting my son to his many activities and parties or play dates.

Earlier this year, I began using our local transportation service to get to my ASL classes at Kent State. I ride on door-to-door service. They pick me up at my house and take me to the exact location I need to go. I'm the first deaf-blind person ever to use this transportation service here. They had a difficult time understanding my needs at first. They have to come into the building and tap me on the shoulder. It's the only way I'll know the bus is there (I have no vision and cannot hear speech now). They also must take me to the exact location and the exact same door every time. Otherwise, I won't know where I am or how to find where I need to be in the building.

We've had so many issues. They wouldn't tap me, so I missed the bus, because I never knew it was there. They took me to the wrong door, so I'd be confused and not able to find my classroom. One time, they took me to the wrong building altogether and left me there.

It's been rough, but they finally seem to be getting the idea. This semester has been fine, no serious problems yet. I love riding the bus to class, because it's something I can actually do on my own. I don't want my parents to have to escort me to the classroom—that's embarrassing. I'm an adult; I can do things on my own. I just need a little extra help. The transportation service makes it possible for me to achieve this bit of independence. And that makes me feel a little bit more like a normal person.

Christian S. Shinaberger

Mostly, I've lived in houses. When I lived in a dormitory for three years at UCSD, I used the cafeteria and going out with friends for meals.

I liked the laundromat on campus. The washers had three choices: cold, warm, and hot, and I could remember which was which without the benefit of vision. Doing my laundry was very easy.

In the dorm, I always got a single, which suited me just fine. I didn't have to worry about my Braille equipment being stolen.

I also had an experience in high school one summer when I lived in an apartment for one month, alone. My mobility instructor helped set it up. I was already familiar with basic laundry and cooking, although I didn't cook much when I was alone.

As for homes, they have so far always been with my immediate family. I currently live at my mom's house.

I help out with cleaning in the kitchen. Cooking isn't something I do a lot of, but I do enjoy cooking with someone else, and I like to use our propane grill. We just got a new dishwasher here, and I don't have it marked with tactile labels yet. I'm sorry our old one finally died after about thirty years. It had real push buttons, which is damned hard to find on appliances these days (as opposed to touchpad buttons that cannot be felt). I still can't read Braille that well, even after the carpal tunnel surgery. Of course, some things just need a few raised marks.

I'm estranged from my sister, and most of my relatives live back east, or should I say, down south (in Georgia).

Yard work . . . well, I don't do much there. But on occasion, I do things alone, like trimming bushes. And sometimes, I help my mom do things outside. She often supervises what I do in the yard. We have gardeners at the present, so we don't have to do too much out there. My regular outdoor work consists of taking the trash out front on Tuesdays. Nothing special involved here. We have three cans: recyclable stuff, general trash, and garden trash. I've tied a shoelace around the one for recycling, so I can identify it. The garden can has a dent in the lid, and the regular trash can is smaller than the other two.

I prefer gas stoves with real knobs when cooking. That is the most important thing for me. I should label things in the kitchen, but I don't cook that much. I'd like to find an easy-to-use talking thermometer for the grill and perhaps the oven. I use the grill more than the oven. But I really don't have any special gadgets for cooking at the moment.

Separating laundry without sighted help is the one task I dread the most. I can't tell the difference between dark and light colors. At the dorm, I had everything pretty much match, so it didn't matter what I grabbed to wear. But at home, the laundry is more complicated. Once someone helps me sort the colors out, I can handle the rest of the job on my own.

Christy L. Reid

After leaving college and beginning my first full-time paying job, I moved into an apartment and lived on my own. The job was located in Baltimore, and my parents drove me from Poplar Bluff, Missouri, to Baltimore to help me find an apartment in an accessible location. We found an ideal apartment complex in a very good location that would make it easier for me to live on my own. The apartment complex grounds were set right next to a subway stop, and tenants received a key to the private gate.

There was a supermarket about a mile down the road from the apartment, and it was easy for me to walk there on the sidewalk. But getting back to the apartment with groceries was a different matter. I usually purchased a good supply of groceries, so my grocery shopping trips would be less frequent. I devised a sign using a big piece of cardboard and wrote my apartment address on it with a black marker. I taped the sign to my front door (I had a ground-floor apartment with a private patio) and left the outdoor light on over my door. Then I set off on foot for the grocery store. After completing my shopping, I asked the person assisting me to please call a taxi for me to take me home. I didn't really like using cabs; I almost always had to wait for them for a long time. But there was no other way to get all those groceries home, so I was prepared to wait. When the taxi finally showed up, I would give the driver a printed note with my address and told him to look for the sign on my door. Thus, the cab drivers always found my apartment without trouble.

I didn't need any special equipment to help with household chores. But vacuuming the carpet and sweeping the kitchen floor were difficult and my least favorite chores. I used a broom to sweep under the kitchen counters and then vacuum up the dirt, but not before I checked the floor with my fingers for anything that might break the vacuum. Cleaning the carpet was a tedious job. Because I couldn't see if there was something that would damage the vacuum, I always had to brush my hand over the carpet first.

I enjoyed cooking and didn't really have any adaptive equipment in the days of my first apartment. I did have an electric wok and liked to stir-fry chicken and vegetables. Using an electric wok was easier to manage than a wok on the stove, and I could use my senses of touch and taste to help me know when the food was cooked.

I also had a crock pot, which was another easy way to cook my meals. In the morning before I left for work, I would put some chopped carrots and onion in the bottom of the crock pot and place a whole chicken over the veggies, add a bay leaf, cover and set it on low heat. This made a delicious, healthy dish that would last for a few dinners.

After living on my own for a few months, I married Bill, and we eventually moved to Silver Spring, Maryland, where we rented an apartment. We found an ideal location that enabled me to travel independently. I got a part-time job at Gallaudet University and also took a few courses in education. I was able to walk to a nearby Metro subway stop from our apartment and travel to Gallaudet. However, there wasn't a nearby grocery store, and Bill, who is hearing and sighted, would drive us to the store, so we could do grocery shopping together. Bill didn't mind cleaning the apartment's hardwood floors, so we had a sort of mutual agreement that he would take care of the floors, and I would do our laundry. Likewise, whenever Bill cooked dinner, I would clean up, and when I cooked, he cleaned up. This agreement has continued throughout our marriage.

After living in an apartment, Bill and I rented a small two-bedroom house near enough to the campus of the University of Arkansas at Little Rock (UALR) for me to reach on foot. I had enrolled at UALR to study deaf education, and the location of our house met my needs.

However, living in a house was different from living in an apartment. For one thing, it wasn't easy to find neighbors whenever I needed help. I had to either cross the street and find someone's front door or walk to the house next door. But most people were friendly and went out of their way to help. For example, I liked to put my son, Joe, in his jogging stroller and go for a walk in the neighborhood. One day when I decided to turn into an alley behind our house, I somehow got disoriented and got lost. I walked on and on, trying to find a familiar landmark. I really felt lost and started looking for someone who might help me. I finally turned onto an asphalt street with a white line near the edge that looked familiar, and as I walked a little further, I passed a woman who was getting something out of the trunk of a parked car. I stopped and asked her if she could please show me my house, telling her the house number. When she took my elbow to guide me, I realized she was a neighbor that lived a few houses down the street from us, and I knew exactly where I was.

As a deaf-blind mom, homemaking became busier. I learned a lot from caring for my first son, Joe. I decided before he was born that I would breastfeed him. I figured that, as a deaf-blind mom, it would be easier to nurse my baby than to make bottles, and I had read that nursing the baby strengthens the bonding between mother and child. Plus, there were the nutritional and immunization benefits of breastfeeding. All in all, it was a very good decision. But it was more comfortable than having to get up, get a bottle, and sit with the baby. As he got older and began eating baby foods, it sometimes got frustrating for me. I couldn't see his mouth and always missed my target, making a big mess. But mother and son learned together. After a while, my baby learned to grab the spoon with his mouth, so he could eat the food.

I had two more babies after Joe, Ben and then Tim. I cared for each baby very similarly to how I had cared for Joe. The main difference was that I got a cochlear implant (CI) before Ben was born, and, thus, I could hear Ben and Tim. When Ben or Tim cried or laughed, I heard it, unlike with Joe. I used a baby cry device to alert me when Joe was crying, though it wasn't that reliable. Usually, Bill would tell me when Joe was crying, or I would keep Joe within arm's reach, so I could check on him. Maybe that wasn't such a good idea, because when he got older, he liked to sneak away. But with the CI, things were less stressful. I could leave Ben in his bassinet near our fish aquarium, which he enjoyed, while I worked in another room in the house. I could hear him if he cried.

When I go shopping on my own, I always go to the customer service counter and request shopping assistance. Even though my speech is good, I give whoever is working behind the desk a note that explains I'm deaf-blind and would like an assistant to help me find the things on my list. Then I show the person my shopping list and wait. Usually, the people working behind the customer service desk know what to do. They pick up a phone and talk into it; then a few minutes later, a store employee approaches me, takes the list, gets a shopping cart, and we're off. In my experience, the assistant usually gave me items that were on my list, so I could put them into the cart myself. After collecting all the items on my list, I would ask the assistant to help me go through checkout and write the cost of my purchases in very big numbers with a black marker on white paper that I always had handy. After paying for my things, I would give the assistant a taxi company's number and ask him or her to call and request a cab to pick me up. This all usually went smoothly, but it also always took a great deal of patience on my part. Having to communicate with people who don't know sign can be a little slow, and then the wait for the cab can take an hour or longer.

But this routine didn't always go according to plan. Once when Bill was out, I used my TTY to call and requested a cab to come and take me to the grocery store. The cab arrived and took me to the store. I got an assistant from customer service, and everything went very smoothly, until after I paid for my purchases and the assistant called the taxi company for me. The assistant spoke into the phone, and I assumed he was requesting the cab. Then he looked at me and took my notebook and black marker, printing in large letters, "Your address?"

To my great embarrassment, my mind went blank, and I couldn't remember my address! Flustered, I told him I couldn't remember. He turned back to the phone and spoke into it some more, while I wondered what in the heck was I going to do? I didn't know anyone to call for help; other family members were out of town that day, too. Gosh, I felt like a fool.

Finally, the assistant hung up and took my notebook again, printing, "Cab company found your address in their records." Whew!

When we lived in Pittsburgh and Ben was almost four years old, I took him to all his doctor appointments at the children's hospital there. Bill was in culinary arts school and working as a cook. I was a full-time stay-at-home mom, caring for Joe and Ben. I used the local transit bus service to take Ben to the hospital, because it was safer than public bus service and cost less than a cab. The driver of the transit bus helped to set up Ben's car seat in the bus and then would leave the car seat in the lobby of the hospital. An interpreter would meet us and guide us to Ben's appointment.

When I was pregnant with Tim, I had help from a woman who worked as a doula, a woman who helps a pregnant woman with prenatal visits and any other things and with labor. She didn't know sign, but I taught her finger spelling. She drove me to most of my prenatal doctor visits, and Ben came, too, if he wasn't in preschool. An interpreter would meet us at the hospital and help with communication.

I first experienced white cane training when I was thirteen years old and a student at the Missouri School for the Blind in St. Louis. I learned basic cane skills, like trailing the cane up and down stairs and sweeping the ground in front of me. I also learned how to cross intersections by following traffic patterns. However, I didn't start to seriously use a white cane until I was in college and went off-campus to restaurants and shopping malls. At first, I found that the white cane was more like an ID, helping other people to understand I was visually impaired. Without the cane, I looked pretty normal—until I bumped into someone I didn't see or couldn't find the handle on a door. The cane helped other people to understand, and I appreciated that.

In the fall of 1997, I went to Leader Dogs School in Michigan, where I met Milo, my first guide dog. He was a seventy-pound yellow Labrador retriever, and he was the guide dog of my dreams. I had read quite a lot of stories about blind people's experiences with guide dogs, and I was very inspired to have one of my own. Milo was a great match, very patient, calm, always wanting to please, and adaptive to different things we encountered together.

For example, Bill and I went on a long road trip along the western coast of Florida to Key West. Joe was about three, and he stayed with my parents. Milo enjoyed the adventure. Wherever we stopped to explore, he was game and guided me along, following Bill. When we finally reached Key West, we went out on a sunset cruise on an old schooner. The sunset cruise trip offered free beer and champagne. It was mid-February, but I hadn't bargained for cold water and wind. The sun had been so warm that I was surprised at how cold it was on that schooner, and the waves were moderately rough, making the boat rock and the ocean spray hit me. Bill was busy behind our video camera, filming the beautiful sight of the Keys as the schooner moved around them. But I couldn't sit still while getting wet and cold. Milo helped me walk from side to side of the boat, trying to avoid the spray. I found the drinks table, and the free champagne helped to warm my blood. It was an exhilarating experience to have Milo guide me to wherever I wanted to go.

Usually, whether I used a white cane or guide dog, people didn't try to grab or steer me. Most people would stop near me, and I knew they were asking if I needed help. If I knew where I was going or if I was just waiting for Bill or someone, I would say, "I'm fine, thanks." If I really did needed help, I would look for someone to help, like with a big intersection. In that case, I'd have a note to show a passerby that would ask the person to please help me cross the street. But I have encountered people who were too aggressive or too persistent with wanting to help me. On a Baltimore subway platform, a woman noticed me with my white cane. A train pulled in, but I knew it was the opposite direction from where I wanted to go. The woman grabbed my wrist and tried to pull me onto the train, but I shook her off and said I was waiting for the other train. Finally, she gave up and ran into the train as the doors closed.

After a little over eight years of working, Milo retired. I got a second guide dog, but unfortunately, he didn't work out, and I had to send him back to Leader Dogs. Now I use my white cane again, but because of my deteriorating balance, I use a support cane more often and feel more confident if someone is guiding me. My younger sons, Ben and Tim, like to hold my left hand, while I hold the support cane in the other, and we walk around in the neighborhood near our home. I may return to Leader Dogs for another guide dog, but for now, my children keep me busy enough.

Judy Kahl

At the age of sixty-four, I can tell you I am independent only in my home. I do not venture out of the house without the aid of a sighted person. I am with my husband, friend, or one of my three adult children. They are all trained and know my limitations. It is difficult, especially in new surroundings.

Restaurants, unless they are fast food places, are normally too dim or too noisy for me. We always ask for their brightest table with the least amount of noise, and most of the time, it is satisfactory. If we're at a new restaurant, my husband will check out the table first before taking me to it. He guides me with his hand on my shoulder, or I hold his hand and walk behind him. I usually take one of my girlfriends' arms and ask them to walk just one or two steps ahead, so I know if they are going up or down a step.

As for shopping, it is best if there is a cart, like in Target or TJ Maxx, so I can stand behind the cart, and my companions pull the cart. This way, I can walk and look side to side so I don't miss anything and don't have to worry about obstacles.

I do find shopping exhausting, and I am always happy to return to my familiar surroundings. I also do not ask to be taken anywhere, but I have friends with whom I go to the manicurist, petite-clothes shopping, bargain shopping, etc. I try to spread myself out, so I am not too much of a burden to any one person—they don't like it when I talk like this, but it's the reality of it. I know it would be a drag to be a sighted person and have to tag someone along, so I try to be a positive, fun person and always pick up the tab for lunch and explain I'm not paying for gas. Sometimes they accept, and many times they refuse, but we very seldom go to a fancy place, as we are too busy shopping, so it could be a drive-thru.

I miss being able to drive (I could drive until my vision became too limited, due to Usher's syndrome), and I miss the independence. But once again . . . what are my choices? So I must make the best of it. This is just another reason I have chosen to keep myself busy and why I am so driven to make my BEE project successful—raising funds for FFB. It is only the funds that slow down progress, and I'm working myself silly, so we can wipe out blindness.

Mark Gasaway

I have lived in the average American home as an adult, This includes a small home on my parents' land, a room rented from the facility I was employed by, several apartments (after getting married), and a condo. At each of the places, except the apartments and condo, I lived by myself. At the apartments and condo, I lived with my wife and a dog. Now I am divorced and share a condo with a friend.

I did not and still do not need any special equipment or technology to help me with any housework. I do everything the old-fashioned way!

I cooked and still do, but again, I do not need any special equipment to help me. I cook like other people might cook. However, reading oven and stove dials and frozen food containers is not easy. To help me with setting the oven and stove temps and reading heating instructions on containers, I use a handheld magnifying glass. I know where all the utensils and cooking things are kept, so it is not hard for me to find things. The kitchen is kept organized, as well as the entire home.

Sometimes, the vacuum cleaner would not work properly, and I had to do some tinkering to make it work. To do the tinkering, I had to rely on what I could feel rather than see to fix things, and did well in that category. At times, my vision was not good enough to see what I was doing, so I had to get down on hands and knees to feel.

Getting around is one thing I do the best! I have been able to get around independently ever since I can remember. As a youth, I walked down to the post office, food store, bank, and anywhere else I needed or wanted to go. I also rode my bike down and around town. My vision was good enough for me to do this safely, and I enjoyed the exercise.

Then I moved to Atlanta, where there is not much space to ride a bike the way I could in the small town. I learned my way around an area near a shopping center near where I lived in an apartment. That area also had a bus I learned to ride, and I still ride the bus a lot. I miss riding my bike the way I used to; I can only ride it when traffic is light on the street I live on. During the day, my street is crazy!

Where I live now (in a condo), there is a shopping center just down the street and a mall not too far from there. The mall has a lot of good stores.

My primary doctor is in a medical center not far from my condo complex, and I have a choice of walking there or riding the bus. If I need to go to another doctor or specialist, I can take the bus to a hospital not too far from my area.

Going out in public for me is a real confidence-booster and helps me learn where to go and remember how to get to certain places. It takes time and practice, but once I learn how to do it, it becomes easy, and no stress is involved.

I do not use any type of paratransit system [a low-cost transportation service for the disabled that provides rides, scheduled in advance, within a limited region] and do not think I will ever use it. I am on the transit authority advisory committee and have heard a lot of unpleasant stories from paratransit users. It is hard for them to use paratransit when it does not arrive on time or get them to a certain destination on time. These users spend a lot of time traveling on the paratransit (because of long routes that are designed to include other passengers, rather than go directly to an individual person's destination). A fifteen-minute direct trip by car can take an hour or more with paratransit.

I use both a cane and a dog, but only one at a time. I do not use the cane too much, now that I have a dog. My dog is a hearing dog but understands the guiding role, too. [Hearing dogs are trained to alert deaf people to certain sounds, such as a knock on the door or a telephone ring, but do not have guide training.] I use a cane when I go out without the dog but only in unfamiliar places. When I go out in familiar places without the dog, I just go as if nothing is wrong with my vision. It is not that I am uncomfortable with the cane; it is that I just know where I am and just want to feel "free." I am quite comfortable with the cane and dog.

Being guided by a sighted person is fine by me, provided this person is able to guide well and knows what to do when something happens. It is important for sighted guides to know sign language, as well, because I want to be able to communicate with them. Not being able to communicate with a sighted guide frustrates me and can lead to problems when something doesn't go the way I expect.

When strangers try to help by grabbing my arm and "steering" me, I simply reverse what they are trying to do and tell them what I want to do by grasping their upper arm or placing my hand on their shoulder for support. I tell them to walk in front of me or to the side so as not to be in my way. If they continue to grab my arm, I stop and just stand there and let them understand what they are doing wrong.

Melanie Bond

My husband does the shopping. Sometimes, I accompany him to the grocery store. Usually, he'll pull the cart along, while I hold onto the handlebar. When I go to DB (deaf-blind) camps and on DB cruises, I do my shopping with the help of an SSP (support service provider).

I don't have a problem taking a bus or paratransit, if a car is not available. I still have two good feet and don't mind walking to wherever I want to go.

I love eating out! I love walking the 17.5-mile riverwalk/rail trail in Bay City, Michigan. I love searching the online library catalog, which allows me to order library books and place a hold on them so that those books are set aside for me. My husband usually takes me to the library to pick up my books and drop them off when I'm finished with them. I always feel confident, as long as I'm with someone. I enjoy knowing that I can get out and do things like everybody else, for the most part.

I used to be real good about taking my white cane everywhere I went. But whenever I go out with my husband, I never take my cane because he loves to hold my hand and guide me. The cane is nothing to be ashamed of, although I do wish we could personalize our canes by choosing our favorite reflective colors. At first, I did feel a little embarrassed about using such a bright red and white cane, but I quickly learned that using my cane was like parting a sea of people, so that the way before me was cleared. I no longer care what other people think about my cane, because safety should be the most important consideration for any person who is blind or deaf-blind.

I do like being guided by a sighted guide. It's nice holding hands with my husband. It's nice being guided by an SSP who knows how to guide deaf-blind people properly to keep them safe.

When strangers grab my hand and start to pull me against my wishes, I shake their hands off and tell them that I prefer to place my hand on the back of their arm, just above the elbow, and tell them where I want to go. It's always so important to educate anyone that you come into contact with, so they can learn more about our deaf-blind culture and ways of doing things in the safest manner possible.

I can see myself moving to a deaf-blind community and possibly to an assisted-living center that would provide me with deaf-blind services and accessible communication, if I ever find myself without a mate. I would not want to depend on my siblings or my grown children to look after me.

Patricia Clark

In my teenage years, my disabilities were not severe enough to limit me in public. I was living at home with my parents so I did not deal with tradesmen or domestic shopping. Job interviews were horrifying and usually did not go well.

The years passed and I left home, and my sight and hearing became worse. The supermarket took care of domestic shopping, although I could not always find what I wanted or read the prices and could not ask questions, as I was unable to hear the answer. I simply found alternatives.

Appointments with the GP went quite well, but it's surprising how many specialist doctors do not understand the word "deaf" and just go on shouting when I ask them politely to write down what they want to say. In hospitals, I wear a badge that says, "My sight and hearing are impaired," as it seems easier for receptionists and others to read the badge rather than listen to what I say.

As well as being deaf-blind, I am now arthritic and can't walk far. Public transport is quite beyond me, but I can fetch a taxi with the telephone relay system. I ask the operator to let the driver know about my special needs. Drivers are almost always polite and helpful. I now rarely go anywhere alone, though.

I use a walker, and when I am out with service providers or even with friends, they may try to "steer" me. It annoys me, and you need to have a chat about it later. Sometimes, the helpers who are supposed to be helping will let a door slam in my face or fail to warn me of obstacles. Some are too zealous. Others don't think ahead at all.

I have spent most of my adult life living alone with increasing disabilities, and it has made me self-reliant. Since the age of twenty-five, I have been too deaf to use voice telephone, and to be alone without help available in an emergency has been frightening. I had a TTY, but very few people had them in the 1970s. The computer with email and the telephone relay system have made life much safer for me.

Now that I'm of retirement age, the difficulties are closing in. My sight loss will soon prevent me from using the Internet for shopping, banking, accessing news (normal print is beyond me), and much more. My Braille display on the computer will give me text files, but it is impossible for a totally deaf-blind person who uses Braille to get training for Window-Eyes. My blind instructor can't write, and I can't hear speech or audio. Without help, my life will soon be very, very limited. I'll have nothing but Braille books and a stuffed toy for company.

Tonilyn Todd Wisner

At different times in my adult life, I have lived in different apartments and a number of homes. At first, I was living in my family's home alone. I had already been diagnosed with Meniere's disease and become deaf but still had sight. I was limited in what I could do only by the fact that the Meniere's disease causes your body to use a lot more energy than normal. I did just basic dusting, really, and washed clothes and dishes. I cooked for myself without any special aids.

When the Meniere's disease became so severe that I couldn't live alone, I moved into my dad's apartment. He did all the cooking, and I helped with laundry and dishes. I also did the housework for the most part, just a little at a time.

Once I rehabilitated but was still limited, I moved away to a different state. My homemaking changed drastically then. I wanted my apartment to be clean, and most people I knew cleaned once a week. But I could only clean for about one hour at the most before I became too dizzy and nauseous. So I started cleaning one room a day. I had four rooms, so I was cleaning four days out of the week. I did my own laundry and dishes. I cooked for myself, but more often than not, it was TV dinners—I didn't like cooking for one person.

I was unable to drive and had my groceries and prescription medications delivered. That was the only help I had back then.

When I moved back to Louisiana years later, I got my own apartment, and everything was the same as in my previous apartment. A few years after that, I met my future husband and eventually became engaged and moved in with him. I had someone else to cook for, so I started cooking again. I did all the housework—dishes, laundry, and housecleaning. The housecleaning became more rigorous, because he had six cats, two large litter boxes, and six medium-to-very-large rooms. I was still just as limited by the Meniere's disease, so I was pretty much cleaning and doing laundry and scooping litter almost every day—five or six days a week! It was hard, but I enjoyed knowing that my house was—hopefully—clean.

A year later, I developed the constant vertigo and was mostly bedridden for two years because of this. I mostly still made my own lunch when I could manage to get out of bed and attempted some housecleaning, but that was all I did. My fiancé, Keith, had to do everything else. It was during this time that I became blind.

After two years, the doctors found the problem and operated to fix it—which worked for a while. I didn't have vertigo, except for occasional Meniere's attacks. After I recuperated, I picked up where I left off. I started cooking again without any special aids. I cooked on the stove, in the oven, and in the crock pot. I cut things by myself. I developed my own safety techniques.

Then we moved to a smaller home, as the large house was becoming a big burden to take care of. It's not much smaller but a little more manageable. I was completely blind by this time. The vertigo returned, coming and going, and began to limit me again. But I continued to do all household chores. I cleaned one room every day, if I felt up to it.

I did the laundry myself, almost a daily chore, and Saturday was bedsheet day. I had my washer and dryer labeled with Braille stickers, so I could do laundry on my own. I used powder detergent, because it is easier to measure by feel. I put Braille labels on my clothes. I pinned the labels that have the colors listed on the front of my clothing with a safety pin, took it off and put it on a shelf by the hamper when I wore the clothes, and then when I got ready for bed at night, I put the pin back on before putting the clothes in the hamper.

I had my oven, stove, microwave, dishwasher, clothes washer and clothes dryer marked in Braille. For some buttons I just learned what they mean, instead of marking them all.

Following my divorce, I moved into a new apartment and have been living alone there. I had to do the Braille labels all over again. My daily routine hasn't changed much, though, except that my dad helps me a lot with groceries.

I do *have* to have my morning coffee, so I use a one-cup coffee-maker. I fill the water container by using my liquid-level indicator and have learned what the buttons mean. I measure my coffee (I drink instant, so I only use the machine to make the hot water, but have used ground coffee in it, too) by leveling a spoon with the amount I need. I can feel when the water is heated by the way the machine feels, so I know when to press the button for water. I can then tell by feel when it is done pouring and know how to turn it off.

When I became completely blind, it changed my previous level of independence—temporarily, because I am *determined* to regain my independence! I am finding it hard to do many things on my own, but I have been able to make certain adaptations in my home that really help me keep some of my independence.

I don't go anywhere out of the house by myself yet. Mostly, it's because I am not very social yet, as I am nervous about being completely blind and not understanding speech very well with my cochlear implant. Any time I go to the doctor or need to go to the store, etc., my dad, who lives close by, takes me.

Wendy Williams

As an adult, I have mostly lived alone in apartments with my dog guides. There were a few occasions when my living quarters were boardinghouses and college dormitories that I shared with other students.

While I had residual vision, I needed little in the way of home accommodations, other than adequate lighting. But it became quite the challenge when I began to lose the rest of both my vision and hearing because traditional methods no longer worked for me. I already had had homemaking training while wearing shades at a blind rehab agency about a decade earlier, and these skills were of later benefit in that I had little fear of the stove without sight. Still, I sustained minor burns, but they were learning experiences. For example, when I removed hot dishes from the oven using oven mitts, I burned my arm against the top of the oven, so I switched to elbow-length mitts.

There were a few occasions when I almost tripped over my dog guide while carrying hot food. So she was banished to the kitchen doorway to observe from that vantage point.

Determining when water was at the boiling stage was through feeling the faint vibrations of the bubbles through the pot handles, along with the steam.

Previously, I had placed Braille Dymo tape on my measuring cups and spoons, and these were now a necessity. I then put Braille labels on spices and other food items. I carefully measured (non-oil) liquid ingredients over the sink to prevent excess moisture in my recipes. It is easier to measure some liquid ingredients, like oil, when it is cold. Also, immediately replacing the caps on bottles prevented me from later potential spills, lest I happen to bump into them and knock them over.

I found I had a poor sense of thoroughly mixing the batter with utensils, so I used my clean hands to complete this step. Parchment paper allowed more uniform cooking and minimized food sticking to the pans.

I learned to use the senses of smell, touch, and hearing (with cochlear implants) to tell me when food was cooked. For example, ground beef changed from big, soft clumps to small, firm ones. I used a talking thermometer to ensure other meat (e.g., chicken) was cooked. One problem with this device is I cannot distinguish between the spoken numbers "150-something" and "160-something" with my implant.

I was willing to tackle sensitive recipes, such as stollen (Christmas bread), from scratch, using yeast, beaming with pride over my finished and tasty product. On the weekends, I prepared hot dishes, so I had nutritious lunches at work to give me the energy to get through my days of employment.

As for housecleaning, I discovered initially going over the floors with a sweeper prior to vacuuming picked up any fallen treasures I did not want to disappear into the vacuum. It also helped ensure that unknown soiled messes (e.g., dog poop) did not make their way into the vacuum.

My sense of feel was a big part in determining if sinks or floors were clean, using the grid pattern. I preferred safe cleaning agents in place of potentially harmful ones that could splash into my eyes or burn my hands. I try to keep up with cleaning, as it is easier and quicker to take care of messes, such as the indoor grill, shortly after it cools down.

As for management of my personal business and duties, I relied on an SSP to help me with reading and responding to mail and doing errands (e.g., grocery shopping). For washing bedding and other large items, the SSP assisted me in going to the laundromat and operating the larger, commercial machines to avoid the many steps up and down the stairs of the apartment building with its standard machines and competing tenants.

Earlier, I had residual vision and wore hearing aids, and upon the diagnosis of Usher's syndrome, I received O&M training to learn to use a white cane. Up to that point, it had been so habitual for me to walk around without the cane, bumping into people and objects, that I continued this means of traveling alone, until I stumbled off a curb in a shaded area and sprained my ankle. After that, I preferred to use the cane, though it annoyed me when its tip lodged in cracks, causing its handle to hit me in the stomach. When I was feeling fatigued or under the weather, the cane hitting things resulted in overstimulation and heightened anxiety.

When I began to have fearful close calls with vehicles coming from the left and right, I applied for a dog guide. Either with or without a cane or dog guide, I thought nothing of traveling anywhere, be it the doctor's clinic, the grocery store, or work. Five days a week, my dog guide and I walked a mile to work and home again, in all four seasons. Occasionally, in adverse weather conditions or distances longer than a mile within the community, we took the small city bus. If I needed to venture out of town to attend continuing education workshops, I paid drivers from a local church.

Within all facilities, I relied on my residual senses to locate things independently. Strangers usually provided me with verbal directions if need be. I would beam with pride if they asked me questions about my dog guide.

As I began to lose the rest of both my residual vision and hearing, traveling became a bigger challenge. It was increasingly difficult to localize traffic at busy, lighted intersections. Turning more to my tactual and olfactory senses resulted in me getting lost, even on familiar routes. I could no longer find my way in buildings or hear people giving me directions in them, causing me to feel insecure, frustrated, and discouraged.

Bilateral CIs obtained in 2000 and 2005 then enabled me to better hear vehicles on quieter streets. Audible and vibrating signals were installed to assist me with busy traffic flows, though distracted and impatient drivers are becoming a concern.

An SSP drove me to businesses, guided me within them, and located desired items and services for me. She also assisted me with participating in some community activities, such as martial arts and the Thanksgiving banquet for deaf-blind people. A hired driver helped me with medical appointments.

I hope, in the future, that accessible cell phones and GPS will be more affordable and manageable to permit me to travel more independently within my community and revive my confidence.

10
Adult Relationships

Given that we humans are social creatures by nature, one of the most important aspects of our lives is building relationships with other people. Deaf-blindness interferes with normal social interactions in a number of ways, such as inhibiting communication and making common social activities difficult or impossible.

Adult relationships include romantic relationships, friendships, and relationships with family members. Each contributor focuses on the relationships that are most relevant to him or her. Here, you will find insights into the social lives of people who are deaf-blind, a taste of the thoughts and feelings they experience, and some interesting approaches to dealing with the social difficulties that arise from being deaf-blind.

Angela C. Orlando

I never really got the chance to develop normal social relationships. I consider "normal" to be like what my brothers had: They went out with friends, they had girlfriends, they went to parties or just to hang out on weekends. I never had any of that.

I was just beginning to "blossom" at age thirteen when I began losing my hearing. I had my first boyfriends and went to junior high dances. I had a group of friends and felt like I belonged somewhere. However, after I started losing my hearing, I lost most of those friends. The boys were no longer interested in me. I was no longer a part of anything social.

There was no difference between me as a teen or an adult. My social isolation never changed. It's so hard to become part of anything when you can't drive or talk on the phone or understand a group of people as they socialize.

I was hurt that my life was so different from my brothers'. I cried often on Friday and Saturday nights when I was all alone. Why couldn't

I have what they had? Why couldn't I have boyfriends and hang out with a group of girls or go to parties? It didn't seem fair. The few occasions I tried to go out with friends were always so awkward and hard. I couldn't understand people. I had trouble walking around because I had no peripheral vision. I couldn't keep up with others. I couldn't see in the dark. I had trouble getting up and down stairs at night.

I was never very close to my roommates in college, either. At first, they asked me to go out with them, but it was difficult. I was embarrassed by the help I needed. I started to make excuses about why I couldn't go out again. Eventually, they stopped asking me. I immersed myself in my isolation. I tried to tell myself that I didn't need anyone else. I was fine alone. It was never true, though.

I was always so depressed and lonely; I was missing out on so much. I didn't know how I could ever develop any relationships while being hard of hearing and visually impaired. No one wanted to try, or else I gave into my fear and hid myself away.

I finally found a place to belong when I discovered the world of online chat groups. Through email and online "conference," I could communicate with people very easily. It didn't matter that I couldn't hear or see well. No one even knew about my disabilities. I was able to form relationships based on who I was or what I liked and how I communicated with people. They knew me as "Angie" and not as "that deaf-blind girl."

My first "real" friend was a guy from California named Steven. We talked in conference every Friday night. He knew more about me than my friends in high school ever did. I considered Steven to be my best friend. We were just friends, though; I never liked him as a boyfriend. Still, it hurt me when he announced he was seeing another girl online. Why couldn't it be me? Why couldn't he love me? Why couldn't anyone love me?

I had a very nice group of women who became close friends online. We exchanged emails and talked in conference. We sent each other cards. We did Christmas ornament exchanges. We talked about our most intimate secrets. Fifteen years later, I am still so close to these women. We have even met in real life.

Eventually, I told Steven and my female friends about my disabilities. They didn't seem to care at all. They already knew me so well. The fact that I had sensory impairments didn't change who I was in their eyes.

When I was twenty-one, I met Greg Howard on a *Star Trek* bulletin board. I wasn't a die-hard "Trekkie," but I enjoyed talking about the show. I told him right away about my disabilities. He responded by telling me he was overweight and battling depression. We began to talk in conference almost every night.

I had never seen this man before. I didn't even have a picture of him at the time. All I knew was what he told me about himself. Yet, things were going so well. He said he loved me. No man had ever loved me in a romantic way before.

Finally, Greg and I decided to meet in real life. It was so awkward at first. Online, my hearing and visual impairments were meaningless. In real life, I couldn't ignore them. He sometimes had to repeat himself or help me walk in the dark. He seemed okay about it. After the first visit, I knew it was true. I was in love, and he loved me back. I never imagined that could happen. We continued our online relationship and visited together once a month or so.

It was an on-and-off relationship. He broke my heart a couple of times. I always took him back. I wanted to be loved so much. I could put up with a little attitude and trouble in order to keep him in my life. The problem seemed to be his mother. When he was at school, we got along so well. When he went home, he'd become cool and distant. His mother didn't approve of me because of my disabilities. She managed to create a wedge between us several times. Once Greg left his mother's home, he would want me back again.

After I graduated from college, I moved to Maryland to live with Greg. We shared an apartment together. He was my first serious boyfriend. I knew nothing of relationships, except what Greg and I shared. I had nothing to compare with.

Greg and I became engaged and then got married. We bought a house together and had a child. It was everything any normal person would ever have. It was a dream come true to me. I felt like a normal person.

My son, Daniel, was six months old when I became ill. Suddenly, I was totally deaf and blind and couldn't walk. Greg had to care for me as if I was a baby. He fed me, dressed me, and put me on a potty chair. It was like he had two kids instead of a child and a wife. Everything changed at this time. What had been a slight temper and a few random acts of violence became daily acts of abuse. Greg was so angry. He was angry at the work and took it out on me.

He slapped and pushed me. He kicked me and threw things at me. He hit me. He forced himself on me sexually. He said the cruelest things to me and made me cry. I was living in a nightmare.

Greg told me that my worsened disabilities didn't matter. He wasn't angry because of that. He didn't mind helping me. He claimed he loved me so much and couldn't live without me. Yet he treated me so badly. I was terrified of him and what would happen next. I didn't dare leave him—I was afraid of losing Daniel. My child was my life; he was the only thing that helped me survive the hard times.

When Daniel was five years old, he said to me, "Daddy is bad because he hurts you." I finally realized I had to leave the marriage in order to save my son. He wasn't being physically abused, but he saw his father hurt his mother each and every day. That had to qualify as emotional abuse. I could not let that continue.

My parents helped me escape with Daniel, while Greg was at work. We moved in with my parents in Ohio. I went to court and won custody of Daniel. I also divorced Greg. He is no longer a part of my life, other than the fact that he is Daniel's father. Our relationship is over.

Living in Ohio is much better. My mother and I are very close. I can't communicate with my dad or brother, so that makes our relationship somewhat strained. I wish they would learn sign language, but I don't think they ever will.

Most of my family lives in Ohio. I'm not close to my aunts, uncles, or cousins. They don't know sign language, either, and I can no longer understand speech. They will pat me on the shoulder to say "hello." They talk about me to my mother but not to me. I don't let it bother me anymore. If a relative really wants to be part of my life, they will figure out a way to communicate with me. They will at least try. I know my relatives love me, but there's no way to have any type of meaningful relationship without a method of communication.

After moving back to Ohio, I still didn't really have any friends. I don't know how to be part of a social group without vision and hearing. I can't see what is going on. I need someone to tell me every little thing. I can't keep up and never feel like I'm part of the group. I'm just an outsider who happens to occupy the same area.

Lack of access to telephone, cell phone, pager, instant messenger, and text messages also make it hard to form relationships. People use technology as part of socialization. I miss out because I don't have that ability. There's no such thing as "I'll call you later" when I can't even make calls.

Last year, I began taking ASL classes at Kent State University. I'm trying to improve my communication skills so I can better understand interpreters. I'm also making connections in the real world. This includes both hearing and deaf people. I'm actually making friends with fellow students. It's so amazing!

Sheila and I go to Taco Bell once a week. Andrea takes me shopping and out to dinner. One time, she took me to a bar. I was thirty-five, and it was the first time I'd ever been out to drink with friends. Farah wants to take me to ASL events. So many people in the deaf community stop to talk to me when we go out to these socials. I'm going places and doing things. I'm having fun. It's what I always wanted.

Knowing the language helps with forming relationships. My new friends either finger spell or use ASL. They can communicate to me in a way that I actually understand. We joke and have fun together.

Thanks to new technology called the DeafBlind Communicator (DBC), I now have access to TTY, text messages, Google IM, and a great face-to-face communicator for people who don't know sign. You could say the playing field has been evened. I'm now part of the modern world. I love to send text messages to my friends. I talk to them using text messages or TTY. I'm having live chats with both my local and online friends. What a huge difference this technology is making on my life!

Last year, I was involved in a short relationship with a man who is also deaf-blind. I met him online, and we eventually had two real-life visits. He was a very nice man, and I was amazed that he loved me. I think that's part of what went wrong: I loved being loved, but I didn't exactly love him. There were warning signs, and I ignored them because I so badly wanted to be in a relationship again. He said he wouldn't rush me, but in reality, he did. He pushed me too hard and fast. I think our relationship was too forced. We were both lonely and wanted something so we tried to make it happen too quickly.

Even as I started to see that things weren't working out, I didn't end the relationship. I thought that I should stay with him because I'd never find anyone else. Being with someone I didn't love would be better than being alone. Eventually, though, I realized that it wasn't right. I wasn't happy. I had to end the relationship.

Christy L. Reid

As a child, I was an outgoing, social kid, in spite of my visual setbacks. I was involved in after-school activities, such as Brownies and dance classes, and I joined neighborhood kids playing games. In my early life, making friends was not a problem. But as I grew older and deafness set in, my social life dwindled to a few friends who were willing to learn finger spelling and some sign language.

As a deaf-blind adult, I relied on one-to-one communication, even in an environment where almost everyone signed. I could not participate in group discussions without someone telling me what the other people were saying. I would join my college sorority group, and we would go out to a restaurant, but someone would always have to volunteer to interpret for me and tell me what the other girls were talking about. This took a great deal of patience on my part and for the person helping me, as it was difficult to interpret for me and participate in group discussions at the same time. Being in a group has become one of my least favorite social outings. Even family dinners, where my extended family gathered, were a little stressful. Even though most of my family members know sign language and can efficiently communicate with me one-on-one, I had to rely on whoever was sitting next to me to sign for me, to help me to know what the group was discussing.

Ben, my deaf-blind son, faces the same problem. Someone always has to interpret for him using tactile sign language to help him be involved in a group discussion. Often, I would sit next to Bill (my husband), while Ben sat on my other side, and Bill would sign into one of my hands; then I would sign into Ben's hand using my other hand. We could be called a "human communication chain."

As an adult, communication was my main obstacle in developing friendships. But if the other person could finger spell, I could usually get along well. I still have good speech, and my CI has really improved my speaking confidence. Most people can understand my speech, but I am unable to understand other people's speech, and those who know some sign are those who I feel most comfortable with.

Bill is a very good signer, and we usually don't have communication difficulties. His training and experience working with deaf-blind people at the HKNC has helped him feel comfortable talking and socializing with me. He knew deaf-blind people could be independent individuals, and he always gave me room to do things on my own. And he has the same attitude toward Ben, encouraging our son to grow and learn and try to do things independently, as long as the child is safe. A good example is when Bill drives our van to pick up a pizza we ordered for dinner. Ben accompanies him, and when they arrive at the pizza shop, Bill gives Ben enough cash. Then Ben, who has his white cane with him, enters the shop. Once inside, Ben walks up to the counter and says something like, "I'm Ben Reid. Can I have my pizzas, please?" Usually, things go smoothly, and Ben hands over the money and is given the change and the pizzas and then goes back to the van. Meanwhile, Bill is watching closely, making sure there aren't any problems.

All three of my children use tactile sign to communicate with me. Joe, the oldest, was two-and-a-half years old when I taught him the concept of tactile sign. We were sitting in the kitchen at the table. I had a bag of cookies, and Joe kept trying to grab the bag from me. I wouldn't let him have a cookie, but took his hand and signed "cookie" into his palm. I held my hand out to him, and after a moment, he put his hand in mine and signed "cookie." I rewarded him with a cookie, and we did this again and again. He probably got five or six cookies, but the concept was set in his mind.

When Joe was younger, I was still using a CCTV (for reading). I taught him to sign "machine," and he associated my CCTV machine as a way I could read books to him. Reading books to Joe was a great way to help my first son to learn signs and for us to share time together.

Later on, I let Ben ride his tricycle on the sidewalk, while I followed close behind with Milo (my guide dog) guiding me. Ben loved to explore the surrounding neighborhood and would always stop in front of a fire hydrant, pointing at it. I would kneel down to be level with his height and sign into his hand, "help fire truck." He would nod and then pedal on.

By that time, I was reading Braille, and Ben was receiving early intervention services from the Pittsburgh public school system. We had quite a number of print-Braille picture books that were given to Ben by one of his teachers. But my Braille reading speed was still slow, and Ben seemed to prefer the stories I made up for him and Joe. Both boys always wanted me to tell them a story before bedtime. Their favorite was a story based on a Scooby Doo character and always involved Joe and Ben Reid. In the stories, Joe and Ben would get lost and encounter some kind of monster. Scooby Doo would always rescue them and use sign language to communicate with them. The monsters didn't know sign, so Scooby Doo and the two boys had an advantage. Ben and Joe loved these stories.

Then Tim was born. Ben was no longer the baby. Suddenly, he had a new, tiny brother. Ben had been very excited and sweet, while Tim was growing in me, kissing and patting my belly. But when Tim actually entered our family, Ben's attitude changed, and we experienced a bit of chaos.

Bill was in school during that time. I hired a woman to come to our apartment every morning to help me out. I had my hands full with the new baby, and Ben didn't go to preschool until the late mornings. The lady who came to help didn't know sign language, but she was very enthusiastic to learn and wanted to help. She learned the finger alphabet, and we could communicate pretty well. She helped start laundry, helped Ben to make his bed, get dressed, and eat breakfast. Meanwhile, I was able to sit and relax while nursing Tim, knowing Ben was being taken care of. But it wasn't a pretty, peaceful picture. Ben grew jealous of Tim and started being difficult for our hired helper. He would throw things and try to run and hide from her. At one point, he locked himself in Bill's and my bedroom where Tim was asleep in his crib. The hired helper could see Ben lying on the bed with Tim on his stomach, rolling the baby from side to side through a crack in the door. She kept calling Ben's name, and, finally, he stopped and opened the door. Later, Bill removed all locks on the doors; we were really shaken up.

The problems with Ben didn't improve, and the hired helper quit. Fortunately, it was near the end of the school year for Joe and Ben. Bill and I had come to realize that living in Pittsburgh wasn't working out for our family. We needed more help, which we couldn't find there. We decided we would be better off moving back to my hometown of Poplar Bluff, Missouri. My parents were able and willing to help us, as well as my sister and her family and my brother.

Moving to Poplar Bluff was a good decision. The children settled down and started to thrive; the small-town life was less stressful for Bill.

I felt more secure, knowing the children were happy and safe. There were trade-offs, too. Poplar Bluff is a small, rural town, and support services, such as SSP and interpreting services, were nonexistent. Bill found that the family needed his help at home. Instead of finding a job outside of the home, he found himself doing most of the grocery shopping and driving the kids to school and other activities. A job for me was nonexistent, too. We had Bill's school loan to pay off, and the money issue became something we had to learn to live with.

Joe entered fourth grade, and Ben started kindergarten at public school. Joe was happy with his new school and new friends, and Ben was happy with his, at first. All was rolling along pretty well. Tim celebrated his first birthday that October. He was a sweet little boy who liked to stay close to my side. That was a good thing for me, as my vision had worsened.

My Braille reading pace improved, and I requested print-Braille books from the library service for the blind. I read to both Ben and Tim, as we all sat together out on the front porch on warm summer evenings.

As Ben grows older, his relationship with Tim has greatly improved. Tim and Ben are like best friends now, playing and communicating together. Tim uses tactile sign with Ben, as well as with me. Joe can be very helpful when asked, and he also uses tactile sign with Ben and me.

While I was in college, I didn't experience the usual girl/boy relationships. Although I attended a college set up for deaf people, and most guys signed, the deaf guys shied away from getting involved with a deaf-blind girl. I satisfied my social needs by joining a sorority and had a number of girlfriends. But even when my sorority mixed with a fraternity at parties, I never got to talk with the fraternity guys.

Then I met a deaf-blind guy, and we became friends. We started going out together to eat at restaurants or to see movies or go dancing. We enjoyed hanging out together, and the relationship lasted for a few years. But he wasn't ready for a serious commitment, and we were more like friends, two people who enjoyed doing things together.

Then I met Bill the summer before my senior year at Gallaudet. Bill was different from other guys I had known. He was lots of fun, and he made me feel like a real woman, instead of a deaf-blind person. I went to HKNC that summer to do an internship, and Bill was working full-time in the residence program. We met at a bar, where there was a small celebration for another intern who had just completed her internship. I was chatting with Bill and found him intriguing. I decided to get myself another beer and walked over to the bar, made my order, handed over the money and thanked the bartender. I walked back to the table with my new beer, and somehow, I had a strange feeling that Bill's eyes had followed me all the way. Later, he commented he wasn't used to seeing deaf-blind people get their own beer, and I thought that was strange. I was used to doing things for myself.

After that, Bill asked me out to eat at a Mexican restaurant he knew in Manhattan. Boy, was I thrilled! Here was the date of my dreams with an exciting guy. I took special care getting dressed for that first date, choosing an aqua green cotton sundress. Bill picked me up in his truck and drove into the city. It didn't bother me when he got lost and couldn't find the restaurant. He drove 'round and 'round the streets, trying to find his way, while I kept staring up at the skyscrapers. Finally, he found the place, and we had our dinner in an outdoor courtyard.

After that first date, we embarked on a fun and wild romance that summer. Then I went back to finish college, and Bill eventually left his job at HKNC, moving back to Cleveland, his hometown. In spite of the distance between us, we kept meeting from time to time over the next few years. I would take the train out to Ohio to visit with him, or he would drive to Washington, D.C., to see me. Whenever and wherever we met, the spark in our relationship was always there. We were good friends, could discuss all sorts of things, as well as two people very much in love.

Bill has a big family—three brothers and three sisters. Only one sister learned the finger alphabet and can communicate with me without Bill's interpreting help. Yet, I always feel welcome whenever we go to visit with his family. At first, when I could read large printed notes, his family members could write notes for me. In the beginning, they were a little uncertain how to interact with me, but as the years have gone by, Bill's family sees me as a capable person.

There are times when I meet someone who will say something like, "You need help. You have your hands full!" The person says this sort of thing to Bill, who is interpreting for me at a meeting and then helping me down some steep steps without a rail. The other day at a swimming party, the lifeguard told Bill that if Ben didn't hear the whistle, he would need to jump in the water fully dressed and get Ben's attention. When we meet people like these examples, we realize they are ignorant of how to interact with a deaf-blind person.

Judy Kahl

Living with deaf-blindness puts one in a mold of one's own. When the disabilities are not bad, I feel one can fit in the hearing-sighted world; however, as things deteriorate, it becomes a withdrawal world, which means one tends to just find excuses not to leave their comfort zone, like their home.

When I was profoundly deaf, I did not make phone calls and would only pick and choose my activities and always avoided parties and big groups. Now, with my CIs, I *love* the phone, but I still have some difficulties with noisy environments. My point is, *yes*, there is a big difference in life when you can hear or can't hear.

It is the same with vision. You are much more active when you can venture out and do like the sighted world; however, when you need to depend on others for your transportation, etc., it limits you. No one likes to feel like a burden, so again, you tend to withdraw.

This is lonely, so my coping skills kicked in, and I decided to help raise funds for research for Foundation Fighting Blindness (FFB) to help find cures for retinal degenerative diseases that rob us of our sight. It is easy to feel depressed, dealing with deaf-blindness, and I'm so thankful that I've found a niche and welcome any and all to join me with my FFB mission. Together, we can make a difference, and together, a cure is in sight.

My relationship has not been affected, as my husband is very supportive, and I have wonderful friends. I still have some central vision, but when I lose that . . . who knows what will happen?

There are struggles every day, but we must pick up and find a way to go on with a smile on our face. No one wants to be around us if we are sad. All we can do is "do our best."

Mark Gasaway

I find it neither harder nor easier to make friends as an adult, as opposed to doing the same while a child. Why I say this is because I still have the child in me, and my outlook on life is still based on how I feel about what I can do, including making new friends. I still use the same approach now as when I was a child in making friends.

There is really a way to making friends easily, but keeping those friends is a bit hard to do. I have been able to make friends easily with a smile and friendly manners that let the other person know I am interested in being friends with them. That is what I did as a child and still do now! However, we all know people come into our lives for reasons. They may be there for support as a friend or make it all the way to falling in love.

I found love after high school and while at Gallaudet University. I did become attracted to several girls in high school but did not have any luck with them because I felt my hearing loss played a part in the feelings of the girl. I did not have any dates in high school, probably because I was not able to drive. Met my ex-wife at Gallaudet, and we fell in love after I graduated because she did not stay at Gallaudet.

I have had problems feeling equal in a social setting with family and friends because of the lack of conversing in sign language. I really need people to use sign language and try to bring me into the conversation. I cannot understand signing that is not directly in my line of vision. It is extremely important to be able to communicate with a deaf-blind person in a way they can understand. Sometimes, in a social setting with family and friends, they are talking by voice or signing when I cannot understand or see their signs clearly. This causes me to feel like I am not important to them. The setting is truly not equal.

I have never avoided a relationship with any woman I was attracted to, whether or not she was disabled. I do not think it would matter if the other person was disabled, because to me, the thing that matters is what comes from the heart. My ex-wife is disabled and uses wheelchairs. However, it did not matter that she had disabilities. What mattered was the love we had for each other.

I believe my disabilities have interfered with good relationships because I know some women are turned off by the fact I am deaf-blind. Even deaf-blind girls have mentioned to me they prefer to find someone who is not deaf-blind.

I think my disabilities have not played a role in how things have gone with family, friends, or lovers because my disabilities have been steady (unchanging) all my life. I have grown to understand how people react toward me but know the role my disabilities have played in my relationships has very little to do with how the family, friends, or lovers really felt from the start.

Melanie Bond

It was easy making friends when I was enrolled in the deaf oral program as a young child. But when I was mainstreamed, I found myself stranded without any friends. Once they learned of my hearing and speech impairments (and unknown to me at that time, I also had visual impairments), I had trouble. It didn't take long for the other kids to figure it out, because I had difficulty understanding their speech.

When I became an adult, I found myself reluctant to cultivate new friends for several reasons. First, my deaf boyfriend, who later became my first husband, pretty much cut me off from having any contact with my family. Over time, he became more abusive with me. The irony here is that he always went out drinking and partying with his male friends, but then I wasn't allowed to have any close friends at all, though there were some deaf friends who visited me occasionally.

For the most part, the more I got to know people, the less I liked most of them. I disliked people who were superficial and those who gloated as if they were superior to me. As a matter of fact, I did suffer from an inferiority complex for many years—through my childhood years, teen years, and adult life, until I finally learned to stand up for myself at the age of thirty-one. That was when I found the courage to divorce my husband after counseling with my minister. By this time, I was free to be "me," and I loved who I was becoming. It didn't matter whether I had friends or not. But for whatever reason, there were some people who felt drawn toward me, and I accepted their genuine friendships, along with their desire to be helpful to me. For two years, I lived on my own and raised my two young daughters named Meilani ("Lani") and Jamie.

I don't know what it is about me that draws other people (both men and women) to me. Maybe it is because they sense my vulnerability or their desire to be helpful to me. My first husband was attracted to me, and after our divorce, a few guys from church asked me out on dates. It was hard for me to know what their motivations were, and whether they had considered my disabilities and/or had wondered about taking on additional responsibilities, such as a ready-made family, I don't know.

But then Harvey Bond came into my life when we met at Niagara Falls in 1987. For whatever reason, he was inexplicably drawn toward me. He told me that when he first saw me, he fell head-over-heels in love with me. He had been on a four-day fast and spiritual quest, looking for a mate. He felt that his quest led him to me. (He is part of the Mi'kma'q native tribe.) He actually became fascinated with the fact that I was going deaf-blind. He felt as if I was carrying a heavy burden by being on my own, and he wanted to help lighten my burden. He had been separated from his wife and two daughters, so when he met my two girls, he felt that he had been blessed. He told me that, even with my disabilities, I was still a real person.

A year later, we were married in Lansing, Michigan.

For the most part, I don't put up with anyone who patronizes me. I think my family has learned their lesson! It's the same with friends, coworkers, etc. I do not like being treated as if I were a child. The way I see it, we all have our abilities and disabilities, whether they are visible or hidden. It's all the more imperative that we treat each other as equals and respect each other's privacy.

I have to admit that, when I first hooked up with the guy who became my first husband, I didn't think I could find someone else because of my disabilities. He was a lot of fun, at first, but then he became more possessive of me. I didn't like what was happening, but I was afraid that I wouldn't be able to find someone "better" if I left him. But when I read the book *How to Break Your Addiction to a Person,* I found the courage that I needed to take a leap of faith and make a clean break from my abusive mate. I needed desperately to move on with my life. By putting my past behind me, I was able to open myself up to the possibility of finding a mate who would truly love and care for me.

I never had anything against serious relationships with other people with disabilities—I married a deaf person, didn't I? That wasn't a problem, because I was also deaf.

After my divorce, I married a hearing-sighted Canadian, and in a way, that became more of a challenge to me because I would learn later that he had spatial disabilities that have prevented him from learning to sign in ASL fluently. It was a major disappointment to me, but he was equally determined to find alternative modes of communication that would work for both of us. For a while, we communicated via Morse code by tapping on each other's body. And when I am really desperate for him to finger spell to me, he finger spells perhaps the first letter, maybe the second letter, and hopes that I'll guess at the correct word, so that he doesn't have to spell out the complete word. That is often frustrating. I do use our FM system when we do some serious talking, and we do email each other.

There is no way to measure whether a handicapped person is more "able" than another person who may not appear disabled. Circumstances change all the time. Forget about disabilities—we all have them! What really matters is love, chemistry, and compatibility to create a lasting relationship, in spite of freaks of nature, illness, and accidents.

Patricia Clark

The conformist society I grew up in was not sympathetic to disability. There was a feeling that difficulties were somehow your own fault for not trying hard enough. I was told that I must stay out of sight and not be a nuisance. This applied to deafness rather than to low vision. I had little confidence.

I did make girlfriends and was comfortable with boys. By the time I reached early adult years, the deafness was worse, and although I had some social life, I realized that marriage, like employment, was not going to be easy to find. I have never married.

When I was eighteen, a steady boyfriend told me that I was a nice girl and we'd have a whirl, but he was not going to marry me. Later, other men made it clear that marriage to me was not on their agenda. They did want sex, of course.

A steady boyfriend I had when I was twenty-one seemed to be just the right person in the eyes of everyone else. We had interests in common and knew each other's friends. He got on well with my family—too well. He shared their patronizing attitude to disability and saw himself as a hero for dating me. So it was the strange reason that he fitted in too well that ruled him out. He did not understand me.

A few years later, another boyfriend, who was about eight years older than me, seemed very keen. After the relationship warmed up (yes, sex), he confided he had a secret: He'd been married previously. I had already guessed this. Then he said his ex-wife was blind, and I went into orbit. Why would any man marry a blind woman and then run after a deaf-blind woman? Obviously, he had something wrong with him. I thought hard about this and decided he wanted to dominate but also to lean on me emotionally. Again, there was the feeling that he was heroic to marry a disabled woman. I turned him down.

After that there were a few more men in my life but no marriage proposals. I mostly parted with men on good terms and even saw them socially after it was over.

Throughout my adult life, my disabilities have become seriously worse. As this happened, it became harder, almost impossible, to make friends. Some of the old friends have stayed with me but not many. I rely heavily on email for any human contact, as I live alone in a retirement village. The deeply ingrained wish not to be a nuisance makes me non-assertive with new people.

I never really found love, partly because the attitudes of the men I met were to look down on me from a great height. This was so, even when they lacked qualities I had, such as determination, focus, emotional stability and the capacity to solve problems, rather than to run from them. The other reason was that I can't respect feckless men who are unable to take responsibility and who just drift through life.

The able universally believe themselves to be morally superior to the disabled. So in any social situation, we are marginal, and don't quite belong.

Tonilyn Todd Wisner

As a child and before my brain surgery, I had many friends. I was "only" hard of hearing and compensated well by lip-reading. I made friends very easily.

After my brain surgery, my so-called friends had a hard time with the fact that one side of my face was paralyzed, and most of them started openly making fun of me in school and encouraged other kids to do the same. I still made some friends, but it was much harder, and I had lost most that I had before.

This was the way it was till I graduated from high school and started working and/or going to college. People at that age were much more mature and didn't care about the way my face was or that I walked like I was drunk (due to poor balance). After I was diagnosed with Meniere's disease and couldn't go out and do a lot—and especially when I had a large hearing loss—I did lose some friends, and it became harder to make friends. But while I was still able to function enough to work and attend college, I had many friends and did more social activities. But when I became completely disabled and was very limited in what I could do and where I could go, and had to cancel plans because of vertigo attacks and also had to use the relay service to talk on the phone, I lost all friends. At that point, I turned to my computer and found that I could make many online friends.

As a deaf-blind adult now, I cannot make friends. People don't want to try to communicate with me. I tell them how they can write in my hand (print on palm), but it's like they are afraid to touch me—like, "Oh, I might catch deaf-blindness!" I love talking to people and making new friends, so this is very hard and hurtful for me. I haven't stopped trying, but the results are the same. I don't live that close to any deaf-blind people and can't drive (obviously!), so I don't have the opportunity to make deaf-blind friends. I do still have many, many online hearing-sighted and deaf-blind friends, however.

Because I was considered a "freak" in school, I was very shy. I never dated because no one ever asked me out, except for one person who was just annoying. I dated a little after high school but was still shy and afraid of a serious relationship.

But things got better, health-wise. I wasn't as physically disabled by the Meniere's disease—I had gotten it under control. I had a hearing aid and could understand most speech and use lip-reading to understand almost 100 percent of speech. I still didn't date much, but I did gain the confidence to date. But I still mostly met people online, but I also started playing Disc Golf again and met people there.

In 2004, I met my now ex-husband, Keith, online. We dated for a little while and fell in love fast. We became engaged at the end of February of 2004. I moved in with him several months later. After being together for just a little over a year, I unexpectedly became bedridden with constant vertigo. Just a few months after that, I became legally blind without a natural cause. After two years, the cause of the vertigo was found to be a right superior canal dehiscence, a hole in one of the inner ear's balance canals, and was fixed, but I wound up completely deaf. My eyesight mysteriously continued to degenerate during that time. All of this was totally unexpected and did put a strain on our relationship.

We were married in 2008. I continued undergoing problems with my CI and vertigo, due to repeated head trauma. I also developed unexplained punctures in both of my eye lenses. The marriage was rocky, and my husband retreated into his own world, which I could not be a part of, and left me to deal with all of this on my own. But I wasn't ready to give up and did my best to make things work. But the relationship had been an abusive one, and I finally found the courage to leave and file for divorce in 2011.

Wendy Williams

As a child, I usually had friends. During this time, I was not as self-conscious of my hearing loss. By the time I was ten years old and in fourth grade, I began to withdraw for different reasons. I became so increasingly clumsy that I wanted to be glued to my seat. I was uncomfortable mentioning my hearing impairment to people. My mother's frustration toward me took its toll on me emotionally so that I had low self-worth and low self-esteem.

In my adolescence, I had a friend or two early on, and then I was a loner. I yearned to be a part of the teen social network, but I did not feel I was good enough.

In my early twenties, I worked in a group home, and I developed wonderful friendships where I felt I was an equal to my peers. I even was a maid of honor at a close friend's wedding. After I returned to postsecondary education, I continued contact with a former colleague for nearly thirty years.

In graduate school, I was in a small program, and we were close to the professors and the students.

In my last employment, I had another circle of great friends, and we have maintained connection in retirement.

Ever since I was a child, I wanted to marry and have a family. My early experience made it difficult for me to get into a trusting relationship with someone. Also, my dual disabilities consumed so much energy and time for basic living, school, and work that I could not consider a serious relationship.

11
Communication

Communication is a critically important issue. While the group of deaf-blind individuals discusses their communication methods throughout this book, some readers may want to focus specifically on understanding how people who are deaf-blind communicate and what problems they face in this area.

This chapter looks at communication on many different levels and in numerous forms. It also shows how some people's communication modes changed as their disabilities worsened or were corrected to some degree.

Angela C. Orlando

Over the years, I have used a wide variety of communication methods. The need to vary was caused by the changes in my condition. These changes reflect both loss and improvement, depending on the time period in question.

When I first began losing hearing, I wasn't able to understand speech. Friends wrote notes to me, because I couldn't understand what they were saying. My parents had to repeat themselves a lot.

Later, I received a CI and was better able to hear speech. I combined what I heard with my CI and the visual cues of lip-reading. That served me very well for twelve years.

Then my illness hit, and I couldn't hear speech or read lips anymore. Sign language was not an option. I had no feeling in my hands. I suddenly found myself totally deaf and blind with no method for receptive communication at all. It was very scary.

My mother came up with the idea of printing letters on my face (with a fingertip). That was the only part of my body that had any feeling. I could feel the letters and could put them together to form words. We used print-on-face for over a year. It was slow and tedious. I'd say I hated it, but I remember having nothing at all. As bad as print-on-face was, it sure beat no communication. I tried to remember that, so I wouldn't get too frustrated.

Both my own family and my in-laws were willing to use print-on-face to communicate with me. Some people out in the world did, too, like my physical therapists. It was hard because everyone seemed to have a different method of printing letters, just like they do with real writing. It wasn't always easy to understand new people.

About a year and a half after my illness, I began regaining feeling in my hands. I already knew the sign language manual alphabet. At deaf-blind camp in 2003 (in Maryland), I learned how to feel people's hands as they signed the letters to me. This is called "tactile communication." I instantly realized it would be much easier to use tactile finger spelling for receptive communication. It's still a slow method, but it's faster than print-on-face. I never did like people touching my face at all.

After camp, my husband, mother, mother-in-law, and a few other relatives learned the manual alphabet. Other people, like my dad, brother, and father-in-law, could not or would not learn to finger spell. They switched to printing letters on my palm. I liked tactile finger spelling better, but print-on-palm worked, too.

I've been using tactile finger spelling and basic sign language for several years now. My son has learned to finger spell, too. He's very good at it. For expressive communication, I am oral and am told my speech is very clear.

There are problems with finger spelling. It's slow. It doesn't work well for classes, meetings, and group events. I always tell interpreters to use finger spelling, but they end up switching to actual sign language to keep up. They also go too fast. Using interpreters won't do any good if I can't understand them.

I also feel that my methods of communication keep me isolated from other people who are deaf and deaf-blind. I have no experience with expressive sign language. I find it so hard to communicate my thoughts using sign language. As a result, when I go to DB camp or a social, I mostly only talk to the hearing interpreters and SSPs.

I'm trying to do better. I'm now taking ASL classes at my local university. I want to be able to better understand interpreters so I can take other classes or attend meetings or whatever I need. I want to be able to socialize with other people who are deaf. Improved communication may help me fit in with both hearing and deaf people. At least that's what I'm hoping for.

I'm in my third ASL class now. It's been a great experience. I'm learning so much and doing better with communication. I still have a long way to go before I'll really feel comfortable with the language, though.

At DB camp, I can now talk with other people who are deaf-blind. I like that. It's not easy, but I'm doing it. It should get easier with more time and practice.

My family still doesn't use sign language or ASL. I have interpreters at school but not with my family or during community events. I miss so much. I don't feel like I am a part of most crowds and gatherings. My mother will finger spell to me a little about what is going on, but I still miss about 95 percent. I sit alone reading much of the time, since I don't have a good way to understand people around me. It's not a good situation, but I'm used to it. I don't let it get me down.

Once I improve my ability to understand ASL, I hope to use interpreters more. Maybe then I'll have a clue about what's going on in the world and can participate in events. Interpreters also give descriptions about the environment and setting. There's more to communication than just the spoken word.

Technology has attempted to address the issue of deaf-blind communication. There is a machine called the Screen Braille Communicator. The sighted person types on a keyboard, and the message is shown in Braille for the deaf-blind person to read. It's a very simple, primitive machine that is prone to much trouble. I've found it impossible to use. I gave up on it and gave mine to a friend.

Now I have the new DeafBlind Communicator (DBC). This is a great machine. The sighted person types on a cell phone keypad, and I read the message on my Braille Note M Power. It works so much better. I've been very successful with the DBC for face-to-face communication.

The DBC has also finally given me access to TTY (telephone) and text messages. I have been without phone access for eight years, and I never got to try text messages before. I love texting people!

The DBC is doing a good job of bridging the communication gap. It's not perfect. The other person has to want to communicate with me or want to make the effort to find out how to use the machine. People seem to mostly be receptive to the idea. Strangers have been willing to give it a try. It's amazing to be able to talk with people who don't know sign language. I can't hear them; I'm reading their message in Braille. But we are still communicating. That's the real issue. *How* we manage to do it isn't as important.

Mark Gasaway

It is imperative for people to approach us who are deaf-blind and make an effort to communicate with us, so we in turn can express who we truly are.

Without communication, the deaf-blind world seems to be a world of its own, where the person who is deaf-blind will find other means to entertain himself or herself. When this happens, people more established in the hearing world will think something is wrong with us deaf-blind folks. The thing that is "wrong" is that the people with normal hearing and vision just do not understand our world and our needs for communication.

My primary communication mode when talking to people face-to-face is sign language with those who know it and speech with those who do not know sign language. Sometimes, I do speech and sign simultaneously. I use both ASL and PSE [Partial Signed English, a mix of ASL and English], using the language I believe is best understood for the person I am talking with. I guess I am more of a PSE-user than ASL-user in expressive mode, because the people I mostly talk to are not too fluent with ASL. I am very good receiving in ASL receptively, but it may take time for me to grasp what is being said because of my vision.

I also can use tactile and tracking modes of signing and use them, depending on circumstances, such as lighting, clothes colors, skin contrast, and other situations when tactile or tracking help me understand better.

I have never been able to read lips, unless maybe one-word commands! Lip-reading is very difficult for someone with nystagmus, which causes my eyeball to move involuntarily because of nerve damage.

I can read written communication as long as people use dark ink or felt marker and write in large letters.

My family will use whatever mode they have to use because of my vision when I talk to them. Most of the time, they will not use sign language but write. They may try to use gestures, and half the time I am able to understand. The other half, when I can't understand, they will write. Family communication is not easy.

Friends, on the other hand, when they are comfortable with me tracking their wrist, will allow me to do so and have no problem with it. ["Tracking" is a technique employed by people with low vision, especially tunnel vision, to "keep track" of a signer's hand by lightly holding the person's wrist.]

With other people, tactile and tracking may be necessary because I may be in a situation where I have not seen their hands before. New signing hands are sometimes difficult to follow, especially when the clothing/background color does not contrast with the hand.

Other forms of communication I use are writing with a bold black marker, erasable whiteboard, print-on-palm, and gestures. All alternative modes work well, depending on the situation. I talk with my vet through writing, and she uses a bold marker without me having to remind her. When I need to use these alternative modes, I will use them.

I also use electronic modes of communicating, including instant messenger, videophone, email, large print display TTY that I can use to call the relay service or another TTY, and a Blackberry pager from Sprint that has large black letters.

I rely on the Internet a lot for communications with almost everyone else who uses Internet communications. Using the Internet is wonderful and fast, but there can be some hang-ups to using it, because technology is not perfect!

Melanie Bond

Well, I started out in my early childhood years learning the deaf oral approach. With my powerful Phonak hearing aids and my Comtek FM system, I've been told that my speech is fairly easy to understand. I have been reading lips my whole life! I often choose not to wear my hearing aids, because I find environmental sounds to be quite distracting when I'm busy working on my various writing projects and reading for fun.

It wasn't until I reached high school that I began to learn ASL. My first husband was deaf, so, of course, we communicated with each other in ASL.

When my second husband, a hearing-sighted man, came into my life, he had the heart to try and learn ASL for my sake, but because of his spatial disabilities, he was unable to sign ASL fluently, although he is able to do some finger spelling. For the most part, we communicate in several ways: through speech, lip-reading, tactile Morse code tapping, emailing, and writing notes. Surprisingly, when I'm not wearing my hearing aids or when I'm lying in bed, I can understand some of what he says directly into my ear. But he has to be careful, because if he speaks too loudly, it hurts my ears. Strange, huh? Maybe it's not so strange. When I am not wearing my hearing aids, my voice tends to revert to an unnaturally loud, deaf-sounding voice. It is only when I wear my hearing aids that I am able to moderate and control the sound of my voice.

My sister might finger spell to me when I don't understand her speech. But everyone who knows me understands that they must get my attention first before speaking to me.

A big part of my life is the Internet. I happen to be the moderator of several DB listserv groups, including DB-Adventures for sharing travel stories and adventures; DB-Authors for those who hope to flesh their stories out and hopefully get published; DB-GoldinLife for sharing humorous stories, jokes, and famous quotes; DB-GoldinPoetry for writing poems; DB-Philosophy; DB-Relationships; DB-Spice-of-Life (as a comoderator); and DB-Women (as a comoderator). Those of us who are fortunate to have access to the Internet are very serious when it comes to good communication. The beauty of DB listserv groups is that it brings deaf-blind people together into a living, breathing, virtual DB community so that there's always someone to talk with, share news with, and so on.

Patricia Clark

I learned to lip-read very young through my own efforts. My mother had elocution lessons as a child, and when she was angry, she spoke loudly and mouthed words in exasperation. So . . . I lip-read!

The years went by; hearing aids came and went and became more advanced as my hearing became worse. My sight also diminished, and now my main form of communication is a thick-tipped pen and paper. I never became fluent in sign language but can finger spell quickly. A few people use finger spelling with me in public for speed, and I am happy with that.

I now have no hearing at all, and when my sight goes completely, I'll be dependent on Braille. Email will be my best form of communication and an Internet newsfeed my only contact with the wider world. My isolation will be horrific. There is no shelter accommodation for people who are deaf-blind in New Zealand, and I will probably be shunted into a rest home where staff are low paid and not skilled. I hope to retain a few friends who can finger spell or who have keyboard skills and can type on the computer while I read a Braille display.

Over the years of losing sight and hearing, I have become accustomed to being alone. But the lack of services for deaf-blind people, who are such a small group, makes my future look very bad, indeed.

Scott Stoffel

When I was a kid, I didn't even know I had a mild hearing loss. All the focus was on my bad vision. I could hear speech fairly well and spoke well. I didn't realize until years later that I mispronounced some words and had trouble with new names. I also had trouble in noisy environments, but I just assumed everyone was the same way.

After my hearing nose-dived when I was eighteen, understanding speech became a living nightmare. My auditory neuropathy caused my hearing to be worse in certain frequency ranges and better in others. The result was that—for a while—I could understand certain people's voices better than others. I needed quiet and one speaker at a time, but I could manage some communication this way for a few more years. It was very frustrating, though. People would get offended if I couldn't understand them but could hear some other person present. I was accused of having "selective hearing" more than once. That always infuriated me—I had no control over what I could hear.

I tried several hearing aids during this time. None were of any real benefit, because the neuropathic hearing loss was "uneven," meaning certain frequencies needed amplification while others became too loud with the same amplification. Also, auditory neuropathy causes sounds to be distorted before the information reaches the brain. Unfortunately, this latter issue is not correctable by current technology.

Nonetheless, I tried some hearing aids. One thing I always did when attempting to hear was try to anticipate what someone was going to say and then associate the sound I heard with what I thought the words would be. If I got a match, it created the illusion that my hearing had improved. And my family was obsessed with saying things to me that were easily anticipated, such as "Can you hear me?" When I said I could, they'd immediately say, "See? You heard that!" And the aids were deemed a total success. Never mind that I did much worse when trying to hear something I couldn't anticipate. A lot of arguments ensued, and the whole business with the aids was monumentally frustrating.

As the neuropathy destroyed my residual hearing, I started using a whiteboard. I carried a whiteboard with a black marker around for a couple of years. Asking people to write down messages in big letters wasn't fun, but it was all I could do to communicate. Some people were okay with the board, while others would wave their hands in the air and walk away.

I learned tactile finger spelling and sign language at the HKNC. With constant practice, I got to where I could understand tactile pretty good and could follow an interpreter at a fair pace. But because of the neuropathy in my hands, I was limited in my ability to sign to other people. I couldn't make signs that required the thumb to move forward or across the hand, such as in making the letters "C" and "O." But I loved tactile. It was great to be able to have comfortable face-to-face conversations again.

My parents learned to finger spell after that. We could communicate some that way. But no one else in the family wanted to bother with it. Other relatives continued to shout in my face years after my hearing was totally shot. I tried to stay cool and explain that I could no longer hear; I needed sign or the board. Some people would say they really wanted to find a way to talk to me—I'd just told them how! They didn't want that answer. They seemed to want me to tell them there was a magic angle they could stand at while uselessly shouting at me that would cause my neuropathy to take a vacation in the Bahamas. Then I'd be deemed a grouch for not cooperating with this admirable effort to interact with me. I reached a point where I disliked get-togethers and avoided them when possible.

The tactile sign enabled me to attend college and earn my degree in engineering. And it enabled me to land a job and function reasonably well at meetings via interpreters—not great, but reasonably well. But the neuropathy in my hands degenerated further, making it harder and harder for me to understand tactile signs. This development was gradual, not sudden. By 2006, it got to where I just could not read signs fast enough to keep up with meetings. The stress ate me up.

In 2007, I took a long shot on a CI, despite being warned by two audiologists that I was unlikely to get significant speech discrimination out of it, due to my auditory neuropathy. I was desperate. I spent a year doing speech recognition exercises with my CI, but my discrimination remained at zero.

When the CI didn't solve my communication issues at work, I stopped using tactile interpreters and tried using CART. An interpreter brought a laptop computer and typed what people said at meetings, while I tried to read in large print. But my vision was inadequate to keep up with real-time speakers. All I saw was a blur of text scrolling down the screen. When someone asked me a question, I needed the typist to just stop and let me read the question. I could save the meeting transcripts and read them at my own speed later, but this mode did not solve my problem with real-time communication.

At the present time, I can read tactile at a very, very slow rate and still use it to communicate sometimes. But I cannot follow it at the same speed a person speaks, and my hand goes dead quickly, so I have gone back to using whiteboards a lot.

Email and instant messages have become my primary modes of communication with most people. With enlarged print, I can access these modes of Internet communication. I also use text messages on my cell phone.

Tonilyn Todd Wisner

My main mode of communication right now is speech. I have a CI and can understand some speech with it. I speak to respond to people because I have a clear voice.

Sometimes, I just can't understand what is being said, though, or I am not wearing or can't wear my CI at the time, so I use tactile finger spelling and sign with a few people who can communicate that way. For others, such as my family and people I don't know well, I use print-on-palm. My family members prefer print-on-palm and haven't learned finger spelling or signs. I find that many people don't want to try to communicate with me directly, so they talk to another person, and that person tells me what they say.

I have one friend who is deaf. When I had vision, we used sign language. Now that I have no vision, we use tactile sign and finger spelling on her part and "regular" sign on my part.

I am not very good at receptive—reading—tactile finger spelling, so it's not easy to use that method. I am trying to practice, so I can get better and faster. I can use print-on-palm very easily. Although I have more trouble with tactile finger spelling, I prefer it to print-on-palm because it is still faster.

I use email a lot to talk with friends and family. A few doctors and nurses have even given me an email address so I can communicate directly with them. I use a Notetaker (a handheld Braille computer), so I can't do instant messaging or texting. Well, to be honest, I do have MSN on here, but I get so confused trying to use it without being able to see it that I never really learned to use it! I also use Facebook and have started using text messages with a cell phone that works with a Braille display.

Something that I do often now that I am completely blind is something only I know about, but I am still embarrassed that I do it. I'll walk into a room where a person *was* and start having a conversation with him or her, only to find out after waiting for a response that I am talking to an empty room. Or the person in the room forgets that I can't see him or her leave and just gets up and leaves, setting me up for that conversation with the air. Ugh!

Wendy Williams

My receptive and expressive communication primarily has been oral, as this was the mode used by my relatives and most friends. For the first eighteen years, I depended on lip-reading to gain access to the environment. As a very young child, I was slow to learn to talk, and only my older (toddler) brother could interpret my vocalizations.

In time, I was able to correct my speech myself, though I always made occasional mispronunciations of words. At age seventeen, I received one month of speech therapy at a camp for hearing and physically challenged children and youth to correct my "s," "sh," and "ch."

I acquired the British two-handed manual alphabet from the campers there and taught it to a few close friends in my hometown.

In early adulthood, I was fitted with my first set of hearing aids. I was prone to verbal outbursts while adjusting to the many loud noises. After several months, I adapted to the sounds and speech. It then dawned on me that the previous reliance on only speech-reading caused me to miss out on incidental learning and seeing the perspectives of others.

While I was in graduate studies at Gallaudet, I was required to master sign language. It was very difficult for me to follow the signs with my limited visual fields, so one-to-one tutoring for tactile sign language was scheduled for me. I well remember my mental and physical fatigue as I tried to convert words into signs and to decipher them on my hands. Most of my deaf friends were verbal, so I only used expressive signing with them. I found myself avoiding receptive tactile sign because it was so taxing.

After a battle with cancer in 1997, I began to lose the rest of both my residual vision and hearing. With that came my increasing inability to lip-read and to hear with hearing aids. There were moments when tactile sign or print-on-palm was my only means of receiving information.

My first (right) CI was implanted in 2000, giving me limited speech discrimination. Along with that CI and with only light perception visually and declining hearing in my other ear, I could no longer localize traffic to make safe decisions to cross busy, dangerous intersections. Thus, I was implanted with a second CI in 2005 with the resultant speech discrimination being close to normal. Now that I am blind, I mostly rely on my bilateral CIs for interactions with others. On a rare occasion, I may need tactile finger spelling or sign or phonetic spelling (e.g., *d* for dog) if I cannot grasp a word.

Using my CI, I hear familiar people on the phone with volume control, provided they speak clearly. I run into problems listening on the phone when the caller speaks fast or has an accent. I have had to wait till an SSP is present to assist with such calls, but in the future, I may need to resort to the relay service for quicker access.

I use the computer speech screen-reader JAWS to do email, surf the Net, and to do Word documents. Daily connection with relatives, friends, and the deaf-blind community on several listservs helps to minimize the isolation within my home.

Reading books was not a pleasurable activity for me visually because I tended to come to the end of a line and lose my place on the page repeatedly. Using a ruler still distracted me from the flow of the material. I now listen to talking books on the National Library Service for the Blind's player, but I have had to forgo "reading" some books because the cassette tapes were not clear to me. Recently, NLS has distributed new digital players, and the improved clarity may make it possible for me to catch up on books I could not understand earlier.

I first learned Braille reading through Hadley in my thirties because I was uncertain of my future with my vision and wanted to be prepared, particularly if I needed it to continue working and for basic reading and writing at home. I was strict with myself by feeling with my fingers as I felt it was a waste of my time to cheat with my eyes. Then I forgot about Braille until I was in a blind rehab program in my forties. I quickly relearned to read Braille and started reading interesting novels.

I continued to use Braille at home, limiting it to reading fiction and writing labels for my personal items (e.g., color labels for clothing). For a time, I still read regular print, followed by squinting through a magnifier, and then I switched to large print. Later, I could no longer read print and had no choice but to use Braille, especially at work to perform my duties. I remember having to read technical books, which were harder than pleasure books, and so quickly, too, that out of sheer exhaustion, I would collapse my head and arms on the desk. In time, it was easier to read technical books, and I was not so tired.

Now that I am retired, I still read Braille novels and nonfiction books at home. I write with the slate and stylus, such as making notes, writing recipes, labeling print pages or other items, and so forth. With learning Braille later in life, I am not as fast and accurate as a native Braille reader, but I love curling up with a good Braille book in an armchair.

12
Cochlear Implants

The advent of the cochlear implant (CI) has had a major impact on the deaf-blind world. While the technology is far from perfect and is less effective with certain types of hearing loss, such as auditory neuropathy, the CI has helped many deaf-blind people improve their ability to communicate and glean information from their surroundings. On the other hand, some people are opposed to the CI for personal or social reasons.

In this chapter, CI users discuss their experiences with the technology, and nonusers explain why they prefer not to try an implant.

Angela C. Orlando

I was sixteen years old when I underwent CI surgery. By this time, I was profoundly deaf. I could hear only the loudest of noises. Hearing aids did not help me. They only seemed to make the distortion of sound worse. I hated my hearing aids and refused to wear them.

I was attending hearing therapy at the Kent State Speech and Hearing Clinic. My therapists were graduate students. Most were studying to be speech pathologists. They didn't have many students who were studying to become audiologists, so I had to work with the speech students. For the most part, they did focus on hearing therapy, like my parents wanted.

The person in charge was an audiologist who had a PhD. Dr. Davis was a strong believer in the "oral movement." He believed deaf children needed to wear hearing aids and learn to speak. He did not want his clients to learn sign language at all. That would make them "lazy" in their attempts at speaking. Dr. Davis told my parents that I wasn't trying hard enough to hear. If I would just try, the hearing aids would work, and I would be able to understand speech. He called it "being a teenager." He insisted I didn't want to look different from other kids, and that's why I wouldn't wear my hearing aids.

The therapists used to stand behind me and say sentences and words. I was supposed to repeat what I heard. I heard nothing, but they didn't believe me. My first therapists were so frustrated that they ended my therapy for that semester. They said I wasn't trying and refused to work with me further.

I was at the region's top ear clinic for my yearly audiology examination when someone finally listened to me. The audiologist there realized that I really could not hear. I wasn't just being a teenager. I couldn't hear, and the hearing aids were not helping. This was when they first mentioned the idea of me getting a CI.

It was 1990. Few people had even heard of CIs back then. It was brand-new technology. The FDA had not yet approved the CI for patients under eighteen years old. At sixteen, I was not a little kid, but I was still underage. I would become one of the first children to receive a CI. My case was also considered special because I had already acquired speech and language skills as a child who grew up with normal hearing. I also had some residual hearing, if only a little bit. Previous to my case, they had only implanted people who were 100-percent deaf and had not yet learned to use speech to communicate.

My case was considered experimental, and it was a huge deal in terms of research. Dr. Davis was completely against me receiving a CI. He still felt I could learn to hear with hearing aids. He was also certain that I would refuse to wear my CI processor for the same reason I wouldn't wear hearing aids—I wouldn't want to look different from other kids. So it would be a waste of time for me to undergo the CI surgery.

The regional ear clinic offered to let Dr. Davis and the Kent State Speech and Hearing Clinic become closely involved in the research and testing for my case. This was an exciting opportunity for Dr. Davis. They had never had a patient with a CI at the hearing and speech clinic before. Although he made his doubts known, Dr. Davis accepted the offer.

I didn't really decide to get an implant; it was my parents who made the decision. They wanted me to be able to hear again. They thought this was a last chance to restore my hearing. I was scared, but went along with it. I wanted to be able to hear again. I wanted a way to escape from this silent and frustrating world that I was suddenly thrust into as a teenager.

I spent the next six months undergoing all sorts of tests—medical tests, brain scans, an MRI, X-rays, blood tests, hearing tests, all sorts of ear scans, speech evaluation—so many, many tests. Since it was experimental surgery and would be used for research purposes, they needed data on absolutely everything.

My parents also had to tackle the tough question of how they would pay for this surgery. I was covered under my father's insurance, but because CIs were still experimental for children, insurance would not pay. My parents believed that if it was meant to be, a way would be found. They were right: One week before my surgery, my grandmother died. Most of my dad's share of her estate went to cover my medical bills.

On June 12th, 1990, I underwent CI surgery. I received the Nucleus 22 CI system. I had to stay overnight in the hospital after my surgery. My recovery was long and hard. I had trouble with extreme dizziness and poor balance. For a little while, I even had to walk with a support cane for stability.

At first, everything sounded so robotic. I compared the sound to a squeaky cartoon voice. Everything sounded so weird. I had my doubts about this thing that was attached to my ear.

Within a few weeks, I was wearing the processor full-time. Sounds soon sounded like real sounds. I was quickly identifying everything I could hear. I was doing well with speech, too. By combining what I heard with my CI and the visual clues of lip-reading, I could understand speech again. I couldn't understand speech without lip-reading. And I couldn't follow lip-reading without sound from my CI. The two together were the key that worked for me.

I continued to attend therapy at the Kent State Speech and Hearing Clinic, until I graduated from college. Dr. Davis was forced to eat his words and admit he was wrong about me. He became one of my biggest supporters. He was so proud of my success with the CI and the change it made in my life.

For the next twelve years, I was very happy with my CI. I didn't feel the need to learn sign language. I was doing well with speech. I considered myself hard of hearing. I did better in quiet environments and often needed a person to repeat what they said. But overall, I was doing okay with hearing, thanks to my CI.

When my illness struck in late 2001, I temporarily lost the ability to hear with my CI. The auditory nerve was damaged, just like all the other nerves in my body. Thankfully, it began to heal, and I slowly regained what hearing I had with the CI. Unfortunately, I was left permanently blind. Unable to lip-read, I could no longer understand speech. That was a rough blow.

I can hear environmental sounds with my CI. It helps me know what's going on in the world around me. I can hear the dog bark, the sound of the TV, my son's video games, the hum of the dishwasher, and many other sounds. I can hear voices, but I can't understand what people are saying.

For eighteen years, I used the Spectra body-wear speech processor with my CI. I had a little box in my pocket and a wire all the way up to my ear. I hated that wire with a passion. Still, it was worth putting up with in order to hear sounds.

Last year, I was finally able to get Medicare coverage to upgrade the speech processor to a Freedom behind-the-ear (BTE) model. I am so pleased to be free of that stupid wire! The sound with the Freedom is a little more distinct, but I still cannot understand people when they talk.

I'm not at all disappointed in my CI. It's nearly twenty years old. For technology that old, this CI has been a grand success. It bothers me when people suggest my CI is a failure because I don't understand speech. Twenty years ago, they didn't expect you to be able to understand speech with just a CI. I love my CI. I still wear it every single day. I feel more blind without it. I know that doesn't make sense. But it's exactly how I feel. I see less without my CI. Or maybe I sense and experience less without it, so it makes me feel blind.

Now I am hoping to get a second implant. If I'm approved as a candidate, I will get the Nucleus 5 system. It's possible I may be able to understand spoken words with the new CI. There are never any guarantees, but I can always hope. I'm very excited about this possibility. [Angela received her second CI recently. She states that having two implants helps with localizing sounds, but she remains without appreciable speech discrimination.]

Christian S. Shinaberger

Since I lost all my vision at an early age and depended so much on hearing aids, it was fortunate that my hearing didn't deteriorate rapidly for quite a few years. I limped through college by using every improvement in hearing aids that was available, along with a Phonic Ear FM system.

But after struggling through the doctoral program at UCLA with less and less hearing, the tinnitus that had plagued me in both ears for years finally became so severe in my left ear that I could no longer hear through it. Then one evening with a prolonged hiss, the left ear became totally deaf.

I'd been a patient at the House Ear Clinic for many years, so I was able to get an emergency appointment for the very next day. Dr. William Luxford, my doctor, did not seem to be terribly surprised about what had happened. After all, we both knew the diagnosis was a steadily deteriorating sensorineural loss. The first question I asked was, "How long will the right ear last?" Of course, I knew that he had no way to determine that, but I was grateful when he recommended that I consider a cochlear implant. Dr. Luxford and my audiologist, Dawna Mills, agreed that the implant was the best solution.

One of the first things I did after making the decision was attend several implant user group meetings. The people who came were all very nice and willing to talk about their choices and their medical experiences. I was relieved to learn that CI surgery is usually done on an outpatient basis.

I also used the Internet to find documents on the two implants that were available at the time, the Nucleus 22 and the Clarion. I chose the Clarion, because it was more programmable, and I figured at least one of those programs would work for me.

I had one hurdle to clear before I could get the first implant: Since my right ear still had about 40-percent speech recognition, I didn't meet the FDA requirements for receiving a CI. At that time, you had to be down to 12-percent speech recognition in order to qualify. Dr. Luxford and Dawna decided to petition the FDA, since I was a special case. First, I didn't know touch sign language, so I was totally dependent on hearing. The right ear could go at any time, just as the left ear had gone with almost no warning. They hoped that I'd learn to work with the implant faster, if I still had some hearing. Finally, as an adult and graduate student, I was aware of the situation and fully understood the risks involved with surgery.

The FDA agreed to the petition. I signed the informed consent, and in August of 1996, I received my first Clarion implant. Five days later, the implant was tested, and I heard various tones. It was exciting to hear the tones, but I had the agonizing wait before the first programming (mapping) session.

I had my first mapping session in September of 1996. The mapping was disconcerting at times. The implant had restored a range of hearing I'd not enjoyed in years. It took quite some time to get used to all the high-frequency sounds. One of the first sounds I figured out in the first mapping session was the telephone time. I couldn't actually hear the time, but I figured out what the message was about. Then on the way home, I heard the turn signal in the car very clearly and almost immediately figured out what it was.

The first few days were spent trying to learn lists of single words. I later learned that is not the best idea. Many short words are hard to understand out of context but can be more easily understood if used in simple sentences. A friend figured out that she could amuse me by reading shady stories to me from the *National Enquirer.* It really helped, and she had me laughing in no time.

I also used a couple of talking books (audio recordings) to help the implanted ear learn to recognize speech.

I discovered just how noisy my clothing was. One day, for instance, I kept hearing a swishing sound and a clicking sound. It kept coming and going, and I was really stumped, until I noticed that it only occurred when I was walking. When you are blind and haven't heard sounds like these in years, it take a while to recognize your pants cuffs rubbing together and your belt pouch clicking.

The implant's ability to pick up sounds at a much greater distance than a conventional hearing aid can cause a real sensory overload at first. I spent a lot of time in our backyard, listening to birds. I really got to enjoy my wind chimes for the first time. On summer nights, the cricket symphony is absolutely fabulous! I have learned to recognize our neighbor's bubbling fountain, which gives me an audio landmark for getting home.

A major, major plus is going out to dinner and to actually be able to participate in a conversation, understanding what is being said. And it's fun being able to eavesdrop on conversations going on at nearby tables.

Music is much more enjoyable for me now. Relearning music with the implant was a little frustrating, but now it's a joy—everything from Mozart to Garrison Keillor and his Prairie Home Companion people. I love and adore the Hollywood Bowl!

A very important benefit for me is that now I can use computers with Windows operating systems because the implant makes using synthetic speech comfortable for the first time. I spend many, many hours at my computer.

About two years after getting the original implant, strange things started to happen with it. It would suddenly cut out. I thought it was just the batteries running out, but sometimes replacing the batteries with a charged one wouldn't get the implant working. At other times, just pulling the magnet away from my head and letting it snap back would get it working again. Then one day, it suddenly just quit altogether.

I met with Dawna at Advanced Bionics (the maker of Clarion) to try to solve the problem. It turned out that I had a defective internal unit that had microscopic cracks. My unit had two cracks in it, and my body fluids had seeped into it and shorted it out.

I was devastated, as the hearing aid ear had further deteriorated. I had become totally dependent on the high quality sound from the CI. Dawna also told me that sometimes re-implants didn't work as well as the first one. I was seriously depressed. My speech pattern changed noticeably. Dawna realized what an impact this experience was having on me and managed to get me into surgery with Dr. Luxford in just four days. I was terrified, to say the least. Not only do I not like being put to sleep, but the very thought of the replacement implant not working scared me to death.

Fortunately, the second implant seems to be working out as well as the first Clarion. I got an upgrade to a newer model of Clarion. An improvement is the rechargeable battery used by the new Clarion external processor.

I am totally hooked on everything that goes with the CI. It has opened up another world for me and has given me a chance to continue to learn and to grow and to participate in the world around me in a warm and personal way. I cannot recommend it highly enough to anyone who can possibly benefit from it. It might be a little trouble to become accustomed to, but the rewards are more than worth it.

Ilana Hermes

One morning, I unexpectedly woke up deaf in my right ear and went to have it checked. That ear became totally deaf, but the left ear still had some hearing. It was thought I had brain-stem cancer. After tests, it was determined that my white blood cells had started to destroy the good cells in my body. I received a tablet form of chemotherapy. My hair fell out a bit, and reality and shock came upon me. My remaining hearing was monitored, but a week later, I was in total silence.

Then it had to be determined if I could benefit from cochlear implants, which took a while. During that time, communication was difficult. I learned to lip-read with my hands (i.e., by touching the speaker's face).

I attended a church and also the church's young adult group. There, I was seen as Ilana and not the deaf-blind Ilana. I met my American friend at that time and place. My one friend introduced us and said I was deaf but forgot to say blind. My American friend started signing to me; then my other friend realized I couldn't see the signs. My American friend put my hands over hers and started to sign again. I had some background in sign language, but ASL (—what she used—differed from SASL (South African Sign Language). So I started to receive ASL lessons from my American friend, so she could sign to me in church.

My ears were deemed acceptable to have CI surgery, but Medical Aid wouldn't pay for it. It took ten months of fundraising before my family could cover the cost. In the time of total silence, I still heard when God spoke to me. But I often didn't (and still don't) understand what He wanted from me.

The surgery was successful. After activation of my first CI, I struggled to hear. When I put my speech processor on after I'd been lying down, it took two hours before I could hear clearly. My audiologist knew about my headaches (due to hydrocephalus), and said the fluctuation in my hearing was caused by my shunt (a device for draining excess fluid from the brain) not functioning well.

I went to the neurosurgeon that did my last shunt placement. My mother also mentioned my loss of sensation all over my body. He said if symptoms got worse then I should come back—that being in a wheelchair. My mother was not happy; I was shocked.

My audiologist made an appointment for me with a different neurosurgeon, and that neurosurgeon said I needed a spinal MRI to rule out a spinal tumor. An MRI is tricky for people with a CI, because the internal magnet needs to be surgically removed if greater Tesla than 1.5T is used—they used 3T. So I had my magnet temporarily removed and got the MRI. No tumor was found!

We then got in touch with a professor of neurosurgery that was my neurosurgeon when I was young. He looked at my brain CT scans and confirmed why I experienced loss of sensation and function: My brain didn't develop fully and was missing brain tissue. Nothing could fix this situation, but with God helping me to be strong, how could I be afraid?

My new neurosurgeon took one look at my CT scan and said that with my headaches and the fact they are less painful when I lie down, my shunt was draining too fast whenever I changed position or any atmospheric pressure change occurred. But he said he didn't want to touch my brain to change the shunt—too dangerous. He suggested an anti-siphon device might help.

Every morning remained a hearing challenge. My audiologist created a "morning" program for my CI, which is a louder (higher current) program for when I experience the fluctuations. I use this program mostly in the mornings and sometimes during the day or when I change posture. This helps somewhat.

I received a second CI in May of 2006, exactly six years after I received my first CI. My second CI also fluctuated, so I used the "morning" program for it, too. The second CI worked out well, and I discovered that having two implants improved my hearing significantly.

I found that when one processor has dead batteries, sounds are cut in half, with respect to volume. With two, it is a comfortable loudness, and with that comes being able to hear sounds that are further away. I use two different model processors, so that can also have an effect when using each one alone or hearing faraway sound. The one processor helps the other processor—together provides the best hearing. When both are on, I have more volume than when I only had my first CI and can understand speech better.

Mark Gasaway

Since I do not have a CI nor want one, I am taking this opportunity to answer the question: Why did you decide not to try a CI?

Before I begin to answer the question, I want to make it known that what any person, whether he or she has a CI or not at this time or is thinking about trying one, reads in my answer, please understand that it is *my* personal feeling. It is not based on how someone else may think or feel about the CI.

I choose not to have a CI because I do not appreciate the idea of an electronic device being inserted into my brain to "mess" with my nerves that were severely affected by encephalitis. I also do not want to get the implant, only to find out the CI does not work and then have more surgery to remove it if it does not work or go around like some freak with part of the device in my brain.

I realize technology is wonderful and improvements in the status of the CI happen perhaps every two or three months or so. But I will say this: I am deaf-blind for a reason, and I do not think it proper to try to reverse the reason for not being able to hear or see clearly. I know there are ways to help blind people regain some or all of their sight, but would I try such a method to regain lost vision? The answer is no. I am not going to think about trying to reverse the effects of encephalitis and trying to "fix" my hearing and vision losses via electronic devices or technology. That is *not* me.

I once had an appointment with an audiologist who told me, after all the testing, that she believed I would be a great candidate for a CI. She said this because all the hearing tests I had just had were showing her that my (auditory) nerves might accept the CI. My answer: "I appreciate you telling me your thoughts and trying to encourage me to try a CI, but I am not interested in the CI." That is how I feel and will continue to feel this way, because I am not interested in regaining hearing or sight through bionic means.

Like I have mentioned, I am deaf-blind for a reason, and my hearing and vision losses have grown with me. It is too much to go through surgery, be implanted, wait for activation of the CI, and go through retraining of the brain and nerves to "hear" or "see" again—not to mention that the CI may not function properly.

Melanie Bond

I am not comfortable with CIs because they involve drastic medical procedures. This includes destroying the cochlea, rendering a person permanently deaf without their CI in place. [The cochlea is not actually destroyed but is "disconnected." While it is true that a person cannot hear with the implanted ear without attaching the external processor, the cochlea can be reconnected to the nerves during surgical removal of an implant and usually restore some of the person's hearing as it was prior to being implanted.]

But it's not for me to judge anyone, if they choose to be implanted. I'm aware that there are problems that can and do occur, and I also know that CIs are continuing to improve and that the quality of sound and music can be quite superb.

We all have the right to choose for ourselves, and I can respect that.

Scott Stoffel

I was cautioned by two audiologists that a CI was not likely to give me good speech discrimination, due to my auditory neuropathy. The implant replaces the function of the ear and cochlea, but it still depends on the natural auditory nerve to deliver the signals to the brain. So if the nerve is defective, the signals don't get through clearly. However, when my weird neurological disorder caused the nerves in my hands to deteriorate to the point where I could no longer feel tactile sign language fast enough to keep up with interpreters during meetings or training at work, I was desperate for a real-time communication mode.

I received the Nucleus 24 implant and Freedom processor in 2006. Stoffel's syndrome was at its hell-spawned best right from the start. Midway through the surgery, the equipment broke down. An engineer had to be brought in to fix it before the operation could be completed. Thus, the usually three-hour procedure took over eight hours.

Recovery didn't go well, either. I developed a severe infection in the eardrum. It felt like someone had crammed a deflated basketball into my ear and then inflated it.

When all the medical mishaps finally subsided and the CI was activated, I responded fairly well to tones. In terms of detecting noise, my hearing was improved. Unfortunately, speech discrimination was zero. After a year of therapy and hearing exercises and a few alterations in the programming, I still tested goose egg in understanding random speech.

It was very disappointing for me but not unexpected. I had been aware all along that speech was unlikely.

The CI has its usefulness for me, despite the lack of speech. I can hear the door with it and have better awareness of things going on around me, like my cats knocking something over. The sounds are definitely helpful, so I continue to use the CI.

Tonilyn Todd Wisner

When I was diagnosed with Meniere's disease, I had already lost a great deal of hearing (was in the moderate-to-severe hearing loss range) and was wearing a hearing aid as strong as I could get. I could understand about 80 percent of speech in my right ear and had been 100 percent deaf in my left ear for most of my life. My doctors kept telling me not to worry, that if my right ear deteriorated to where an aid was not sufficient, I could get a cochlear implant. I had done a little reading about them but did not want one. I did not mind being deaf, and I didn't like the thought of having this "thing" in my head.

When I lost all of my hearing from inner-ear surgery in my right ear, I had already lost much of my vision and was far past legally blind. But I could still read lips up close and was OK with that. But as my vision got too bad to read lips and I had to use tactile communication, I came to the conclusion that I had nothing to lose and a lot to gain by getting a CI. So I talked to my otologist and neurotologist about getting one. I was tested and was a candidate. Since I had only been deaf for about five months at the time (seven by the time I got the implant), there was great hope of getting good speech discrimination from the CI. The problem came when Medicaid refused to pay for it. I had gotten my hopes up, and that was a big letdown. There was just no way I could pay for it myself.

It just so happens that, before I decided to get the CI, the infamous Hurricane Katrina wiped out the only CI facility in Louisiana, which was in New Orleans. They rebuilt it and were just looking for an audiologist to map (program) the CIs, and then they would be ready for patients.

My doctors, Justin Tenney, otologist, and Moses Arriaga, neurotologist, believed that since I was blind also, I was definitely a perfect candidate, Dr. Tenney fought for me, and the Earl K. Long hospital in Baton Rouge performed the surgery free of charge and donated the CI. I was the first patient to receive a CI at the new facility. Dr. Tenney wanted to promote the new facility, so I was to be the spokesperson in return for my CI. Dr. Tenney set up an interview with a local news station, WBRZ. It was to be a two- or three-part series to educate people about the facility and show through me how they can help. The first one was to concentrate on the CI operation, how the CI is placed, and how it works. But when the series aired, it was more of a story about me, my brain tumor, and how I became deaf and blind.

Because the CI was donated, my doctors picked out the CI that they thought I would do best with. I received the Med-EL implant with the Tempo Plus processor. A new processor was coming out a few months later, and I would exchange mine for the new one.

I was implanted on August 30, 2007. I was doing great with healing up, waiting for my surgical site to heal, so I could receive my processor and be "turned on." I received my processor and a first mapping on October 10th. At first, I was disappointed because I couldn't understand anything. And everybody sounded like a robot on helium! But just a few hours later, I was able to understand most of what my (then) husband said! He had to be close to the processor, but I could understand him! I never thought I'd hear a voice again, so I was on cloud nine! I also ran around the hotel room like a kid on a sugar high, turning water off and on, zipping and unzipping my purse, tapping my cane. Everything made a noise again. It was *so* awesome to hear these things again that I didn't want to take the processor off that night. For days, I would make sounds just to hear sounds. I could recognize some sounds but not all that many. One funny thing I do remember was that dogs barking sounded like ducks!

Everything went well, and people's voices were sounding more normal, and I could identify more sounds every day. My doctors and audiologist said I was a miracle patient because I was understanding speech so well and so quickly. But I wound up in the hospital in December with a bad staph infection on the surgical site that had also gone into my right ear.

Once that was cleared up, after about a week in the hospital, I could wear my CI again. Things weren't as clear as they were before the infection, although I could still understand a good deal of speech. It was possible that the infection had damaged the implant, but my doctors didn't think it did. In March of 2008, I began having vertigo with sound (that darned Tullio phenomenon, again!) and getting "shocks" to my head when wearing my processor. So I had to stop wearing it, until we could find the problem. Tests were done. They couldn't say for sure that the internal implant was damaged, and I had some tests done that showed my inner ear—already severely damaged over the years—was acting up with sound. My doctor didn't want to re-implant me if it was not absolutely necessary, and with my history of vertigo, it was decided best to try changing my medication. So we went through a lot of medication trials and eventually, in January of 2009, I was able to wear my CI again.

I still have days that I can't wear it, and my doctor may still re-implant me, but we are just waiting to see what happens.

Anyway, in June of that year, I received my new processors, the Opus 2, which I *love!* It has a remote control, instead of everything on the processor. The remote is very thin and palm-sized, and has very tactile buttons (raised and with a texture). It has four program buttons, volume buttons, sensitivity buttons, and a default button in case you make changes you don't like. It gives you so much control and is easy. The Opus 2 also comes with a rechargeable battery pack and three batteries, so you always have some charged. The battery lasts a good ten or eleven hours. I keep one in the processor, one in the charger, and one fully charged battery in a pouch I have on my long white cane. Since the cane goes everywhere I go, I always have a spare with me.

Because of the setback, I am still on a low-power program, but I am understanding speech again and getting better with each map.

I don't get any formal listening therapy. But I try to listen to my TV shows, music I know, and books on tape. I don't understand much from these—*yet*. I keep plugging away because I am *deaf-blind and determined!* I do feel like I am understanding more and more slowly. I am very happy with my CI.

I cannot have a CI on the left side because the hearing (auditory) nerve was cut by the brain tumor, and you must have a healthy hearing nerve for a CI to work.

An embarrassing thing that has happened because of my CI is when someone clears their throat or coughs. To me, it sounds like they said something, so I say, "Excuse me, what did you say?" or something to that effect, and the person is either confused, thinks I'm nuts, or both.

And a *really* embarrassing one is when I misunderstand something someone says, but to me, it seemed perfectly understandable, so I don't know that I misunderstood—and the other person doesn't realize it, either. We are essentially having two different conversations but think we are on the same subject until something just doesn't fit!

Wendy Williams

In my earlier years when I had residual vision and wore hearing aids, I frowned on the use of CIs because of the poor outcome reports I received by word of mouth. My parents had been told upon diagnosis of my hearing impairment that, if I lost more hearing, it likely would be when I was elderly. Since learning of the Usher's syndrome, I knew my vision would deteriorate but not my hearing loss.

Prior to returning to Seeing Eye to obtain my second dog guide, I noticed a hearing drop in my right ear. I assumed it was due to my old hearing aid, and I had had no time to see the audiologist before going to New Jersey. As soon as I returned to my home, I scheduled an audiology visit. Both my audiologist and I were astounded to discover I actually had lost hearing. She inquired if I had a Finnish background, and I replied, "Not to my knowledge." [At the time, it was thought that people with Usher's syndrome Type 2 should not experience further deterioration to their initial hearing losses and that additional loss was a characteristic of Type 3, which was believed to be most common among people with Finnish heritage. However, it is now known that those with Type 2 may experience continued deterioration of hearing.] Over the course of the next six months, I had a series of audiology tests, documenting my fluctuating but decreasing hearing. Meanwhile, my right vision was going downhill, too, confirmed by the eye doctor.

A CI center agreed to see me, and more tone and discrimination tests were conducted. A hindrance to the CI candidacy was my better hearing in the left ear. I pleaded with the audiologists that basic functioning had become such a struggle, compounded with the simultaneous visual and hearing deteriorations. The CI team decided to proceed with the CI. I was implanted with the Nucleus 24M in 2000.

At activation four weeks later with the Sprint (body-worn processor), I was distraught to initially only hear static. Then I connected a noise to my dog guide's collar. Thereafter, I heard other noises, sometimes associating them with different environmental sounds, other times being clueless as to the source because of my limited vision and poor localization. Squeaky noises occurred when people spoke, but there was no speech comprehension.

Over a period of several months, all voices from toddlers to men changed from Mickey Mouse to Darth Vader. During this period, my left hearing was deteriorating, plus the vision in my left eye. With my poor sight and localization, it was hard for me to recognize who was talking to me, and I was embarrassed to ask who the person was.

It was at least a few years before the natural voices kicked in and enabled me to better know who was talking to me. I was frustrated my CI discrimination was near 70 percent. My repeated requests for speech rehab for this CI were denied, since insurance did not provide this service to adults. I had to rely on daily listening practice that occurred in everyday interactions with people, the radio and TV news, and talk shows.

When it became impossible for me to make safe crossings at intersections, I received the Nucleus Freedom CI in 2005. I was pleasantly surprised to understand a soft, deep, robotic voice very soon after activation.

Upon turning on the two CIs together, I was blown away by the richness of the sound. I achieved speech discrimination close to 100 percent with the second CI. The bilateral CIs allowed me to better localize sounds and to communicate with others in quieter settings without tiring as easily. Noisy environments, fast talkers, and heavy accents still pose challenges for me, though.

13
Coping

The previous chapters of this book have dealt with coping primarily in a physical sense. Here, the contributors talk about how deaf-blindness affects them psychologically and how they cope with this. Being able to manage physically does not guarantee a person is at peace with the disabilities on the inside. In truth, it is rare for a deaf-blind person to be completely accepting of the disabilities. Many people will say, "I accept being deaf-blind," but in reality, most do not. There is frequently a constant inner struggle to cope and be content.

People with degenerative losses in particular struggle to cope with the worsening problems and the changes these force on the way they live. Remembering things that one once enjoyed but can no longer do or experience, such as driving a car or listening to music, can cause depression that is not easily remedied.

A possible gauge of a person's ability to cope is the way in which people dream. Often, a deaf-blind person will be able to see and/or hear in dreams and do things that are not possible in their real lives. This can be a sign of nonacceptance of the disabilities. It can also add to depression and frustration.

Angela C. Orlando

Does anyone ever achieve full acceptance of their disabilities? Is it truly possible to live this life without depression? I really don't know, but I think I'm doing well with my own coping. I've come to accept my disabilities and the way in which they limit my life. I don't dwell on that, though. I focus on what I can do and how I can compensate for what I am unable to do.

I'm not saying it was easy or that it magically happened all at once. It's been a long struggle to find peace and acceptance in my life. I've stood at the very edge, ready to give into hopelessness and despair. Yet, something would always pull me out, and I'd find a way to move on.

Many people who are deaf-blind find strength in God and their religious faith. "God gives you only what you can endure." "Jesus loves you." "There will be no deaf-blindness in Heaven." If it helps someone cope, then I guess those sentiments are good for them. It's all empty words to me. I don't have any religious background. I don't even know that I believe in God. I've had to find other sources for my own inner strength.

I have no doubt of what got me through it all. I have achieved this sense of peace in my life through being Daniel's mother. The love I have for that child has allowed me to triumph over everything that life has thrown in my way. I feel as if nothing can stop me now.

I was hard of hearing and visually impaired when Daniel was born. That seemed hard enough. When he was only six months old, I became so incredibly sick. I lost all hearing, all vision, the use and feeling in my hands, arms, and legs. I couldn't walk, and I was in so much pain. Add that I was trapped in an abusive marriage. My husband kept me completely under his control, living in a pigsty of a house. He hurt me physically and emotionally. There was sexual abuse, as well.

And there was Daniel . . . my son. My baby. He was everything to me. He gave me the power and strength to endure it all.

At times, I wanted to die. It was the abuse more than the disabilities that made it so hard. But I couldn't allow myself to give up. I knew that Daniel needed me. Or maybe I needed Daniel. Just his existence was enough to save my life. I just kept on going. One day at a time. One problem at a time.

Somewhere in the middle of all that horror, I realized that I had found acceptance of my disabilities. I was mentally coping with the challenges of deaf-blindness. I found new ways to do what I needed to do. I figured out how to be Daniel's mother. I realized there was hope for a future again, and I would do everything I could to make it happen. It wasn't the future I originally dreamed of, but it would still be a good and happy life. As long as Daniel and I were together, everything would be fine.

It was Daniel, too, who gave me the strength to leave my abusive husband. I went to court and won custody of my son. That was the toughest battle of them all—and the most important.

Now I'm living a very comfortable and pleasant life. I'm not deliriously happy. I'm content. There is no more abuse in my life. I can deal with my disabilities and the way they have changed my life. Daniel is a wonderful and happy child. That's what really matters to me.

I still can't hear, see, or walk very well. I hope for a "cure" someday. Stem cell research or visual implants may give me back some sight. With so many medical advancements, I won't give up hope. I dream of the day I will be able to look at my son's face and actually see him smile . . . to see his brown hair and crystal blue eyes . . . to look at his freckled face. Everyone says he looks just like me. Maybe someday I'll see that for myself.

That doesn't mean I haven't accepted my disabilities. I'm not fooling myself or putting too much foolish hope on the future. I just refuse to give up dreams, even if they never come true. . . . Life without dreams would be too dreary to endure.

Christy L. Reid

My deaf-blindness occurred very gradually over several years during my youth, giving me time to adjust and learn ways to cope with the dual disabilities. I guess I gradually came to accept the loss of my vision and hearing. I don't recall spending much time thinking about the past when I could hear, though I recall that, for a short period of time when I first started college at Gallaudet, I would turn the radio on, hoping I could hear it. I really believed a miracle would occur. But it never did. And after a time, I stopped thinking about it.

I never really had time in my life, especially my adult life, to dwell on things I couldn't do anymore. Instead, I focused on things I *could* do. I always had a desire to get involved with people and enjoyed doing things with friends, like traveling and exploring new places and shopping. I did not really enjoy big group activities where I had to depend on someone to interpret for me, but when I could not avoid having to be involved with a group, I had to muster a lot of patience. Sometimes, I would even bring a book to read, instead of depending on an interpreter. After I learned Braille and had better Braille reading skills, this was a convenient solution to cope with restlessness, especially in family gatherings.

As a mom and wife, I sometimes felt frustrated that I could not drive a car. With three kids who needed to be driven to school and sports and other events, not to mention errands and shopping, it can be really difficult for my hearing-sighted husband who has to shoulder these responsibilities. If only I could drive . . . or if only I had an SSP to help. . . . And sometimes, it crosses my mind that, if I had normal vision, I could see my sons playing soccer or could see them in a school Christmas program.

But it does me no good to live in a dream world, dwelling on things I can't do. I can't drive, and who knows if I ever will? And unfortunately, our town doesn't have services for deaf-blind people. I believe in facing the reality of my life and accepting my limits, trying to find ways to overcome the feeling of inadequacy.

I look for things I can do to help balance Bill's burdens, like cleaning the kitchen or doing the laundry. I always appreciate other people's help—friends or family members, when they offer to go shopping with me or pick up something from the store for us or meet us at the ballpark and help involve me in one of the boys' soccer games.

Several times while living in Poplar Bluff, I have volunteered to teach ASL. First, I volunteered a few times at the local Independent Living Center, and this experience led to being invited to speak to students at local schools. I also taught ASL at the church my family attends, and several people can now use basic sign language to communicate with me. These volunteer experiences have led to a paying job as an ASL instructor at the local college in the continuing education program. The pay I earn is like the jam to our family income, and it really helps reduce the stress on Bill and me. I am hoping this part-time job will develop into a full-time position somewhere in town.

In the meantime, while I teach ASL once a week, I spend a lot of time, using my computer and Braille display, preparing stories and articles, which I hope to sell and earn a little more jam. Working at serious, professional writing helps to further satisfy my self-respect—I'm trying to do something productive that contributes to the family.

An advantage of writing is that I can let go and enjoy the make-believe world of fantasy. I can create characters that hear and see, drive cars, talk on phones, etc. This type of writing is fun, and I allow myself to indulge, but I also spend time writing nonfiction articles. I also find writing poetry a challenge and hope it will lead to further publishing opportunities.

Since other deaf-blind people or deaf people who understand deaf-blindness don't live in or near our town, I have found that getting involved with online groups designed for deaf-blind people to be a great social outlet. Here, I can share with others who understand and have similar experiences. Furthermore, these online groups often offer helpful information about deaf-blind social events and other issues, like adaptive kitchen techniques. The online deaf-blind groups are like a lifesaver where I can chat with others and just have a good time, which really helps to break the feeling of isolation that comes with living in a rural town.

Mark Gasaway

Coping is an excellent way to figure out how you really feel about who you are and what your limitations might be. You learn to understand your mind and body as it relates to your disabilities. You come to terms with how you feel about things—love, hate, growing old, staying young, being happy, getting depressed, and so much more. Learning your skills of coping can be a most rewarding experience because the way your mind and body cope with the disabilities can result in a healthy or unhealthy lifestyle.

Being able to fully accept your disabilities has nothing to do with depression. I have fully accepted my disabilities but still get depressed now and then—not because I have not accepted what has been given to me, but because getting depressed is normal and happens to everyone. Even hearing and sighted people get depressed.

I have felt at times that I did not like what was going on with my life and felt I needed to change things. That is a good sign of how we cope and does not necessarily mean we do not like who we are because of our disabilities.

Dreaming when I sleep is something that really helps me cope a lot. The dreams can be about me with fewer or no disabilities, but I also have dreams where I am still deaf-blind. Sometimes, I dream of being only deaf. I have some dreams where I am not disabled, but they do not stay long. I guess dreaming that I am still deaf-blind helps me deal with the issues of life better. Dreaming of a nondisabled life is an unwanted distortion of reality for me.

I am not haunted by many things I once was able to do, but I do wish I were able to drive a car at times. Wish I were able to take a girl on dates.

The memories I have of times past have not been a problem for me. I may get depressed or somewhat angry—more about my balance than about my hearing and vision loss, because my balance, when it is bad, completely makes me look like an idiot at times. That makes me feel like I am not in control of the balance issue. If you have bad balance, you will understand what I mean here.

Things that may help me cope better are going for a walk, reading a book, cleaning house, maybe playing cards by myself, and watching TV (especially sports). The most important thing, though, is I can cope just fine by myself. But when the feeling of depression is too strong, I will seek counseling.

Melanie Bond

I have come to fully accept my disabilities. If you think about it, it's really a great opportunity to explore a different way of life, apart from mainstream society. I know in the past that I didn't feel good about myself for various reasons, but somehow, I found the courage and the strength to overcome whatever false values I had been taught to believe in. I truly love myself for who I am, and I will always strive to be open and honest with everyone. In fact, I usually tell everyone that my life is an open book. I have nothing to hide, no guilty conscience, and I believe the best in everyone.

I believe in a power greater than all of us, and I put my trust and faith in that power to guide me through life. I do not espouse any particular religion, but I do embrace my soul and my spirituality.

Somehow, it is the nature of life to challenge each and every one of us to overcome whatever difficulties we may face in life. Yes, there are barriers, but there's a reason and a purpose for them, and that is to help each and every one of us to advance to a higher spiritual level. It means having to change the way that we think about things. It means having to cultivate new thoughts and possibilities for dealing with our disabilities. Find out what works for you. When you succeed in your goals and have learned to be content with your lot in life, then you can be truly at peace with yourself.

I find it interesting that people (and cartoonish characters) in my dreams sign to me, although I don't always understand what they're signing. Same with people who try to talk to me in dreams—I don't understand them, either. Sometimes, I'm aware that I'm deaf-blind (in dreams), and I will tell others that I cannot hear or understand what they are trying to tell me. Other times, I'm aware that I can hear and speak, too. Twice in a dream, I heard someone speak my name, "Melanie," in a loud, clear voice. Then I'd wake and look around my room to see who had called me, but no one was there!

For the most part, I do not have disabilities in my dreams. I slip in and out of my body; I fly; I do astral traveling; I have vivid dreams that are real, and I have seen my doppelgänger—someone who looks just like me—in my dreams.

I'm not haunted by memories of things I can no longer do as efficiently as I once did. I got to drive for twenty years without a single ticket and without killing or maiming anyone. I used to play racquetball (loved it!), was quite good at playing ping-pong, and I bowled in several bowling leagues. I played the piano until I could no longer read the musical notes. That is one thing I hope to remedy, because I enjoyed playing the piano, which can often be calming and helps to relieve stress. I enjoy listening to Kenny G's instrumental music, but there's not much music out there that I can truly enjoy, especially music with lyrics that, to my ears, sound so discordant and rackety that it gives me a headache!

I stopped watching my 27-inch TV screen for at least two to three years because I couldn't read the tiny closed-captioned words very well. Sometimes, when the captioned words aren't synchronized properly with the words that are spoken, that can be very annoying! Usually, when that happens, I end up understanding nothing! But in 2008, after I came home from Seabeck Camp, I walked into my house and found a huge 40-by-30-inch TV standing in my living room. My husband had bought it at a garage sale for $250. I frowned at him, knowing that he had bought it just for me, hoping that I might be able to get some enjoyment out of watching TV again. I was rather skeptical, but when I put on my FM system and my ugly telescoping glasses, I was shocked but pleased to discover that I could once again enjoy watching TV! Sometimes, details on the TV screen (like a person's facial features) seem to fade out on me, but, overall, I'm glad that my husband took a big gamble on me when he bought the TV for me.

I can honestly say that, with the electronics technology that we have today, I have been able to delay what would be the inevitable progression of deaf-blindness. Technology has bought me time to enjoy sights and sounds for a little while longer, and I intend to take full advantage of that!

I will never give in to depression or anger, if I can help it. It only delays the inevitable process of healing. No matter what happens to me, I can only hope that I will remain gracious, in spite of any setbacks I may face in the future.

I don't mind pity parties, as long as they don't last more than a day or two. I don't think non-DBers can truly sympathize with what us DBers are going through. A rare few might be able to empathize truly. Speaking for myself, I really do not want sympathy from anyone because of my disability issues. I'm glad that there are people and SSPs who are willing to be supportive of DB people.

I seldom ever feel depressed because of my deaf-blindness. I've got so much to live for! Oh, my gosh, there are so many things I enjoy doing and new things I'd like to learn to do! I cannot get enough of life! There's never a dull moment, unless I'm caught in a waiting room somewhere! Seriously, I love reading and writing, going for walks, talking with my husband who's my best friend, traveling, going to the beach, going to deaf-blind camps and, occasionally, deaf-blind cruises, flower gardening and landscaping, crocheting, visiting with my kids and grandkids, watching TV, eating in, eating out, and enjoying all the comforts of home.

Patricia Clark

As a disabled child and young person, I longed for acceptance by the able. This led me into seeking cures, but they were not available. I believed that, if I were like the able, they'd include me or value me. This never happened, and as I lost more capacity, such as being unable to use the telephone, I became more unlike them.

As an adult, I wanted my own home, which had to have all the facilities of a family home, so that the able would respect me. This was financially impossible, and I came to realize that it would make no difference whatsoever to the way the able saw me.

Eventually, I gave up on this idea and switched over to believing that the able were at fault for rejecting me or looking down on me. In short, the failure was theirs, not mine. This change of outlook made a big difference to my quality of life. Self-respect does not depend on the able.

Reading, playing the piano, and listening to music provided transcendence in my youth. These things are now lost to me. Television and going to the movies never really got off the ground. I had a small yacht and greatly enjoyed sailing, but increasing age put an end to that.

Self-discipline is needed when others speak of things they can do and I can no longer do. I don't want to be unkind and pour cold water on their pleasure, but I do get a bit angry and must control it. I'm not angry with others but with the circumstances that put me here.

The thing that would most surely improve my life would be the company of people who are kind and patient. I do know people like this, but for reasons of geography or infirmity on their part, I see little of them.

Tonilyn Todd Wisner

I have had a much harder time coping with my deaf-blindness than any of my other disabilities, even "just" deafness. When I became deaf, both when I could use a hearing aid and when I could no longer hear anything, being deaf was not a big problem for me. I guess because I grew up hard-of-hearing, I knew quite a bit of ASL, and even when my eyesight started going, I was still able to read lips well. So the total blindness in itself was a very hard thing—and still is—for me. You see, I have always had a fear of not being able to see what was around me, especially behind me. I don't fear the dark; I have this fear in light, also. I have always had to sit or stand with my back to a wall, so I knew nothing was behind me and could see in all other directions. I know it's odd, but that's me! So you can see how becoming blind plays on that fear. Since I went blind in increments and not overnight, I have tried to deal with this fear as I lost more and more vision. I am now completely blind, and I am not over that fear yet.

Even though the deafness was not too hard on me, the combination of deafness and blindness has been very hard. I can no longer read lips, and that makes the deafness hard, too. Because of my brain damage, I process things slower than most people, and that makes tactile communication slow and usually frustrating for the other person. And, of course, it hurts my feelings when people get frustrated with me, even though I understand why, because I am doing the best I can. Even now that I have a CI, I can't understand a lot of speech, especially in noisy places or if there is a TV on or something like that. These things make it hard to cope with, but just the change it has made to my life is the hardest thing to deal with.

I loved to read and was a very fast reader, but I am a very slow Braille reader, which makes it less enjoyable sometimes. I loved to play cards, and, again, I still can with Braille cards, but since I have the memory problems, I can't remember what is in my hand or what has been played, so it is slow and tedious. I can no longer enjoy TV or movies. I can't draw or relax by feeding and watching my fish in the pond. I have to depend on people to take me where I need to go and to make phone calls for me. Most things I once enjoyed doing are now either too hard and frustrating or lost to me.

At first, when I became too blind to read regular print and struggled to read large print, I coped by educating myself. I taught myself Braille and was reading books and magazines in contracted (Grade 2) Braille in three months. Being able to read again, although very slowly, helped me cope a little bit—like I said, reading became frustrating, but at least I *could* still read and knew I would get better the more I read. I taught myself to use a long cane, so I could get around on my own.

I found support groups and got advice. I could still use my computer by enlarging the text, so at that point, I hadn't lost communication through emailing and instant messaging. I also enjoyed doing online research on anything and everything, so I had that, too. When it became too hard on my eyes to use the computer, a Notetaker, a handheld Braille computer, was purchased for me, and I still had email and the Web through that.

Even though I had these things, these adaptations, I would still get angry at what I couldn't do any more like a "normal" person. Then I would get very depressed. I found that I was not really coping with my increasing deaf-blindness. My doctor put me on antidepressants, and that helped me from having breakdowns, but I was (and still am) somewhat depressed. It gets to me sometimes, and I just have to let it out. Some times are harder than others. I am lucky to have my close-knit family.

I really have not coped all that well with complete deaf-blindness, and losing my eyes for prosthetic eyes just makes coping that much harder. I don't really know what would help me cope. I am at a loss and in such inner turmoil that I just don't know where to turn. I would like to find a therapist to talk to, but I am not sure how to go about doing that and finding one that will use manual communication, if I can't understand their speech, or who is willing to take the time to talk slowly and clearly enough for me to understand with my CI.

I am not a social person and have become less social because of my disabilities, so I don't think talking to other DB people will help much. But I would not be unwilling to try, if I could find some people to hang out with.

I can admit I am scared. I know I am not alone, and on my good days, I know I *will* make it through this, but I think it's just going to take time and patience. At this point, I can only hope that one day I will get through this grieving process, for that is what any loss like this puts you through.

One thing that you may not think has anything to do with coping is dreams. Maybe for most, it doesn't, and maybe for some, it has just a little to do with it. But if you think about it, your dreams, if you remember them, can have an impact on you. Have you ever had a dream or nightmare that was so real that you just couldn't shake the feeling that it was real? Has something you dreamed haunted you and stayed with you for a long time? Have you had recurring dreams or dreams that continued where they left off when you went back to sleep? So you see how dreams *can* affect you psychologically. In most of my dreams, I am hearing and sighted and have no balance problems, physical ailments, or facial paralysis. It is rare for any of these things to be an affliction of mine in my dreams. And for me, that makes it harder to cope because I remember most of my dreams. So in everyday life, I am trying to cope with my disabilities, but I "live" in my dreams as "normal," which just multiplies my feelings of loss when I wake up. I expect to see when I open my eyes, but I don't. I expect to hear when I yawn, but I don't. I can remember how easy life was without disabilities in my dreams, and that makes me yearn for that life. But every day, I have to get up and face reality.

Wendy Williams

My perception of the deaf-blindness depends on the kind of day I am having. If I am able to complete tasks independently with accommodations, I hardly notice the disability. If I am faced with a situation in which the deaf-blindness prevents me from solving it myself, I curse the disability.

Recently, the Internet server was down. I encountered difficulty understanding the tech support with a heavy accent directing me to type in a visual code inaccessible to my speech screen-reader. Some days when I crash into a wall, I think nothing of it; other times it angers me greatly.

In some dreams, I struggle unsuccessfully to get auditory information from people (deafness). In other dreams, I am lost, and I cannot obtain help from people (blindness). In one dream, I recall my surprise in being able to see an individual from head to toe, something I have not been able to do in decades. I was touched by the vividness and peacefulness of one dream about my beloved turtle waving to me as he drove away in his tiny vehicle.

I do mourn the loss of my residual vision, which had enabled me, along with my dog guide, to travel the country independently. I miss window shopping to see what is new on the market. I miss watching some TV programs (e.g., the Olympics) and movies. A few friends are empathetic about these haunting memories of mine, and thus I am comfortable to share my dashed hopes with them. It is hard when they are not available. I try to distract myself with a good book or go for a walk, but sometimes, I carry this great sadness through the day and to bed, waking up to a new, sunnier day.

I am thankful for the services of an SSP, which allow me to handle my personal correspondence, to do errands, and to participate in the community. These services are limited, though, and I sadly had to forgo events in the community, such as the church's luncheon or the city's pet parade.

Afterthoughts

The following are poems written by the contributors of this book. There are no particular themes for this section, though much insight can be gleaned from a person's creative works.

Do You See Me?

Melanie Bond

I'm NOT playing by your silly hearing rules anymore . . .
I haven't been in your hearing world for a long time . . .
Do you SEE who I used to be?
Please don't!

I've learned to play a totally different game . . .
I'm getting used to playing by deaf-blind rules . . .
Do you SEE who I'm BECOMING?
Please do!

SEE me . . .
FEEL me . . .
Are you LISTENING?
Please do!

Thoughts of a Deaf-Blind Woman

Tonilyn Todd Wisner

Silence is for the hearing,
Not the deaf;
A deaf world is full
Of many, many sounds.

Darkness is for the sighted,
Not the blind;
For the blind see
Many wonderful things.

The world of the deaf-blind
Is a wondrous place.
We are not limited
By our eyes and ears.

Everything we touch,
We see.
Everything that moves within our touch,
We hear.

To smell a flower
Is to see it,
To hear it,
To know the mystery of it.

We feel the breeze
And see the leaves
As they sway
To Nature's music.

The sun on our faces
Shows us the sunshine
And the brightness
Of the day.

Our lives are fulfilled,
And filled with a multitude
Of sights, sounds,
Feelings and living.

Don't mourn the deaf-blind,
For we have some of the
Most fulfilled lives
Of anyone that ever lived.

Share in our joys,
Experience life to the fullest.

What Is It?

Scott Stoffel

What is it? What is it?
That thing with three legs,
lurching and tottering along?
What grave spat it up,
as if Death rejected it, too?
The living watch it suspiciously,
never letting the children out of their sight.
Greetings mumbled or shouted
glean no reply
from the approaching abomination.
Its eyes see little
but dart like the eyes of evil,
full of malice and mischief,
no doubt.
Guard yourself,
draw back,
lest you be poisoned!
A bold soul might step forward,
dare he even touch the thing!
Egad! That gained its notice!
A single eye ablaze swings about
to bear like a Howitzer upon him.
Stay 'way from it! Stay 'way!
Perhaps his greeting was kind enough,
but the thing's face speaks of war,
the one eye bidding him withdraw
to the ranks of the glorious living,
while the other uselessly withers
the daffodils to his right.
No word comes from it,
the usual explanation having been exhausted

long ago.
Neither can cross the line
between the living and the dead.
In silent fury, it staggers on,
hideous in gait,
but large enough to evoke caution.
What is it? What is it?
What a horrid thing,
belched from the guts of Hell.

Touch Me Softly

Angela C. Orlando

Touch me softly,
As I sit here.
I do not stir,
When you draw near.

My eyes are closed,
As I read.
You stand beside me;
I pay no heed.

My hands glide quickly;
I feel each word.
They are not printed;
They can't be heard.

My book has dots,
With fingers I feel.
I touch them all,
Words become real.

Do you understand,
As you gaze at me?
I am looking,

But I can't see.

No light or color,
For I am blind.
Eyes unseeing,
But sharp of mind.

Touch me softly,
Feel with love.
Sweet, gentle hands,
A pat from above.

Touch me softly
With tenderness.
Together we'll find
True happiness.

Touch me softly,
For that's not all.
I will not hear you,
When you call.

I am deaf;
I cannot hear.
I live in silence,
But I don't fear.

Did you speak?
Was that you?
The words are gone,
Away they flew.

But I can listen
With my hand.
In that way,
I understand.

Touch me softly,
Feel with love.
Sweet, gentle hands,

A pat from above.

Touch me softly
With tenderness.
Together we'll find
True happiness.

Deaf and blind,
Silent and black,
I trudge alone
This endless track.

It is my life;
It is my way.
I can do it;
Forever, I'll stay.

Strong and true.
With touch to guide,
Always with passion,
Spirit inside.

Fear me not,
Believe I can.
I'll change your life;
You'll understand.

Touch me softly,
Feel with love.
Sweet, gentle hands,
A pat from above.

Touch me softly
With tenderness.
Together we'll find
True happiness.

Deaf-Blind and One of a Unique Kind

Mark Gasaway

When I was a kid, I discovered the unique world
That comes with no normal hearing and sight,
Unique because I could still do things I loved,
Rode a bike, walked my dogs, played football
And enjoyed being who I truly was—a funny guy.
Yeah, I am deaf-blind and one of a unique kind!

When I reached adolescence, I had an interest in girls,
Showing an interest like other boys my age;
School was good for me, as I did well,
Graduated with a high grade average,
Went on to college and into the work world.
Yeah, I am deaf-blind and one of a unique kind!

I do not hear with my ears, as sound is not there;
I hear with my hands and heart.
I do not see well with my eyes, as everything is a blur;
I see with my hands and mind.
The heart, mind and hands belong to the deaf-blind.
Yeah, I am deaf-blind and one of a unique kind!

Someday, the world will understand,
And we will all be known and respected in turn.
The deaf-blind will stand with you and share
A life that is full of living and harmony;
Just sit a spell with us and learn.
Yeah, I am deaf-blind and one of a unique kind!

Mother Goose and Her DB Gosling

Christy L. Reid

I laid an egg, and
Into the world,
A young gosling broke free.

His name is Ben,
But he's dubbed Bob the Destroyer,
Because he takes things apart
And doesn't put them together again.

This young gosling—
He was in perfect health—
All was in good order,
We geese family's blessings
Deep in wealth.

But when he was little,
He caught a bug;
I don't know how,
But it wouldn't be tugged.

It made his skin
Break into a terrible rash
And bumps grow on his skull,
And I felt Fate's lash.

We put up a fight,
And so did Ben;
Doctor gave him chemotherapy
That kept the bug at bay and eventually win.

We are so thankful;
The bug never returned,
But it took a toll on his nerves,
And his eyes and ears got burned.

Today he is a DB gosling,
And he has an advantage:
His DB Mother Goose doesn't
Wrap him in a protective bandage.

We share a bond that
Is mighty strong;
It's unbreakable,
Even when things go wrong.

Because we are so alike,
Sharing the same challenges,
The same frustrations, the same needs,
Together, we ride the same flight.

He is already growing
Into a fine DB goose;
He reads with his fingers faster than me;
He follows communication with his hands better than I;
I am a thankful, pleased Mother Goose!

Passing through the Night

Melanie Bond

There are days when we are like two ships,
Passing each other in the darkest of nights;
You are the sun, and I am the eclipsing moon;
I am the shadow that passes over your light.

Though my eyes and my ears are dimming,
In my mind's eyes, I can see you so clearly;
You are like an exploding star for all to see,
And I am the dark lady who remains hidden.

DB in the Race

Scott Stoffel

It's time to go;
Let's start the drive;
Soon we will know
Who can survive.
Roads twist and turn,
Climb to the sky;
Skid, crash and burn—
A soul will die.
'Gainst those who see,
'Gainst those who hear,
What ease to be
Consumed by fear.
Cliffs tall and stern,
The edge so nigh,
Make one wrong turn—
A soul will die.
Race with no light,
Wheels with no screams
Roar through the night;
Hope barely gleams.
Faint hearts won't go,
Perilous strive;
Soon we will know
Who can survive.